LONDON RECORD SOCIETY
PUBLICATIONS

VOLUME LIII

THE DINNER BOOK OF THE LONDON DRAPERS' COMPANY, 1564–1602

EDITED BY

SARAH A. MILNE

LONDON RECORD SOCIETY
THE BOYDELL PRESS
2019 for 2018

First published 2019

A London Record Society publication
Published by The Boydell Press
an imprint of Boydell & Brewer Ltd
PO Box 9, Woodbridge, Suffolk IP12 3DF, UK
and of Boydell & Brewer Inc.
668 Mt Hope Avenue, Rochester, NY 14620–2731, USA
website: www.boydellandbrewer.com

ISBN 978–0–900952–60–9

A CIP catalogue record for this book is available
from the British Library

The publisher has no responsibility for the continued existence or
accuracy of URLs for external or third-party internet websites referred to
in this book, and does not guarantee that any content
on such websites is, or will remain, accurate or appropriate

This publication is printed on acid-free paper

Typeset by www.thewordservice.com

Printed and bound in Great Britain by
TJ International Ltd, Padstow, Cornwall

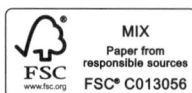

MIX
Paper from
responsible sources
FSC
www.fsc.org   FSC® C013056

CONTENTS

ACKNOWLEDGEMENTS

I first viewed the Drapers' Dinner Book in 2009 as a postgraduate architecture student. That archival encounter changed the trajectory of my working life. It is therefore a particular pleasure to thank the people who have supported the decade of research that has underpinned the production of this volume. Dr John Bold, who supervised my doctoral research out of which this volume grew, carefully read the introductory essay and has been an especially important supporter of the project from the outset. I am very grateful to the Drapers' Company for their financial support of this publication, for granting access to their records over many years, and for their permission to publish an edition of their Dinner Book. Penny Fussell, Archivist of the Drapers' Company, has been unfailingly generous with her time and in sharing her knowledge with me. Archivists of the Clothworkers' Company, Mercers' Company, Merchant Taylors' Company, and Fishmongers' Company, as well as the staff of the Guildhall Library, have aided me in my consultation of various livery company records over many years. I also owe thanks to the Committee of the London Records Society for their support and would like to acknowledge their admirable commitment to ensuring that documents from London's archives are more widely enjoyed and accessed. I am most indebted to Dr Robin Eagles as Honorary General Editor for his astute advice and general encouragement in bringing this volume to completion.

ABBREVIATIONS

Beaven, *Aldermen*	A. P. Beaven, *The Aldermen of the City of London Temp. Henry III – 1912*, 2 Vols. (London: Corporation of London, 1908–13)
Boyd, *Roll*	P. Boyd, *Roll of the Drapers' Company of London* (Croydon: J. A. Gordon, 1934)
DCA	Drapers' Company Archive
GL	Guildhall Library
HP Commons 1509–1558	*The History of Parliament, 1509–1558, 3 Vols*. S. Bindoff (ed.) (London: Secker & Warburg, 1982)
HP Commons 1558–1603	*The History of Parliament, 1558–1603, 3 Vols*. P. W. Hasler (ed.) (London: HMSO, 1981)
Johnson, *History*	A. H. Johnson, *A History of the Worshipful Company of the Drapers of London, 5 Vols*. (Oxford: Clarendon Press, 1914–22)
LMA	London Metropolitan Archives
MCA	Mercers' Company Archive
Oxford DNB	*Oxford Dictionary of National Biography*
Survey of London, xvi	*Survey of London, St. Martin in the Fields I: Charing Cross*, xvi, G. H. Gater and E. P. Wheeler (ed.) (London: London County Council, 1935)
Survey of London, xxv	*Survey of London, St. George's Fields*, xxv. I. Darlington (ed.) (London: London County Council, 1955)
TNA	The National Archives
VCH, *Hants*	*A History of the County of Hampshire*, iii. W. Page (ed.) (London: Victoria County History, 1908)

INTRODUCTION

Dinners have been central to the corporate life of London's livery companies for centuries. Formed primarily to regulate trades and promote the interests of members, the first of London's companies met in City taverns in the twelfth and thirteenth centuries, but as companies grew in size, wealth, and authority, newly acquired halls came to accommodate a round-robin of formal dinners, the centre-point of which was the Election Dinner. On the Election Day, company leaders formally received endorsement for their roles, participating in ceremonial set-piece choreographies in front of an elite group of members and selected guests who enjoyed lavish spreads of food and drink. The annual Election Day Dinners were held in the highest esteem by those within the companies as well as by those outside of them. The act of eating and drinking together, as in a familial setting, was a strong symbol of a united body; the produce on offer, a litmus test of prosperity.

Though a wide range of trade and craft guilds proliferated in medieval Europe and beyond, London's livery companies were especially plentiful, powerful, and therefore visible in the urban environment. Their distinctive moniker recalled the ceremonial clothing that members of the Livery were required to wear on corporate occasions, whether in public marketplaces or at exclusive meetings held inside company halls. By the middle of the sixteenth century, there were at least forty City livery companies, ranked in order of precedence according to their wealth and importance, each bearing the name of their specialisation. These companies were granted monopolies by the monarch to supervise the City's trades and crafts, and members were eligible to obtain Freedom of the City. Forming an exclusive group at the top of the pile, the 'Great Twelve' were companies of the highest prestige and shared a culture of sociability.[1] During the sixteenth century, membership of these companies became more diverse and mercantile in character as ambitious citizens benefited from London's increasingly important position as a lynchpin of international trade, importing all kinds of goods. Election Dinners of the Great Twelve tended to be correspondingly

---

[1]   In order of precedence the Great Twelve consist of: 1. Mercers, 2. Grocers, 3. Drapers, 4. Fishmongers, 5. Goldsmiths, 6. Merchant Taylors/Skinners (alternates annually), 7. Skinners/Merchant Taylors (alternates annually), 8. Haberdashers, 9. Salters, 10. Ironmongers, 11. Vintners, 12. Clothworkers.

impressive. High-stakes corporate issues of honour, hierarchy, and submission were culturally negotiated as business was mixed with pleasure in the context of a flourishing city.

Ranked third in order of precedence, the Drapers' Company regulated the production and exchange of woollen cloth in the City of London, having acquired its Royal Charter in 1364 and Incorporation in 1438. In the sixteenth century, as one of the Great Twelve, the Drapers' Company hosted one Election Dinner and three Quarter Dinners in the corporate year, which ran from August to August. Quarter Dinners were served to the upper tier of the Company (known as the Livery) at intervals throughout the year following the reading of the Company Ordinances by the Clerk and the payment of membership fees (paid quarterly and therefore known as 'quarterage'). The Election Dinner was held only once yearly and represented the high-point of corporate conviviality.

The Dinner Book is a rare account which records a series of such events. It details thirty-six dinners hosted by the Drapers' Company between 1564 and 1602, when foreign trade was intensifying and City growth accelerating. Some fragmentary evidence of similar contemporary dinners can be found scattered in other livery company records, but the Dinner Book presents an organisational and financial reckoning of a number of corporate dinners that is apparently unmatched in its coherence and survival. It escaped the destructive 1666 fire on account of the quick-thinking Company Clerk who deposited many corporate records in a sewer in the Hall's garden.[2] The document broadly follows the form of an itemised expenditure account for the annual Election Day Dinner and smaller Quarter Dinners, which were the responsibility of four elected Wardens. Unusually, two entries describe the service of the dinner itself, detailing the roles of specific employees and their placement within the Company Hall, and one entry identifies the exact tables at which specific guests sat.[3] These aspects of the Dinner Book illuminate the production of the dinner from the point of view of the Steward, an official engaged specifically to oversee the smooth running of such high-status events.[4]

The Dinner Book is stored in the Drapers' Company's Archive which is located in their Hall on Throgmorton Street, close to the Bank of England. The document provides insight into dining practices in a critical period of the Company's history, for by the turn of the seventeenth century, like many other mercantile companies, the Drapers' regulatory power was diminishing and the diversity of business interests of

---

2   Johnson, *History*, iii. 274.
3   DCA, DB1, ff.12r–16v, ff.86r–f.89r.
4   For discussion of the growing bureaucratisation of dinners in an Italian context and 'salco' literature, see K. Albala, *The Banquet: Dining in the Great Courts of Late Renaissance Europe* (Urbana and Chicago: University of Illinois Press, 2007), 139.

its members threatened further corporate dislocation from the trade of drapery.[5] In recent decades, there has been a sustained scholarly debate surrounding precisely how companies were unsettled by large-scale economic and social change. In contrast to the conventional view that the early modern period represented one of 'continuous decline' for these bodies as existing City economic structures were superseded, two leading revisionist scholars have emphasised the prosperity of the livery companies in this same period, stretching as far as to call it a 'golden age'.[6] The years in which the Dinner Book was produced are of particular interest if the complex interplay of decline and prosperity in the context of London's livery companies is to be more fully understood. As such, the 1560s and 1570s can be seen as a tipping point of sorts, when the tension between the old order and the new 'global' future begins to be more clearly discernible in archival documents.

Though the extent of the transformation of London's livery companies in the sixteenth and seventeenth centuries is contested, the enduring significance of the social life of the companies is undisputed. Sociability and 'jollification' had been an intrinsic part of guild life since their formation. Despite this, the dinners of livery companies remain surprisingly under-examined.[7] Scholarship into the cultural history of food and dining has grown in recent years and, through the lens of material culture, research into domestic hospitality in early modern England has been reinvigorated.[8] The relative lack of evidence of urban dining patterns has however hampered progress with regard to London, though Richard Stonley's diaries offer some valuable insights.[9] In a complementary strand of enquiry, the use of ceremony and ritual as a rhetorical device in the Lord Mayors' shows of the early seventeenth century has

---

5   Johnson, *History*, ii. 239–41; J. P. Ward, *Metropolitan Communities: Trade Guilds, Identity and Change in Early Modern London* (Stanford: Stanford University Press, 1997).

6   S. Rappaport, *Structures of Life in Sixteenth-Century London* (Cambridge: Cambridge University Press, 1989), 213; I. Archer, 'The Livery Companies and Charity in the Sixteenth and Seventeenth Centuries' in I. A. Gadd and P. Wallis (ed.) *Guilds, Society and Economy in London 1450–1800* (London: Centre for Metropolitan History, 2002), 15–28 (15). These two studies stand in contrast to earlier publications such as G. Unwin, *The Gilds and Companies of London* (London: Methuen, 1908), who states that European guilds in this period 'expired in giving birth to progress' (4).

7   One exception to this is W. Herbert, *The History of the Twelve Great Livery Companies* (London: privately printed, 1834). Gervase Rosser's important essay discusses traditions of dining in English provincial guilds: G. Rosser, 'Going to the Fraternity Feast: Commensality and Social Relations in Late Medieval England' in *Journal of British Studies* 33, no. 4 (1994), 430–46.

8   For example, see S. Pennell, *The Birth of the English Kitchen, 1600–1850* (London: Bloomsbury, 2016); A. Buxton, *Domestic Culture in Early Modern England* (Woodbridge: The Boydell Press, 2015); P. Findlen (ed.) *Early Modern Things: Objects and their Histories, 1500–1800* (New York: Routledge, 2012); T. Hamling and C. Richardson (ed.) *Everyday Objects: Medieval and Early Modern Material Culture and its Meanings* (Burlington, MA: Ashgate, 2010); C. Richardson, *Domestic Life and Domestic Tragedy in Early Modern England: The Material Life of the Household* (Manchester: Manchester University Press, 2006).

9   See Z. Hudson, 'Food, Dining and the Everyday Life of Richard Stonley' (Unpublished MRes thesis, University of Kent, 2014).

received much attention. Most notably, Anthony Munday's shows for the Drapers in the 1610s and 1620s indicate that the Company was by then fully conscious of the propagandist potential of civic theatre.[10] In his essay on civic consciousness, James Knowles argued that 'we lack an account of London that locates civic ritual firmly within the cultural ethos that fostered an explosion in civic ceremony after 1603'.[11] Facilitating the symbolic transferral of power from one set of Company governors to another, the early modern Election Dinner acted as a vehicle for the promotion of corporate and consequently civic harmony under the Company's elected leadership. In this context, company dinners merit closer inspection, for the performative aspects of the Election Dinner were as important, if not more so, than the food itself. On account of the increasing level of attention given to its ceremonial aspects, Election Dinners can be read as incubators for representational strategies used by mercantile men on a larger City-wide stage in the early decades of the seventeenth century. The Dinner Book therefore presents an opportunity to assess the significance of these dinners in relation to guild history as well as to broaden access to civic dining practices in the context of urban food history. This introduction further explores the purpose of the Election Dinners, firstly contextualising the production of the Dinner Book, then moving to describe the organisation of Election Dinners and the food presented, and finally considering the effects of such costly hospitality on Company Wardens.

PRODUCING THE DINNER BOOK

This edition of the Dinner Book has not been published with only early modern historians in mind. It is equally intended to serve the present-day membership of the livery companies, for in the twenty-first century, companies are still very much embedded in City life and company dinners continue to punctuate the corporate year. While some aspects of the company dinners contained in the Dinner Book may resonate with current members, for the modern-day reader the preoccupation with hierarchy and the ritual nuance that imbued the sixteenth-century dinner with meaning may prove a stumbling block, especially for those unfamiliar with the internal organisation of the companies. The outline below aims to aid orientation to the Drapers' Company in the early modern period.

[10] T. Hill, *Anthony Munday and Civic Culture: Theatre, History and Power in Early Modern London* (Manchester: Manchester University Press, 2004). Also see S. Trevisan, 'The Golden Fleece of the Drapers' Company: Politics and Iconography in Early Modern Lord Mayor's Shows' in J. R. Mulryne, M. I. Alivertie and A. Testaverde (ed.) *Ceremonial Entries in Early Modern Europe: The Iconography of Power* (Abingdon and New York: Routledge, 2016), 245–66.

[11] J. Knowles, 'The Spectacle of the Realm: Civic Consciousness, Rhetoric, and Ritual in Early Modern London' in J. R. Mulrune and M. Shewring (ed.) *Theatre and Government* (Cambridge: Cambridge University Press, 1993), 157–89 (157).

Regarding membership, in keeping with other companies in the sixteenth and seventeenth centuries, women were excluded from full participation in the Company on equal terms to men, though wives and widows were counted as 'sisters' in the wider corporate family and single women were sometimes bound as apprentices.[12] On the other hand, husbands, brothers, and sons could gain full political rights and admission to the Company either after completion of a seven-year apprenticeship, by patrimony (through membership of their father), or by redemption (through payment of a fee). The internal structure of the Drapers required that every member was then classified on account of their experience, success and wealth. Movement up through the ranks of the Company was possible in order to reflect growth in these attributes. As the largest group in the Company, the Freemen of the Yeomanry, also known as the Bachelors, were entry-level members and were consequently not granted the privilege of invitation to the main Election and Quarter Day Dinners as guests. Notably, however, twenty to thirty waiters for the Election Dinner were regularly drawn from the Company Yeomanry. In 1564, the Wardens of the Bachelors were given responsibility for selecting 'the best and comeliest [Bachelors] that could be found and best apparelled' to serve as waiters.[13] Indeed, by this time, the Yeomanry were far less connected to the mercantile Company oligarchy than they had been just a few decades before, and the divide continued into the seventeenth century. At the same time, whereas in the mid-sixteenth century the Yeomanry was made up primarily by retail drapers, by 1624, only about 5 per cent of this group were practising drapers, in keeping with the diversification of Company membership at all levels.[14] Reinforcing an element of independence from the upper-level merchants, the Bachelors were given permission to hold their own smaller-scale Election Dinners in 1547, purposed 'to the end most chief, that each of us should get a loving acquaintance of other, as becometh all honest men to wish for'.[15]

Typically numbering between forty and seventy members, the Livery were ranked above the Yeomanry Bachelors, and progression to this tier was dependent on election by a small number of elite Drapers.[16] Liverymen possessed the privilege of wearing the 'clothing' of the Company. Holding a year-long term spanning from one Election

---

[12] For further discussion of the issue of gender and the livery companies, see H. Smith, 'Gender and Material Culture in the Early Modern London Guilds' in H. Greig, J. Hamlett and L. Hannan (ed.) *Gender and Material Culture in Britain since 1600* (London: Palgrave, 2016), 16–31; L. Gowing, 'Girls on Forms: Apprenticing Young Women in Seventeenth-Century London' in *Journal of British Studies* 55, no. 3 (2016), 447–73. For the Drapers' Company, also see L. C. Orlin, *Locating Privacy in Tudor London* (Oxford: Oxford University Press, 2009), 294.

[13] DCA, DB1, f.16v. See also earlier examples of Bachelor waiters in the 1530s: DCA, MB1B, f.391, f.418, f.577.

[14] R. Ashton, *The City and the Court* (Cambridge: Cambridge University Press, 1979), 49.

[15] DCA, MB4, f.59.

[16] Johnson, *History*, i. 111, 147, 149, 151, 153; ii. 194–6.

Dinner to the next, four ranked Wardens directed Company business and were presided over by the Company Master. Only Liverymen were eligible to take up these senior positions, and men commonly served as a Warden several times once elected, assuming different responsibilities as they progressed from fourth to first Warden, and then perhaps to Master. Intended to counteract any instability resulting from the changing roster of office-holders, the Master and Wardens were advised by a group of experienced governors, known as the Court of Assistants, which was mostly composed of former Wardens. The position of Master was prestigious though financially costly, election to this role indicating that a certain level of recognisable socio-economic success had been reached. Though the Master was the figurehead of the Company, it was the Wardens who bore the brunt of corporate manage-ment, incurring their own significant expenses in dispensing hospi-tality and attending to other duties. Among other things, the Wardens conducted searches to seek out substandard drapery, controlled admis-sions to the Company, distributed alms and oversaw the Company's financial affairs. Supported by the Clerk, the Wardens were responsible for the organisation of Election Day Dinners. The production of the Dinner Book was therefore closely associated with these men, though it is not the sole source of dining information for the period.

Supplementary information relating to earlier dinners can be found in other records in the Drapers' Company Archive. Preceding the Dinner Book, the Company's Minute Books (from 1515 onwards) and Wardens' Accounts (a complete series runs from 1475 onwards) offer some insight into the form of dinners and their administration. Brief accounts of some dinners were included sporadically in the Minute Books, while disbursements of corporate funds, individual payments for goods, receipts and salaries were interspersed with other expenses in the Wardens' Accounts. In the 1530s and 1540s a handful of more complete financial reports for a few dinners were recorded in the Minute Books, but these accounts ceased after the Company relocated to the former hall of Thomas Cromwell on Throgmorton Street, having purchased it in 1543.[17] The Minute Books do not hold any information relating to dinners held between 1543 and 1564, the year the Dinner Book begins. This suggests the Book may not have been the first initiated by the Company, but was rather the second in a new series of accounts dedicated entirely to Company dinners, with a shake-up of record-keeping practices spurred by a physical relocation. The document's lack of a title page or introductory note and the rela-tively consistent entry format adds to the sense that there could have been at least one predecessor to the presenting volume. There is in

---

[17]   The Drapers' Company purchased the Throgmorton property from the Crown after Crom-well's attainder and execution. See Sarah A. Milne, 'Merchants of the City: Situating the London Estate of the Drapers' Company, c. 1540–1640' (Unpublished PhD thesis, Univer-sity of Westminster, 2016), 70–7.

fact another Dinner Book in the Drapers' Archive, but it contains only two brief accounts of Bachelors' Election Dinners in 1658 and 1662, two descriptions of royal processions through the City (in May 1660, April 1661 and November 1697), and one special entertainment held for Lord General George Monck in March 1660.[18]

Although in layout and language, the sixteenth-century Dinner Book is similar to other fair copy account books in the Drapers' Archive, its materiality is not entirely consistent with the make-up of most other journals for it was originally bound in a limp vellum cover with a fold-edge flap for protection.[19] Inside, the dinner records are arranged sequentially in chronological order and follow the charge and discharge system, reflecting the combined expenses incurred by the four Wardens in respect of the feast. Item lists are grouped under headings by type or supplier, with titles such as 'Wine', 'Spice', 'Poultry' or 'The Pewterer'. Earlier dinners are the most comprehensively detailed, while one later dinner is marked simply with a title, wholly lacking in any substantive detail.[20] Although between 1563 and 1575 there is a continuous but uneven series of accounts, after 1575 only four further dinners are included, namely the Election Dinners in 1578 and 1580, and two small Quarter Dinners in 1601 and 1602. Throughout the Dinner Book, the Election Dinners are best described. Quarter Dinners sometimes fall outside the scope of the account, reflecting their more modest nature.

In contrast to other Company accounts, it appears that the Dinner Book is unaudited. There are many incorrect footings, peculiar subtotals, and gaps in expenditure lists, suggesting bills for some items had been lost or the expected information was not provided. As a financial record, the Dinner Book could not have been terribly important. Its principal value lay elsewhere, as a supplementary reference document for the Wardens as they undertook the organisation of the Company's dinners. As a compilation of previous events, the Book most likely served as an *aide-mémoire*, intended to ensure that nothing was forgotten or overlooked in their planning. A certain level of competitiveness between incoming and outgoing Wardens can also be assumed; a document such as the Dinner Book would allow the Clerk, however new to the job, to advise Wardens on best practice. At the same time, the production of the document may have been coloured by the desire to protect against malpractice, misbehaviour and loss (especially in relation to venison pasties). Such 'surveillant' documentation was a tool for the effective stewardship of resources. The Dinner Book can be positioned as symptomatic of the broad-ranging expansion of record-keeping practices in the sixteenth century, a trend that saw the records of London's livery

18   DCA, DB2.
19   It is similar to only one other document in the Archive: DCA, DB5.
20   DCA, DB1, f.117r.

companies increase in scope and importance, propelled by a post-reformation anxiety for greater accountability.[21]

Though the Dinner Book is unusual within the Drapers' Archive, the question of how particular it is to the Company requires more attention. In the sixteenth century, most of the Great Twelve at least occasionally recorded accounts relating to their dinners piecemeal in the pages of their Wardens' Accounts and Minute Books. Useful for reasons of comparison, the Clothworkers' Company Wardens' Accounts contain records for three Election Dinners in the years 1560 to 1562.[22] With regard to the seventeenth century, more information can be found scattered through livery company archives, especially for the so-called 'lesser' companies. Two extraordinary dinners are finely rendered; these are the Merchant Taylors' reception for King James in 1607, and the Grocers' account of the Lord Mayor's Banquet in 1617.[23] Moving closer in conceit to the Drapers' Dinner Book, the Pewterers' Company hold three disjointed and thin 'Entertainment Books' (c.1609–51) which contain brief summaries of Court Dinners, Quarter Dinners, Yeomanry Banquets, and Election Feasts.[24] A further smattering of seventeenth- and early eighteenth-century dinner bills, partial accounts and papers of other companies can be consulted at the Guildhall Library.[25] None of these companies holds a document with the strategic intent or scope of the Dinner Book, which, as a compilation of detailed accounts for many consecutive years of dining, appears to stand alone.

As an account, the Dinner Book is abundant in payment details, but it does little to illuminate the ceremonies that defined the Election Dinner. This key aspect of the dinners was attended to in the Drapers' Company Minute Books where repetitive reports of these corporate set-pieces offer a clue as to the initiator of the Dinner Book. For fifty years from 1538, five consecutive Drapers' Clerks included a detailed

---

21   J. Bishop, 'The Clerk's Tale: Civic Writing in Sixteenth-Century London' in *Past & Present*, ccxxx, Issue supplement 11 (1 Nov. 2016), 112–30.

22   These accounts have been helpfully transcribed by the former Company archivist David Wickham and published by the Clothworkers in D. Wickham, *All of One Company* (privately printed, 2004).

23   Merchant Taylors, Court Minutes (GL, MS 34010/4). Grocers' Lord Mayor's Dinner reprinted in: A. Munday, *The Fishmongers' Pageant on Lord Mayors' Day, 1616: Chrysanaleia*, J. G. Nichols (ed.) (London: privately printed, 1844), 27–31. For comparison also see the seating plan and menu relating to the Lord Mayor's Dinner of 1634, organised by the Clothworkers (LMA, MSS 88.8a).

24   Pewterers, Entertainment Books and Papers, 1609–15, 1634–62, 1637–51 (GL, MS 22181, MS 7104/1, MS 22191).

25   See, for example, Armourers and Brasiers, Yeomanry Quarterly Supper Expenses Accounts, 1604–16 (GL, MS 12079/2); Barbers/Barber-Surgeons, Dinner Accounts, 1676–83, 1698–1790 (GL, MS 5271/1–4, MS 5272/1–3); Brewers, Dinner Bills, 1669–1746 (GL, MS 6818); Haberdashers, Feast Accounts, 1729–1825 (GL, MS 15871); Painter Stainers, Bills of Fare, 1743–1815 (GL, MS 30640); Skinners, Election Day Papers, 1646–1780 (GL, MS 30989, MS 31322); Tallow Chandlers, Extraordinary Dinner Expenses Book, 1705–25 (GL, MS 6170), Entertainments and Ceremonies Papers, 1624–39, 1662–75 (GL, MS 6163/1); Turners, Dinner Bills, 1751–1830, 1837–73 (GL, MS 3818, MS 24161, MS 24166); Vintners, Entertainment and Dinners Papers, 1702 (GL, MS 15378).

description of the election ritual (described below) at the end of the corporate year, amending the general outline of the 'Election Ceremony' preserved in the Ordinances of the Company to record the exact form of the ceremony in the presenting year. (A transcription of four sample narratives is included for reference in the Appendix.) This type of ceremonial record is not altogether extraordinary in the context of other companies but notable nonetheless for the consistent intensity of interest in the symbolic transferral of power from the outgoing Master and his Wardens to the incoming. The investiture ceremony involved a carefully choreographed procession at the end of dinner, including the proffering of cups of hippocras (a spiced wine) and the bestowing of garlands. The time-span of these ceremonial reports overlaps with the period covered by the Dinner Book (and its possible precursor), and the detailed narratives of election rituals act as a useful complement to the Dinner Book's straightforward practicality.[26]

Though the first of these narrative descriptions appeared years before his employment, the practice of recording the precise form of the election ceremony began in earnest with the appointment of a new and likely over-zealous Clerk, Thomas Upton, in 1538.[27] His fastidiousness may have been spurred by the need to prove himself, for Upton was initially required to serve a probation period in which it was hoped he might convince the Court of his sufficient learning, behaviour and knowledge. Fortunately for Upton, any doubts the Court nursed were dispelled. The Clerk appears to have been consistent in his custom of fully documenting the dinner rituals throughout his term, a practice that was followed by his four successors, ceasing only in 1588.[28] Based on his enthusiastic record-keeping practices, it is conceivable that Upton instituted the first Dinner Book in 1543, if such a thing existed.

Documentation relating to the election ceremonies of other companies confirms that the Great Twelve shared a common culture of dining and a concern for their orchestration. Coinciding with the Drapers' ceremonial accounts, the Grocers recorded the manner of their election ceremonies from 1556 to 1585, while other companies took a more selective approach.[29] As in the provision of the dinner itself, companies were keenly attuned to the ceremonial innovations of each other. The Drapers, for example, took a keen interest in the practices of the Merchant Taylors in 1554, while the Mercers were so intent on

26   Though the Drapers' Company Minute Book for the years 1561–7 has not survived and therefore the election ceremony for these years is not recorded.
27   DCA, MB1B, f.586. For an account of the 1522 order of ceremony, see Herbert, *The History of the Twelve Great Livery Companies*, 440–4.
28   Clerks of the Drapers' Company from 1539 to 1603: Thomas Upton (July 1539–Sept. 1546), William Bere (Sept. 1546–May 1557), Edward Messenger (May 1557–June 1569), Bartholomew Warner (July 1569–May 1587), Stephen Wilkinson (May 1587–Sept. 1603).
29   Grocers' Company, Court Minutes 1556–1591 (GL, MS11588/1). An inconsistent approach was taken by the Merchant Taylors: see Merchant Taylors, Court Minutes 1562–1574 (GL, MS34010/1).

the form of the Goldsmiths' election ceremony that they dispatched their employee 'Stockbridge' to observe it in 1567.[30] This reconnaissance led to the production of 'A view of the choosing of the Wardens of the Goldsmiths and the order thereof' contained in the Mercers' Company's Register of Writings, which instructed new officers as to the Company's specific dinner practices. Taking the form of a checklist for new Wardens, the Mercers' order of election was followed by a list of organisational items to be remembered in advance of the dinner. The account began by entreating Wardens 'to remember' to invite external guests six or seven days in advance, to 'remember' the baker, pikemonger, waterbearer, burdens of rushes, the purchase of meal, and 'four trusty servants of your own to take charge of things and to go of your own errands and business'.[31] Including a diverse range of information, much of which did not pertain directly to the dinners, the Mercers' Register of Writings acted as a sort of manual, intended to ensure that accumulated management expertise was not lost from year to year or decade to decade. A similar instinct must have underpinned the Drapers' Dinner Book and the ceremonial narratives included in the Minute Books. The clustering and consistency of documentation surrounding the Drapers' Election Dinner reflected a growing consciousness of the potential of such occasions to reinforce corporate honour.

THE ORDER OF SERVICE

Originally corresponding with the Lammas Day harvest festival, the Election Dinner of the Drapers' Company was held on the first Monday in August, but the full complement of events extended one day earlier and one day after. During the sixteenth century, festivities began on Sunday at 3pm when the Livery gathered at the Hall in their Company clothing, returning there after having heard a sermon at their patronal church, St. Michael's on Cornhill.[32] Quarterage and a dinner fee (16*d.* in the 1560s and 1570s) was then paid, and, depending on the will and purse of that year's Master and Wardens, a small informal banquet or potation was offered.[33] The next day at 9am, the Livery voted for new officers. Prior to 1573, this vote was generally made on Sunday evening or even before, but latterly pushed over into Monday for fear that the results were made known before the dinner, robbing the election ceremony of the element of surprise as those elected were

---

30   DCA, MB5, f.72; MCA, Register of Writings, ii. f.117r. Also see the order of the 1551 election reproduced in the Appendix of this volume.
31   Ibid. f.119r.
32   For a more detailed description of this order and the stipulations about the dress to be worn, see DCA, MB8, ff.113v–114r.
33   DCA, OB1, Ordinance and Oath Book, c.1460–1576.

revealed.[34] If voting occurred on Monday, after privately making their choices known, Liverymen again lined up in the courtyard of the Hall dressed for the occasion and processed together behind the Master and Wardens, two by two, sweet-smelling herbs strewn before them, to hear another sermon at church and to partake of holy communion. After contributing to the Parish poor box and repairing back to the Hall, dinner was served. The results of the election were revealed after the second course. Then, on Tuesday morning, the outgoing and incoming Masters and Wardens met in the parlour, and the new officers received keys to the Hall and its money boxes after taking oaths of office. A small group of the Company elite enjoyed another small dinner or banquet. The events ensured that the legitimacy of corporate leadership was broadcast and assented to at a range of scales.

While the parlour was the site of exclusive governance, the Drapers' great hall was used for sizeable corporate gatherings, and the Election Dinner took place in this impressively large space, likely constructed in 1535–9 by Thomas Cromwell and positioned on the first floor.[35] Following the form of a later-medieval courtyard house, the Throgmorton Hall was inward-looking, its grandeur focused on a four-sided courtyard accessed through a prominent street-facing gate. The new compact house grew in favour with urban elites only later and was rarely taken up by the companies, who preferred to reinforce the associations inferred by the perpetuation of a more 'ancient' building form.[36] Having passed through the southerly great gate, attendees of the Election Dinner gained access to the grand courtyard lined with elevated galleries and topped with symbolic statuettes and weather vanes, before being invited to progress up to the hall through the main processional staircase in the south-eastern corner of the courtyard. Overlooking the courtyard to its east, with the parlour to its north, the great hall was entered by walking along a screens passage, which ran parallel to its south wall and then by turning ninety degrees to pass under the arches of a wooden screen and to face the north end of the hall. The dinner was arranged around three tables set up to form a U-shape around an open central hearth. The high table was positioned on a dais at the furthest north end of the hall, while two larger tables ran down the longer eastern and western walls of the hall in parallel to each other.

---

[34]   For a description of the order of events after the nomination and 'secret election' was moved to Monday, see August 1574: DCA, MB8, ff.269v–270r, and August 1575: MB9, ff.49r–49v.

[35]   N. Holder, 'The Medieval Friaries of London: A Topographical and Archaeological History, Before and After the Dissolution' (Unpublished PhD thesis, University of London, 2011), 168.

[36]   B. Cherry, 'John Pollexfen's House in Walbrook' in J. Bold and E. Chaney (ed.) *English Architecture Public and Private: Essays for Kerry Downes* (London and Rio Grande: The Hambledon Press, 1993), 80–105 (90); A. F. Kelsall, 'The London House Plan in the Later Seventeenth Ccentury' in *Post-Medieval Archeology* 8 (1974), 80–9; Milne, 'Merchants of the City'; J. Schofield, *The Building of London: From the Conquest to the Great Fire* (London: Colonnade Books, 1984), 115–16.

Reflecting its status, those seated at the high table were served by the Chief Master Bachelor and five specially selected Yeomanry waiters. The high table was embellished with green cloth while the others were bare; two resplendent sideboards bearing the Company plate upon fine tablecloths marked with a 'D' were also positioned near to the special table.[37] Behind it, a decoratively painted wall with a north-facing round oriel window separated the hall from the parlour, which constituted a smaller gallery space and connected to the jewel house and the book-house (also referred to as the hippocras house).[38] Symbolic imagery was therefore clustered around the high dais end of the great hall, reinforcing the honour of those seated there.

After two courses, the outgoing Master and his Wardens retired out of the main hall, usually into the parlour, and organised themselves to re-enter with garlands and cups of hippocras, preparing themselves to make the election results publically known. Firstly, the Master re-entered with a garland' (a special cap) on his head, a cupbearer and minstrels before him. Having made a show of tendering his garland at both ends of the high table, the outgoing Master settled the garland on the head of the new Master and made a toast to him. The election of the four new Wardens was announced in a similar fashion, with a great deal more processing around the hall and interruption by the minstrels but with the focus of attention turned to the second and third tables. Performative moments of jest were expected, with Wardens deliberately offering their garlands to those unable or unsuitable to take up office, tendering the symbols of office to female guests or to elite men from outside the Company. These 'playful' exchanges might be seen to represent external endorsement of the corporate patriarchy, though Phythian-Adams helpfully noted that civic ritual in the late medieval period was 'lived rather than studied or articulated analytically'.[39]

The repetitive nature of election ceremonies was a key component of their stabilising intent and changes to the status quo were treated with attention in the Drapers' records.[40] A clear upturn in hierarchical language in the ceremonial accounts is discernible from the middle of the sixteenth century. Bows or 'obeisances' to those seated at the high table were first noted in 1555, while two years later the increasingly

[37] DCA, MB13, f.43r, f.44r; RA6, 1612–13, f.19.
[38] DCA, WA5, 1569–70, f.7v, f.9r; 1580-1, f.3r.
[39] C. Phythian-Adams, *Desolation of a City* (Cambridge: Cambridge University Press, 1979), 170; C. Phythian-Adams, 'Ceremony and the Citizen: The Communal Year at Coventry 1450–1550' in P. Clark and P. Slack (ed.) *Crisis and Order in English Towns 1500–1700* (London: Routledge, 1972), 57–85.
[40] For example, in 1576, the Clerk reported that: 'The open election of the new master was not *as in times past* for that our master being blind could not do *as in time past.*' (emphasis added). On this occasion he remained seated, receiving the garland placed on a cushion 'between his hands' before directing others to perform his duties on his behalf (DCA, MB9, f.49v).

elaborate manner of vacating the main hall after the election ceremony was described:

> all the four Wardens orderly reporting to the upper end of the high table and standing in course one by another before the old Master they had executed their turns made low obeisance and reverence to the highest guest at the middle of the table and the rest of the lower end and likewise to the old Master and gave thanks and departed.[41]

This type of honorific language and action continued to imbue the accounts for the next twenty years, coinciding with a greater cultural consciousness of codes of manners.[42] Important guests at the high table were referred to as 'superiors', Masters and Wardens became 'Right Worshipful', and the form of livery to be worn received greater yearly attention.[43] The maintenance of status and authority depended far more on these extraordinary ritual acts of symbolic submission than it did on the everyday interactions between different members during the corporate year.

The matter of who should be afforded the privilege of observing these investiture ceremonies through attendance at the dinner was the point of some debate. The exclusivity of Election Dinners needed to be protected if attendance was to be seen as an advantage of membership, but Company leaders weighed up such concerns against aspirations to strengthen corporate connections with an influential network of associates through participation in the dinner. Invitations to Election Dinners routinely extended beyond the Livery of the Company to include members of other companies serving in civic capacities, Aldermen, Sheriffs or the Lord Mayor, as well as to those of the courtly or political elite, and sometimes their wives. These prominent guests were seated at the high table, while the second and third tables, positioned easterly and westerly respectively, accommodated Liverymen of the Drapers' Company, often with at least one Warden assigned to each table. The account of the 1564 Election Dinner includes an edited list of those in attendance that year, providing a sample of the range and distribution of invited external guests.[44] In all eighty-nine people were served dinner, with twenty-five at the high table and sixty-four equally divided between the second and third tables. Among others, the high table accommodated Grocer and Lord Mayor, Sir John Whyte, Grocer and Sheriff, Alderman Edward Jakman and his wife, as well as Sir Richard Sackville, cousin of Queen Elizabeth, Sir Thomas Offley, Merchant Taylor, Master of the

---

41   DCA, MB5, f.187; DCA, MB7, f.16.
42   A. Bryson, *From Courtesy to Civility: Changing Codes of Conduct in Early Modern England* (Oxford University Press: Oxford, 1998), 12.
43   Johnson, *History,* iii. 200.
44   Useful comparisons can be found for the years 1516 (DCA, MB1A, ff.26–8), 1521 (DCA, MB1A, ff.182–3), 1538 (DCA, MB1B, f.576), and 1539 (DCA, MB1B, f.608).

Staple and former Lord Mayor, and Lady Granado, likely the widow of Sir Jacques Granado, former Equerry of the Stable. This mix of the City elite with a select number of courtly external guests was typical for such dinners, as exemplified by Henry Machyn's account of the Merchant Taylors' Election Dinner of 1562.[45]

While responsibility for the selection of external guests rested with the Wardens, the Court intermittently issued resolutions that sought to moderate affairs. In 1530, the Court advised that 'according to old custom' the sisters and wives of Drapers were to be invited to the Election Dinner, but 'no outward guests' were permitted. Invitees to the Quarter Dinners were to be decided upon 'at the Wardens' pleasure'.[46] In 1548 and 1554 the Court restricted invitations to citizens of London only, excluding 'strangers' without membership of the City companies.[47] Two years later this decision was revisited and the Wardens were given freedom to invite strangers such as Sir Roger Cholmley, former Recorder of London and Lord Chief Justice of the King's Bench, 'or such like'.[48] These changes in policy were characteristic of a wider corporate anxiety around the extent to which it was appropriate and profitable to include outsiders in these events, partially in respect to the difficulties of negotiating precedence as internal and external hierarchies collided inside the hall, but also in relation to concerns over expenditure and exclusivity. The Mercers' checklist reminded Wardens that, '[depending on] what number you would rest upon ... stranger guests to be bidden six or seven days before your supper'.[49]

At Election Dinners, competing courtly, civic, and corporate orders of precedence were negotiated through the assignment of guests to particular tables and then the seating arrangements within them. The livery companies were not alone in their sensitivity to such matters, for participants in the meetings and dinners of English Town Corporations and the London Inns of Court were also increasingly becoming preoccupied with the placing of individuals in relation to their status or power.[50] Corporate and personal honour were closely guarded, and arrangements at dinner did not always satisfy all parties, with complications relating to the correct order of seating evident in the Drapers'

45   H. Machyn, *A London Provisioner's Chronicle, 1550–1563*, R. W. Bailey, M. Miller and C. Moore (ed.) (University of Michigan), published online http://quod.lib.umich.edu/m/machyn/ [accessed online 3 Feb. 2015], Merchant Taylors – f.151v, Goldsmiths – f.138r, f.150v, Barber-Surgeons – f.153r, Grocers – f.56v.
46   DCA, MB1B, f.386.
47   DCA, MB4, f.51; MB5, f.72.
48   DCA, MB5, f.181.
49   MCA, Register of Writings, ii. f.119r.
50   R. Tittler, 'Seats of Honor, Seats of Power: The Symbolism of Public Seating in the English Urban Community, c. 1560–1620' in *Albion: A Quarterly Journal Concerned with British Studies* 24, no. 2 (1992), 205–23; W. Prest, 'Readers' Dinners and the Culture of the Early Modern Inns of Court' in J. E. Archer, E. Goldring and S. Knight (ed.) *The Intellectual and Cultural World of the Early Modern Inns of Court* (Manchester: Manchester University Press, 2010), 107–23.

records.[51] Tensions ran especially high when Company officers or Assistants rejected City offices, as they frequently did, but were still entitled to a seat closer to the centre of the high dais simply on account of their nomination. On one occasion, after consulting City officials and other companies on their practice, it was ruled that prosperous Drapers who had rejected a civic position would sit just below any junior members who served as Aldermen at dinner. At this time, the number of men in this category was so plentiful that their exact order below the Aldermen was left open for negotiation. Those involved were advised to seat themselves so that they might 'receive better contentment by their own agreement and placing of themselves' and more broadly that the Company would maintain 'loving and brotherly respect of every of them'.[52] Other aspects of dining furniture and material culture supported the communication of status. The flurry of activity surrounding a new Master's chair inscribed with the Company's arms and the upgrading of the garlands used in investiture ceremonies are only two examples of a glut of self-fashioning that characterised much of this period.[53] In contrast, at the second and third tables diners continued to sit on long unadorned wooden benches. In structuring social relations through carefully considered seating arrangements and investing in greater material embellishment of the high table, the Election Dinner was intended to model an ordered society where honour was visibly and spatially enacted.[54]

While women were excluded from participating in the governance of companies and from holding office, they were not devoid of agency or honour in the corporate system. One expression of this was in their attendance as guests at dinners as widows, wives, and daughters. A description of an elaborate Election Dinner in 1515, held in the old St. Swithin's Hall, recorded three tables of women positioned in two rooms connected the main hall.[55] Dinners in the early sixteenth century noted tables for ladies, gentlewomen and maidens, and it seems a child joined the maidens in 1530.[56] In the early 1560s wives of the Assistants and other elite women external to the Company were seated within

---

[51]   DCA, OB1 and OB2; DCA, MB10, ff.407–9; DCA, MB13, f.80r, f.81r. For context, see A. J. Fletcher, 'Honour, Reputation and Local Office-holding in Elizabethan and Stuart England' in A. J. Fletcher and J. Stevenson (ed.) *Order and Disorder in Early Modern England* (Cambridge: Cambridge University Press, 1987), 92–115; R. Kelso, *The Doctrine of the English Gentleman in the Sixteenth Century* (Urbana: University of Illinois Press, 1929).

[52]   DCA, MB13, f.332r, f.336r. Also see discussion of the Goldsmiths' Election Dinner of 1612 in J. Ward, *Metropolitan Communities: Trade Guilds, Identity and Change in Early Modern London* (Stanford: Stanford University Press, 1997), 85.

[53]   DCA, WA5, 1569–70, f.7v, f.9r.

[54]   R. M. Berger, *The Most Necessary Luxuries: The Mercers' Company of Coventry, 1550–1680* (University Park: Pennsylvania State University Press, 1993), 204.

[55]   DCA, MB1A, f.183.

[56]   Ibid. ff.181–2; DCA, MB1B, f.391, f.410, ff.420–1, f.471, f.575. The child is inferred from DCA, MB1B, f.391.

Introduction

the great hall, but in the second half of the decade they were seated separately at a special table positioned either within the parlour or a gallery.[57] The practice of providing a specific space outside the main hall for women to dine in continued through to 1570, though it seems the attendance of wives and widows at the Election Dinner was not always routine. The presence of Wardens' wives at smaller Quarter Day Dinners was however more or less assumed.[58]

Despite the careful negotiations relating to the allocation of dinner invitations, some lesser events were more informal, and there is evidence that dinners could even be prone to intrusion. In 1564, for example, the Drapers' second table on Tuesday, the day after the Election Dinner, included guests 'bidden and some unbidden', though this did not seem to cause alarm.[59] Incursions into Monday's Election Dinner, however, would have been perceived as a threat to the corporate ideal of a harmonious and ordered household. Such incidents were treated with concern across the companies. In 1611, the Barber-Surgeons unhappily complained that 'children, servants, apprentices' as well as other uninvited attendees to their dinner had caused 'much disorder' to the 'disparagement and discredit' of the Company.[60] In 1612, the Carpenters ruled against any external guests and warned their porters to keep a tighter watch on those admitted. The Beadle was especially instructed not to invite his friends and neighbours into the Hall at the time of the dinner. Later, in 1634, the Company ordered a reduction in the number of servants in attendance at corporate meetings, recalling that 'great disorder used to be by the admission and letting in of young men into the Hall to wait and attend upon their masters at feasts and dinners'.[61] Similar rhetoric was deployed by the Drapers in 1629, when the Company noted that, at every meeting (and dinner) of the Court of Assistants, 'of late years' there had been a 'needless number of hangers on'. These people claimed to be employed on the business of the Company, serving those attending the hall, but had caused 'unnecessary expenses and many abuses'.[62] The Dinner Book noted the positioning of employees at strategic thresholds; one porter was stationed

57 DCA, DB1, ff.12v–12r, f.41v.
58 For confirmation of their attendance at the Election Dinner after 1570, see DCA, MB8, f.83r, f.93v; MB9, f.19v, f.274v.
59 DCA, DB1, f.14r.
60 C. Chamberland, 'Honour, Brotherhood, and the Corporate Ethos of London Barber-Surgeons Company' in *Journal of the History of Medicine and Allied Sciences* 64 (2009), 300–32 (321). Giles identified a similar rhetoric in the York Guildhall of St. Anthony's where, in 1622, the Court decried that 'great numbers of people have resorted unto the same feasts and very many not invited or bidden to the same'. So many flocked to the hall that, 'by such disorder', many of the invited guests had to be turned away for lack of space. K. Giles, 'Guildhalls and Social Identity in Late Medieval and Early Modern York, c.1350–1630' 2 vols (Unpublished PhD thesis, University of York, 1999), i. 181.
61 T. Girtin, *The Golden Ram: A Narrative History of the Clothworkers' Company, 1528–1958* (London: privately printed, 1958), 185–6.
62 DCA, MB13, f.230r.

at the gate, two at the foot of the staircase while another kept the main hall door.[63] Meanwhile, in 1604–5 a new door was installed at the top of the main stairs of Drapers' Hall, leading up into the hall and screen gallery, presumably an increased security measure to protect against the threat of incursion.[64] Around the same time, as Sleigh-Johnson has reported, a similar addition was made to the Merchant Taylors' hall, a new door designed to 'prevent many annoyances which happened by reason as the same lieth too common to all commers'.[65] Disorder was to be avoided at all costs.

The pressure to maintain standards at City dinners is evident in the measures taken to ensure that the quality of goods was controlled and the allocation of food monitored. The Dinner Book recorded that in 1564 one of the Warden's servants was given the task of keeping 'a book of all the meat and vessels that was spent out of the house by whom it was sent, and to whom it went', while another servant of a Warden was positioned in charge of the drinks in the pantry, presumably deemed to be more trustworthy than a general labourer.[66] When a member of a company was elected to serve as Lord Mayor, that company took special responsibility for the provision of the annual 'Lord Mayor's Dinner' held in Guildhall. If Election Dinners are taken to be occasions for strict surveillance and quality control, this City dinner should be regarded thus even more so, for competition between the companies was common. In 1588, when Draper Martin Calthorp was invested as Lord Mayor, eight senior members of the Company were nominated to oversee the receiving of the poultry for the feast, ensuring that this be 'good and sweet'. These elite men also acted as Stewards to individual tables, making sure that the food assigned for their table was actually delivered to it and not 'bribed and conveyed away'.[67] At Drapers' Hall, the slovenly and disrespectful service of one Election Dinner was criticised in 1629. Food was reportedly 'unmannerly and unfittly' taken away from guests before they had even reached halfway through the course. This left only an embarrassment of emptiness on display at tables. Servants were suspected of attempting to save this food for themselves. To correct this shameful attack on corporate hospitality, the servants were reprimanded and Wardens were given strict instruction to see that no food was taken from tables until the diners had finished and had risen from the tables. Only the Under-Cook and Scullion of the kitchen were to be allowed a dish allocated directly by the Cook for their dinners. After dinner, food remaining on the side tables was

---

63 DCA, DB1, f.15v.
64 DCA, WA 1604–5, f.23.
65 As quoted in N. J. Sleigh-Johnson, 'The Merchant Taylors Company of London 1580–1645, with special reference to politics and government' (Unpublished PhD thesis, University of London, 1989), 67.
66 DCA, DB1, f.15v.
67 DCA, MB10, f.334.

to be divided between the Beadle, Porter, Butler, and Scowerer, who were given permission to eat in the hall, provided they were seated in order, presided over by the Beadle.[68]

A variety of musicians and actors entertained guests during dinners. A trio of minstrels, often playing a harp, lute, and shawm, was involved in the election ceremony and played at interludes, sometimes from the step of the high dais. Official musicians of the City, the Waites of London performed frequently, playing diverse instruments at dinners in the 1560s and 1570s, as they did for other livery companies.[69] A small group of boy choristers, 'the Children of Westminster', sang in 1566.[70] In October 1658, it was reported that the City's trumpeters, mistakenly assuming their presence was required, 'came of their own accord and sounded in the yard but were rebuked for it, it being not allowed', Cromwell, the Lord Protector, having died just a month before.[71] Reinforcing the performative nature of the dinner, and the hall as a kind of theatre, the custom of employing a company of actors to present a play in the hall at the time of the Election Dinner was long established in the Drapers' Company, and can be traced back to the early fifteenth century, when their first hall was acquired. In the first half of the sixteenth century, the Drapers tended to hire companies of about four actors with royal or aristocratic patronage, but no players are referred to in the Dinner Book suggesting that plays had fallen out of use by the 1560s.[72] Payments were however made to 'them that made speeches at the bringing in of the boar's head' and specifically 'to the child who took pains therein' in 1570.[73] The election ceremony itself seems to have been entertainment enough by this time.

THE THEATRE OF HOSPITALITY

The miscellany of the food and drink served on tables added to the visual drama of election events. For William Harrison, writing in

---

[68]   DCA, MB13, f.230r.
[69]   Waits and musicians are noted: DCA, MB1B, f.389, f.417, f.478, f.489; DB1, f.8r, f.48r, f.72v, f.97v, f.121v, f.123r, f.126r. See also C. M. Clode (ed.) *Memorials of the Guild of Merchant Taylors of the Fraternity of St. John the Baptist in the City of London* (London: 1875), 120–3; Wickham, *All of One Company*, 46. For a discussion of early seventeenth-century corporate entertainments at dinners, see G. Heaton and J. Knowles, '"Entertainment Perfect": Ben Jonson and Corporate Hospitality' in *The Review of English Studies*, new series, liv. no. 217 (2003), 587–600.
[70]   DCA, DB1, f.48r. They also performed at the Parish Clerks' dinner in 1562: E. W. Brayley, *The Beauties of England and Wales: London and Middlesex* (London: W. Wilson, 1814), 441.
[71]   DCA, DB2, unfoliated.
[72]   For full discussion, see Anne Lancashire, *London Civic Theatre: City Drama and Pageantry from Roman Times to 1558* (Cambridge: Cambridge University Press, 2002), 71–80.
[73]   DCA, DB1, f.98v.

1577, the luxuriousness and variety of the food on offer at an English merchant's feast could be quite overwhelming. He enthused:

> it is a world to see what great provision is made of all manner of delicate meats, from every quarter of the country, wherein, beside that they are often comparable herein to the nobility of the land ... In such cases ... jellies of all colours, mixed with a variety in the representation of sundry flowers, herbs, trees, forms of beasts, fish, fowls, and fruits, and thereunto marchpane wrought with no small curiosity, tarts of divers hues, and sundry denominations, conserves of old fruits, foreign and home-bred, suckets, codinacs, marmalades, marchpane, sugar-bread, gingerbread, florentines, wild fowls, venison of all sorts, and sundry outlandish confections, altogether seasoned with sugar, do generally bear the sway...[74]

Harrison's remarks drew attention to the merchants' conspicuous consumption of widely sourced goods as well as the wonder such a manifold spread was intended to induce. As imports entering the City more than tripled between the 1560s and the 1600s, merchants of the Great Twelve companies positioned themselves in close proximity to a diversity of goods arriving at the Port of London and possessed the skills to negotiate a good price for items required for corporate use.[75] But, while the Wardens of the Drapers' Company were advantageously positioned in relation to luxury imports acquired through new or expanded trading routes, the Dinner Book indicates that service of the feast tended towards the conventional and conservative. Dinners were broadly organised in accordance with the prescriptions of contemporary diet books and only slowly incorporated new food items.[76] As with the election ceremonies, continuity was prized and legible changes to the status quo were suppressed.

In line with other elite dinners of the period, sweet and savoury dishes were intermixed and an emphasis was placed on game.[77] The sequence of foods served at the Election Dinner of 1564 provides a good template for the other dinners contained in the Dinner Book. The first course consisted of brawn, boiled and roast capons, swans, venison pasties, and pikes. Custards, taking the form of a flan or tart, were presented as part of this course. While the first course frequently centred on roasted red meat like brawn, beef or venison, the second course was smaller and lighter, consisting of quails, sturgeon, and

---

[74] W. Harrison, *The Description of England*, G. Edelen (ed.) (2nd edn, Toronto: Dover Publications, 1994), 129.

[75] B. Dietz, 'Overseas Trade and Metropolitan Growth' in A. L. Bier and R. Finlay (ed.) *London 1500–1700: The Making of a Metropolis* (London: Longman, 1986), 115–40.

[76] See J. Fitzpatrick (ed.) *Three Sixteenth-century Dietaries* (Manchester: Manchester University Press, 2017).

[77] J. Fitzpatrick, 'Diet and Identity in Early Modern Dietaries and Shakespeare: The Inflections of Nationality, Gender, Social Rank and Age' in *Shakespeare Studies*, xlii (2014), 75–90.

marchpanes in 1564. The final 'banquet' course was a lighter affair still, focused on the drinking of hippocras and sweet items.

Given the size and number of items served during the first and second courses as well as the quantity of guests sitting around comparatively narrow table boards, it seems unlikely that all the dishes could have fitted on the table at once, yet diners were expected to be able to choose from anything on offer, so the constant attention of servers was necessary. English playwright Thomas Nashe observed of his countrymen: 'we must have our tables furnished like poulter[ers] stalls ... Lord, what a coyle have we, with this course and that course, removing this dish higher, setting another lower, and taking away a third.'[78] With such abundant quantities of food, a sense of order was critical to proceedings, and food was apportioned in relation to status. What and how much of it was allocated to whom mattered greatly, as did the visual impression of generosity and wealth. Unsurprisingly, the Dinner Book confirms that the high table was always given priority in respect of the value of food served.[79] For instance, in 1564 fifteen swans were presented at the high table, only two to the second table, and none to the third. One swan was sent 'abroad into the town' to the home of Lord John Graye.[80] Although there was some variation in the sort of food served, overall quantities or 'messes' served to those both at the high and lesser tables were similar.

Some items were presented in unusual forms in order to attract special attention, though not all 'show' items that resembled food were edible. For example, in 1570, a Wax Chandler was commissioned to make a model of a boar's head (see below), the helm and crest of the Company and the Company arms too. These wax pieces were likely presented at the beginning of each course and placed on the high table.[81] A forerunner of marzipan, marchpanes featured in the second course and were often fashioned into models ('sotelties') or presented as highly decorated flat disks. The possibilities for embellishment were described by Hugh Platt in 1609 as he instructed his readers to:

> garnish [the marchpane] with pretty conceits, as birds and beasts being cast out of standing moulds. Stick long comfits upright in it, cast biscuit and caraways in it, and so serve it; gild it before you serve it: you may also print off this marchpane paste in your moulds for banqueting dishes. And of this paste our comfit makers at this day make their letters, knots, Arms, escutcheons, beasts, birds and other fancies.[82]

---

[78] T. Nashe, *The Anatomy of Absurdity* (London, 1589), as quoted in L. Picard, *Elizabeth's London: Everyday Life in Elizabethan London* (New York: St Martin's Press, 2004), 179.

[79] There could however be some variation. For example, at the 1568 Election Dinner the high table was served four 'double' messes, the second table was served one double mess and four single messes, and the third table was given one double mess and seven single messes. It is not clear why the second table was served so scantily in this year.

[80] DCA, DB1, f.13v, f.16v.

[81] Ibid. f.98v.

[82] H. Platt, *Delightes for Ladies* (London: Humfrey Lownes, 1609), ff.21r–21v.

Comfit-maker and sugar baker, Balthazar Sanchez, supplied march-panes of all sizes alongside cinnamon, ginger, orange, coriander, and clove-infused comfits to the Drapers from 1565 to 1578.[83] Allegedly arriving in the royal entourage of King Philip in 1554, Sanchez was one of several Spanish confectioners who arrived in England in the sixteenth century, bringing with them the secrets of producing these fashionable and luxurious sweetmeats. Most conspicuously he supplied pineapple comfits in 1568.[84] Contemporary chronicler, William Bedwell considered Sanchez to be 'the first confectioner or comfit maker and grane master of all that professe that trade in this kingdom'.[85]

Marking the end of the dinner, the banquet course was consumed standing in the hall, the high table having been folded away, allowing for more informal conversation and the possibility of further entertainment.86 This sweet course was centred on the drinking of hippocras, a spiced wine mostly made in-house by the Butler but sometimes bought in. A small room, also referred to as the 'hippocras house', was situated behind the dais and used for the storage of this high-status drink, which filled the cups used in the election ceremony and was partaken of more liberally at the end of dinner. In 1564 three servants (two men and one woman) were stationed in the 'hippocras house' and charged with keeping various types of drink, spicebreads, fruits and green, yellow, red and crimson wafers for the banquet, representing the range of items typically served alongside the hippocras. Fruit such as pears, plums and apples as well as various nuts could also be served at this time.[87]

Beyond their use in the banquet, home-grown fruits such as apples, gooseberries, barberries, cherries, pears, and plums were well-used in cooking sauces and in pies, adding to the sweet and sour flavour of dishes. Filberts grown in the Drapers' own garden were noted in 1564, though it is highly likely that more fruits from the Throgmorton Hall garden would have been utilised in the making of the dinner than were recorded. According to John Stow, the Drapers' productive great garden had been created by Thomas Cromwell.[88] Its reputation is suggested by a report that a servant of one of the King's courtiers demanded a damson plum tree be taken out of the garden in order for it to be set up instead in the King's own garden.[89] The Drapers' garden already claimed roses, gooseberry, and plum trees, white thorn and privet hedges as well as

83   DCA, DB1, f.24v, f.95v, f.128v.
84   Ibid. f.69r.
85   J. Thirsk, *Food in Early Modern England: Phases, Fads, Fashions 1500–1760* (London: Hambledon Continuum, 2006), 321, 325; *Oxford DNB*; Bedwell's *History of Tottenham* (1631), as quoted in C. Berridge, *The Almshouses of London* (Ashford: Ashford Press Pub., 1987), 1.
86   DCA, DB1, ff.13r–13v.
87   Ibid. f.16r, f.128v.
88   J. Stow, *A Survey of London, reprinted from the text of 1603, 2 Vols.* C. L. Kingsford (ed.) (Oxford: Clarendon Press, 1908), i. 89.
89   DCA, MB1C, f.395r.

a herb garden when it was purchased by the Company, but the Court elected to continue to invest in it.[90] Strawberry, damask rose, coriander, thyme, hyssop, and rosemary plants were all purchased in the second half of the sixteenth century to furnish the garden.[91] Access to the Drapers' garden and the distribution of its produce was a near continual bone of contention for the Court. In the 1580s it was decided that fruit, flowers and herbs were to be used only for 'dressing of meat and drink for such honest persons of the fellowship' during recreation in the garden or at Company dinners.[92] In the 1590s, eighteen new apple trees, two 'pear plum' trees, four cherry trees, three filbert trees, and three unidentified trees were planted.[93] In 1607–8, 142 bay trees were set up alongside four plum trees, one apricot and three other new trees.[94] No doubt these trees proved a worthy investment at the time of the dinner. Vegetables were absent from the garden, and indeed were only minimally used in Election Day Dinner. Appearing in the lists of purchased goods in the Dinner Book, carrots, cucumbers, onions, radishes, 'salad herbs', and spinach seem to have been purchased from local producers rather than cultivated in-house.

Although some suppliers are named in the Dinner Book, a fair proportion of goods were purchased from unnamed providers, likely acquired at any one of London's markets. The Stocks Market was most convenient to the Hall and specialised in fish and meat, though no specific markets are mentioned in the accounts.[95] Many of the named individuals suppliers were returned to year on year. Cakes and buns were purchased from Joan Wall at Abchurch Lane for nearly every dinner detailed in the Dinner Book.[96] Key suppliers could even be prefixed with a possessive pronoun 'our' to indicate a pre-existing relationship. Robert Mason, 'our Poulterer', was a member of the Drapers' Company, while William Smyth, 'our Grocer', was a tenant of the Company in Cheapside.[97] Alongside ale and beer frequently purchased from the Company's tenants, Gascon, French, and Rhenish wines were served during the dinner, while fortified wines such as sack, muscadel, and malmsey, originating in the Iberian Peninsula or the Mediterranean, would have been on offer during the sweet banquet.[98] Other imported goods such as currants, dates, and prunes were routinely featured as

---

90   Ibid. ff.383r–383v.
91   DCA, RA4, 1556–7, f.11r; RA5, 1571–2, f.8v; RA5, 1595–4, f.22v, ff.23r–23v.
92   DCA, MB1C, ff.383r–383v.
93   DCA, RA5, 1595–4, f.22v, ff.23r–23v.
94   DCA, RA6, 1607–8, ff.13–14.
95   For more details, see *Hugh Alley's Caveat: The Markets of London in 1598*, I. Archer, C. Barron and V. Harding (ed.) (London: London Topographical Society, 1988).
96   DCA, DB1, f.6v, f.26v, f.46v, f.59v, f.80v, f.95v, f.120r, f.122r, f.124v, f.128r, f.130r.
97   Ibid. f.5v, f.25r, f.58r, f.69v, f.70r, f.92v, f.94r, f.95r, f.103v, f.104v, f.109v, f.120v, f.122r, f.125r, f.128v, f.130r.
98   Martyn, a tenant at the Bull in Smithfield, was particularly regular in his provision of ale (for example, DCA, DB1, f.26v).

part of the dinner. Olives were purchased intermittently. Lemons were used alongside oranges to dress meat and fish.

In spite of the range of items employed in the making of the dinner, the focus was always on high-status meats that were fitting for the quality of the guests. Brawn, likely of a tame boar, was served with some regularity, often purchased 'ready-sodden' or pre-boiled and afterwards gilded by a painter to fit it for presentation at the table. In 1565, a boar was selected and fattened up in East London (St. Katherine's) in advance of the election. Boiled boars' heads could be restuffed with meat, laced with mustard and dressed up so as to act as one of the centrepieces of the dinner. At the Drapers' dinner of 1570, the payment to the Wax Chandler for reconstituting a model of a boar's head, possibly having used the boiled head of a real boar as a base, and its subsequent bringing in by a child actor, suggests the level of prestige ascribed to this item.[99] Swans were popular for their distinguished associations, though prices in the Dinner Book indicate that a single boar cost as much as ten swans in the mid-1560s. In 1564, eighteen swans were purchased for £5, and oats were supplied to feed them, suggesting they were kept alive at Drapers' Hall in advance of the dinner.[100] Swans seem to have fallen from favour by the 1570s, but on the other hand, offal was becoming more of a delicacy in England around this time, and neats tongue baked in butter prominently appears in Drapers' dinners from 1575.[101] Joan Thirsk has argued that early modern households developed a taste for veal in this period, and that it was in high demand in London. Although the Dinner Book includes a few notations relating to the meat, it was not a staple for the Drapers, being served only occasionally at secondary dinners or on the lower tables.[102] The Company's consumption of capons, pullets, partridges, turkeys, larks, geese, and pigeons was fairly consistent throughout the 1560s and 1570s. Excepting salmon, fish was considered to be inferior to meat and was not served frequently at the dinners, unless they coincided with a fish day.[103] Somewhat remarkably, the Drapers ensured the provision of fresh and pickled sturgeon in most years. This fish was a sought-after and expensive product, which was often imported from the Baltic countries. Mr Blage of the King's Head at New Fish Street was an important supplier of both sturgeon and hippocras to

---

[99]   In 1521, Wynkyn de Worde published a song to accompany the bringing in of a boar's head at a prominent Christmas dinner. The dish traditionally was the first to be served on the day amid much fanfare. Wynkyn de Worde, *Christmasse Carolles* (1521), as quoted in P. Brears, *All the King's Cooks: The Tudor Kitchen of King Henry VIII at Hampton Court Palace* (2nd edn, London: Souvenir Press, 2011).

[100] For the swans, see DCA, DB1, f.5v. For the boar, see DCA, DB1, f.24r.

[101] P. Lloyd, 'The Changing Status of Offal' in *Food, Culture & Society*, xv. Issue 1 (2012), 61–75.

[102] Thirsk, *Food in Early Modern England*, 184.

[103] DCA, DB1, f.3r.

the Company for several years.[104] Reflecting their status, sturgeons were gilded for the 1566 Election Dinner, and flowers were purchased specifically to garnish them in 1564.[105] Isinglass, a derivative of sturgeon, was used in the making of jellies, which were almost certainly moulded into diverse shapes and sizes, and also gilded for presentation at four dinners in the 1560s.[106]

The wide-reaching mercantile connections of many members of the Drapers' Company cannot have failed to benefit the Wardens as they sought to acquire all the foodstuffs and drink necessary for the dinner. Although it is hard to trace direct links between their commercial activity and the Drapers' dinner table, it is clear that Liverymen and Wardens of the Drapers' Company were closely involved in a number of trading companies in the sixteenth century, most particularly the Merchant Adventurers of London (established 1407), the Spanish Company (established 1530 and again in 1577), the Muscovy Company (established 1555) and the Eastland Company (established 1579).[107] One indication of the strength of these connections can be found in 1557 when the Drapers' Hall was used by the Muscovy Company to host an important dinner with the Russian ambassador, marking the end of a period of negotiations regarding Anglo-Russian trade. While the Muscovy Company had its own base in the port of London, the trading company held that Drapers' Hall provided the more appropriate setting for an impressive show of hospitality, with two principal members of the Drapers' Company leading the preparations as Muscovy investors.[108] Despite intensifying global connections and their proximity to risky 'adventures', Wardens preferred their dinners to adhere to well-established models of service. In fact, it seems that corporate culture drew ever more consciously on the Company's 'ancient' origins in the face of substantive change.[109] At Election Dinners, the fare served at tables a hundred years earlier would have been broadly similar to that served in the 1560s.

The most obvious example of this culinary conservatism was the focus on meat, and although brawn, sturgeon and poultry were served, in terms of significance, venison trounced them all. The ultimate status symbol at any dinner, attention to the acquisition, treatment, and disbursement of the meat bordered on obsessional in the Dinner Book. Sourced through their extended networks, outgoing Wardens were expected to provide as many red deer (bucks) as possible to mark the culmination of their term, the number of bucks acquired being a

104 Ibid. f.4r, f.4v, f.24v, f.45v, f.59r, f.71v, f.95v, f.106r.
105 Ibid. f.9r, f.48r.
106 Ibid. f.25r, f.46r, f.58v, f.70r.
107 Johnson, *History*, ii. 454–60.
108 Ibid. 185; S. Alford, *London's Triumph: Merchant Adventurers and the Tudor City* (London: Allen Lane, 2017), 88–90.
109 Orlin, *Locating Privacy*, 150.

point of honour. The position of the Drapers' dinner in August, the height of the hunting season, no doubt aided the acquisition of bucks and stags. As the Dinner Book details exactly who sent gifts to which Wardens, the Company's connections with the country and courtly elite are quite clearly represented, though bucks could also be purchased directly from hunting grounds around London.[110] Plainly the gifting of food was still a widely practised means of social exchange during the term of the Dinner Book.[111]

The quantity and type of incoming and outgoing meat was carefully recorded, allowing for some comparison across the companies. In total, in the eight years between 1564 and 1572, an average of twenty-two bucks were received on account of the Drapers' Election Dinner. Although this was a respectable number, the Drapers apparently lagged behind some of the other great companies, whose quota could rise even higher when a company member served as Lord Mayor. When one of the Merchant Taylors served as Lord Mayor in 1562, the Company's Election Dinner was furnished with sixty bucks and four stags.[112] In 1567–8, when a Mercer served as Lord Mayor, John Isham, Renter Warden for that Company, 'welcomed the opportunity to advertise [his] status' by laying out all the bucks he had sourced in a gallery within the Company Hall. He invited 'diverse of his company' to view all thirty-three of them.[113] In contrast, the Clothworkers' accounts suggest only seven bucks were presented at the 1560 Election Dinner when their Master was Lord Mayor, and twelve were acquired the year after in 1562.[114] In the 'ordinary' year of 1567, the Drapers secured forty bucks and stags, a total achieved through a collective effort, for the greatest number acquired by any one Draper in that year was only nine bucks and one stag.[115] In 1565–6 and 1578–9, when the mayoralty was held by a Draper, the Dinner Book intriguingly withheld any detail regarding the acquisition and allocation of bucks.

In advance of dinners, haunches of meat from the bucks were cooked in tough rye-based pastry 'coffins', which could reach up to one metre in length, ensuring the meat inside remained succulent and tender. The outer pastry was not eaten, with the meat inside spooned out after breaking through the patterned pastry lid. Owing to the size of pasties and the quantity of meat, bucks often had to be cooked

---

110 Bridgestock Park (DCA, DB1, f.72v); Eltham (DCA, DB1, f.98r).
111 Archer, *Pursuit of Stability*, 117; Orlin, *Locating Privacy*, 139. For more discussion about significance of early modern gift-giving, see I. K. Ben-Amos, *The Culture of Giving: Informal Support and Gift-Exchange in Early Modern England* (Cambridge: Cambridge University Press, 2008); F. Heal, *The Power of Gifts: Gift Exchange in Early Modern England* (Oxford: Oxford University Press, 2014); C. Woolgar, 'Gifts of Food in Late Medieval England' in *Journal of Medieval History*, xxxvii. no. 1 (2011), 6–18.
112 Machyn, *A London Provisioner's Chronicle, 1550–1563*, f.151v.
113 Archer, *Pursuit of Stability*, 117.
114 Wickham, *All of One Company*, 48–51, 58.
115 DCA, DB1, f.62r.

'out of house' because of the scale of the operation. Roughly coinciding with the years in which a Draper held the mayoralty, when greater demands were placed on the Company's capacity for hospitality, corporate accounts show that the Drapers invested in two large rebuildings of their ovens. Probably in anticipation of securing great quantities of meat in their mayoral years, the new brick ovens at Drapers' Hall were constructed in the year preceding the 1565 dinner and a further oven was added in 1576–7.[116] During the term of the Dinner Book, the cooking of the pasties and indeed all the products procured by the Wardens for the dinner was overseen by a member of the Company of Cooks, Stephen Treacle. In the kitchen, Treacle headed up a team of about eight, which included assistant cooks, scullions, and turnbrochers (boys who were responsible for turning the spit to roast meat).[117] An Englishman, Treacle appears to have served the Drapers up until 1580. He was employed by the Star Chamber at Westminster in the 1590s, and may also have served the London household of courtly Draper, Lord Giles Paulet, indicating the cook's proficiency in catering to the tastes of the urban elite.[118] In the 1560s, Treacle was paid £2 10s. for his service at the Drapers' dinner, £1 more than the Cook of the Clothworkers' and the Carpenters' even at the turn of the seventeenth century.[119]

Although a number of venison pasties were served at the dinners, the Dinner Book shows that there was usually a remarkable surplus. Bearing a resemblance to an almery, the hippocras house received uneaten meat during the dinner, with Bachelor waiters strictly charged to ensure that 'none to be carried elsewhere'. In the small but secure room otherwise used for the storage of banqueting stuff, meat from the high table was safely set on shelves and the 'broken' was sorted from the 'unbroken' by two trusted women.[120] At other times meat was transferred to the larder for safekeeping.[121] In 1569, six porters monitored different thresholds into the hall, but a further man was positioned at the top of the kitchen stairs to check that 'meat accord-

116 DCA, RA5, 1564–5, f.26v; RA5, 1576–7, f.20r.
117 DCA, DB1, f.15r.
118 L. Scofield, 'Star Chamber Dinners' in *American Historical Review*, v (1899), 83–95. For the employment of Master Cooks in livery companies, see A. Borg, *A History of the Worshipful Company of Cooks* (Huddersfield: Jeremy Mills Publishing Limited, 2011), 36. Treacle is noted in R. G. Lang (ed.) '1582 London Subsidy Roll: Broad Street Ward', *Two Tudor Subsidy Rolls for the City of London: 1541 and 1582* (London: London Record Society, 1993), 169–76 [online text], http://www.british-history.ac.uk/london-record-soc/vol29/pp169-176 [accessed online 24 Oct. 2013]. Paulet's admission to the Company is recorded: DCA, MB7, f.176. The transferral of one of his apprentices to his neighbour, Treacle, and the Company of Cooks implies at least a mutually beneficial relationship between Treacle and Paulet (DCA, MB8, f.96v).
119 Wickham, *All for One Company*, 55; Carpenters, Court Minutes 1600–1618 (GL, MS4329/3, f.17v.)
120 DCA, DB1, f.16r, f.88v.
121 Ibid. f.88v, f.100r.

ingly went to furnish the house and that nothing was purloined'.[122] In 1565, the quantity of meat left over from twenty-five bucks filled 162 pasties – the distribution of each one extraordinarily accounted for in the Dinner Book, reinforcing the social and symbolic value of venison. The number of leftover pasties ranged from 184 in 1567 to fifty-eight in 1570. The privilege of directing the distribution of these small food parcels was afforded to the Wardens, who allocated their pasties to servants, businesses, taverns frequented by the Company, family members, neighbours, and other notable persons unable to attend owing to infirmity. The widespread distribution of these pasties to both rich and poor recipients within the City broadcast corporate wealth to a large audience.[123] In this way, the feast was an opportunity to display the 'allocative authority' over provisions both within the great hall at the tables, and without the hall throughout the City.[124]

In 1570, the Drapers' Clerk solemnly noted in the Minute Book that 'the nobility and gentlemen about the Court are much offended at the great number of bucks being consumed in the halls of companies within London at their feast dinners'. This complaint was made in spite of the status of courtiers as regular attendees at livery company dinners, as bestowers of venison, and as recipients of pasties. In light of this the Drapers' Court resolved to limit the Wardens to the 'bringing in' of only ten bucks between them. If this total was exceeded, an internal fine of 40*s.* was to be levied.[125] That same year a clear downturn in response to the courtly criticism is observable. In 1569, twenty-seven bucks were noted. In contrast, 1570 saw only nine.[126] However there is little evidence that the Company scaled back consistently, for the total had risen up to eighteen in 1572.[127] Given the visibility of the livery company dinners, it is no surprise that their lavishness drew critical attention. The excess associated with successful merchants was roundly condemned by preachers such as Edward Hake, who complained in 1579,

> Yea, who are they but marchauntmen that have the costly fare? Who now in banquets with these men are able to compare? For such straunge store of divers meates and dishes finely wrought? Who hath the lyke? No man besides. Welnigh it costes them nought.[128]

[122]   Ibid. f.88v.
[123]   Archer, *The Pursuit of Stability*, 117.
[124]   A. Giddens, *The Constitution of Society: Outline of the Theory of Structuration* (Cambridge: Polity Press, 1984), 32.
[125]   DCA, MB8, f.91r.
[126]   DCA, DB1, ff.84v–85r, f.99r.
[127]   DCA, DB1, ff.115r–115v.
[128]   E. Hake, *News Out of Paul's Churchyard* (London, 1579), 4th satire.

THE WARDENS' BURDEN

The extravagance of City dinners did not only vex corporate outsiders; insiders were also concerned about the consequences of these entertainments and sought reform. John Strype's 1720 edition of Stow reflected that 'our ancient wise forefathers' had 'many times attempted the redress and amendment of the great excess in fare and other things, in Mayors' and Sheriffs' houses' on account of which 'almost all good citizens fled and refused to serve in this honourable city'.[129] City offices were not the only ones plagued by avoidance as entertainment costs grew. From the later sixteenth century, the cost of serving as a Warden in London's great livery companies proved to be a consistent stumbling-block. Many of those nominated refused to take up office, preferring to pay a fine rather than invest the time and money necessary for the performance of their duties.[130] Even Assistants were less inclined to involve themselves in Company business. With this in mind, modest Court Dinners were instituted in 1598, designed to follow meetings of the group and intended to counteract a lack of attendance, but also encourage timeliness, for late arrivals to the meetings were not offered a meal.[131] In 1602–3 nine dinners were had throughout the year at a charge of just over £20 altogether. They seem to have had a positive effect.[132] Participation in the dinners was seen as a privilege of membership, and appears to have inclined members towards service and corporate engagement.

The organisation of dinners presented Wardens with an opportunity to build their own reputations and strengthen networks, though the burden of corporate hospitality was heavy. The responsible Wardens invested their personal resources in the maintenance of the quality of dinners. Securing food gifts, such as bucks, from associates and tenants certainly could defray some of the more substantial costs.[133] At the same time, the Company allocated a proportion of corporate funds towards the costs of entertainment, and nominal sums were collected from Liverymen attending the events. Wardens were however anxious to keep up standards and uphold corporate as well as individual honour by putting on as good a show as they could afford.

---

[129]   J. Stow, *A Survey of the Cities of London and Westminster*, J. Strype (ed.) (London: J. Strype, 1720), i. 246.

[130]   Johnson, *History,* iv. 417–27.

[131]   DCA, MB11, f.242.

[132]   DCA, WA5, 1602–3, f.13v. Six dozen trenchers were purchased to serve these dinners in 1601–2 (DCA, WA5, 1601–2, f.18r).

[133]   See, for example, John Chaloner, a Haberdasher and tenant of a property of the Drapers', who promised the reversion of the lease to John Gill, a Salter. The Drapers' Wardens agreed to honour Chaloner's wishes on condition that he deliver one hogshead of 'good claret wine such as the Masters the Wardens shall like well' so that it could be stored in the Drapers' cellar. Gill was required to offer 'one buck of season' at the time of the Election Dinner (DCA, MB8, f.89v).

The cost of dinners in the sixteenth century appears to have reached its peak in the years 1565, 1566, and 1571, when expenditure came to over £100 each.[134] The least extravagant came to a total cost of £41.[135] Yet these great sums were offset against corporate contributions, which were progressively increased in the latter half of the century. Broadly speaking, the sum of £10 was granted by the Court to support Election Dinners in the 1550s, and £20 thereafter.[136] In 1605, the Wardens requested a further increase in the house allowance for the Election Dinner on account of the higher numbers of Liverymen and the inflated prices for food and drink; the allocated sum was duly raised to 100 nobles (equivalent to around £33).[137] Allowances for Quarter Dinners increased from £6 13s. 4d. to £8 in the same year, and then were raised further to £10 in 1595. One year later the support for View Dinners increased from £6 to £10 on account of a rise in food prices.[138] Extra corporate funds were granted to support more elaborate dinners when a Lord Mayor or Sheriff was drawn from the Company. During 1589, when Draper Martin Calthorp acted as Lord Mayor, the Wardens were benevolently granted an additional £8 above the usual allocation for a dinner that cost a little over £64.[139] Proving that there were exceptions to the rule and indicating that the 1560s was an important decade for corporate dining, the Election Dinner of 1565 was an especially exuberant affair, costing over £100, with no extra corporate support provided on account that Company members did not hold civic offices in that year.[140]

Although it was expected that Wardens would spend far more than the corporate funds allocated to them, some Wardens showed reluctance to contribute to costs. In 1556, two Wardens spent £20 of corporate funds on three Quarter Dinners over the course of the year. As this was £5 over the house allocation, the Wardens were required to

---

134 DCA, DB1, f.29r, f.49v, f.108r. The sum of £100 in 1570 is equivalent to roughly £24,000 in 2018 according to the National Archives, *Currency Converter* [website], https://www.nationalarchives.gov.uk/currency-converter/ [accessed 12 May 2018]. In comparison, the costliest dinner in the 1530s was in a year when a Draper served as Lord Mayor. In this instance, just over £75 was spent by the Company (DCA, MB1B, f.457). Costs for the Lord Mayor's Dinner served at the Guildhall in 1575 had spiralled to £400, of which the Lord Mayor was required to pay £200 (Munday, *Chrysanaleia*, Nichols (ed.), 10).

135 DCA, DB1, f.124r.

136 Johnson, *History,* ii. 222; DCA, WA4, 1551–2, 1552–3, 1553–4.

137 DCA, MB13, f.28v. In 1618, probably in recognition of his efforts in servicing larger dinners, the Cook's annual fee doubled from £2 to £4 (DCA, MB13, f.139r). For a full discussion of food prices, see J. Boulton, 'Food Prices and the Standard of Living in London in the "Century of Revolution", 1580–1700' in *Economic History Review*, liii, no. 3 (2000), 455–92.

138 Johnson, *History*, ii. 222.

139 DCA, MB10, f.416. Each Warden personally contributed £13 to this dinner. Masters were expected to contribute a buck or the equivalent in money (40s.) to the Election Dinner. In 1638, Clement Underhill refused, much to the annoyance of the Wardens, who were forced to increase their contributions to cover his lack of c-operation (DCA, MB13, f.323r).

140 This was, however, the year in which the Merchant Adventurers were granted their Charter of Incorporation by Queen Elizabeth. Johnson notes that relations between the Adventurers and the Drapers at this time were 'very intimate' (Johnson, *History*, ii. 179).

foot the extra sum out of their own pockets. The first offered a ring to cover his expenses. The second was less amenable, and 'vehemently denied' that he owed the Company anything. The assembled Court almost resorted to force to obtain the remainder. Having already sent the Clerk, they summoned the Beadle and an 'officer' to apprehend the unrepentant Warden. Before events escalated, the disgruntled Warden appeared in the parlour 'of his own mere will' with a gilt goblet in lieu of payment.[141] Taking on responsibility for their own lesser Election Dinner, Wardens of the Bachelors were not exempt from such difficulties. In 1613, Bachelor Warden Francis Martin refused to pay what was due for his part of the Bachelors' Dinner as his post required. He was dismissed from his office, and another more willing was selected in his place.[142] While a successful event reflected well on the individual organisers as well as the Company, not every dinner met corporate expectations. House funds designated for the provision of dinners could be withheld if the quality of the fare was not deemed up to standard. In 1617, Mr Ladbrook, a Liveryman and steward responsible for the Drapers' proportion of the Lord Mayor's Day Dinner, 'came short in providing ordinary cheer and provision as other stewards formerly have done' according to the Court, and was not as generously subsidised as a result.[143]

Even though house allowances increased to service dinners, the expenses incurred were still significantly burdensome to Wardens and, by the early decades of the seventeenth century, resentment towards these monetary contributions was increasing. In 1639 the spiralling costs of providing for dinners prompted a wide-ranging assessment of the role of Warden. Acknowledging the difficulties of identifying suitable Liverymen to serve in these offices, the Court noted that Wardens were personally expending £120 each per year in the provision of Quarter Dinners, View Dinners, and the Election Dinner. Concerned about these large sums, the Court attributed the growth in expenditure to the 'extraordinary price of victuals' but also to 'the great addition of fare and number of dishes to every messe', which was more than the Company had enjoyed in 'former times', though there are no dinner accounts from this period to confirm this. Most anxiously, the Court observed that the Wardens' work in service of the Company was undertaken to the detriment of their own businesses, and noted that the particular costs of serving as a Warden in the Drapers' Company dissuaded relevant men 'who might have proved hopeful and profitable members' from joining the corporation. Some prospective members preferred instead to join the Mercers, Fishmongers, Goldsmiths, and Salters, where Wardens were lumbered with lesser charges. The dismayed Court noted that some men

---

[141]   DCA, MB5, f.183.
[142]   DCA, MB13, f.98v.
[143]   Ibid. f.132v.

even elected to join 'inferior' companies outside London that required no fees to be paid. In order that the Wardens went about their duties 'with like cheerfulness as in other companies', they resolved that the ordinary allowance of the house towards the dinners should be increased significantly, and indeed it was. The contribution towards the Quarter Dinners was raised from £10 to £30, and the allocation for Election Dinners rose from £40 to £80.[144]

For all their exuberance, Charles M. Clode considered that, 'the feasts of the citizen were ... always made subordinate to the higher law of charity'.[145] While dinners in the sixteenth century could be passed over in favour of building projects (such as for enhancements to the Hall), livery company dinners were more often passed over in times of dearth or crisis – for with notoriety came moral responsibility and the fear of negative judgement if this was not effectively exercised.[146] The decade of the 1590s was especially challenging for the Company as normal proceedings were consistently disrupted on account of scarcity and economic instability. In 1591, a year of severe plague, the Drapers were apprehensive about the response of afflicted merchants within their own ranks to their continued feasts. Moreover, they feared that partaking of their dinner in the usual way would lead to requests for further contributions towards City projects. A great number of the Assistants 'earnestly requested' the Election Dinner to be withheld in that year, 'lest by their public show, they might be had in suspicion of wealth'.[147] Their requests were satisfied, and the house funds allocated for the dinner were redirected towards the poor.

While decisions to forgo or scale back dinners could be taken corporately, external interference was not unusual. Clearly aware of the significant sums spent on livery company dinners, through the Lord Mayor, the Privy Council issued a precept in 1593 that forbade Election Dinners altogether. Associated funds were distributed to the poor suffering as a result of the plague. Coinciding with these trying circumstances, the Drapers purchased a new press for their Hall so that 'more meat shall be set unto upon the same press at any feast day'.[148] This was likely to have expanded the Company's ability to store leftovers for later deployment to those in need. It was far from uncommon for the Lord Mayor himself to issue a prohibition of dinners in years when it was felt that their performance might cause disgruntled criticism or draw unwanted attention to the prosperity of the companies. It is in fact unlikely that an Election Dinner was

---

[144] Ibid. f.336r.
[145] C. M. Clode, *Early History of the Guild of Merchant Taylors, 2 Vols.* (London: privately printed, 1888), i. 8.
[146] For example, cancelled dinners are mentioned in DCA, MB1B, f.522; DCA, RA5, 1575–6, ff.17v–19r.
[147] DCA, MB10, f.534.
[148] DCA, MB11, f.191.

undertaken in 1563, the year prior to the start of the Dinner Book, for this was a year of plague and company dinners were suspended.[149] In July 1596, a similar exhortation was received from the Lord Mayor to the effect that the companies should refrain from their dinners, contributing part of the assigned budget to provide bread for the poor. The Drapers obeyed, handing over at least £40 for this purpose.[150] Again, in 1603 on account of another bout of plague, 'all public feasting and common dinners' in the City ceased, and a third of estimated costs were directed towards the needy.[151]

A few decades later in 1635, a harvest failure resulted in an extreme scarcity of food. As was to be expected, the Lord Mayor prohibited corporate dinners, but, on this occasion, rather than abandon the election completely, the Drapers agreed to hold a streamlined version of the usual course of events. All events were to be condensed into one day instead of the accustomed three. The whole Livery would still meet and attend a dinner during which the garlands would be bestowed on the new officers, but the concession was that no musicians would play. Attempting to avoid the gaze of outsiders, the Court stressed that the dinner was to be undertaken in a 'private still manner'.[152] In spite of their half-hearted restraint, the displeased Court conceived the charges for the dinner were 'overmuch'.[153] This anxiety about the response of citizens to such displays of prosperity correlates with Braddick's argument that 'early modern office-holders engaged in ... attempts at impression management ... their credibility depended on the reception of their performance'.[154] Yet the Court's desire to be perceived as morally upright was balanced with the desire to continue to meet as a corporate community to promote cohesion, a matter of understandable significance for a group of men with sometimes conflicting commercial interests. If the Company dinner was designed to promote the 'myth of virtuous common purpose and distinctive moral worth', the circumstantial cancellation of a dinner deprived companies of a key means of manifesting the image of corporate harmony.[155]

When a dinner was passed over, so too was the opportunity to choreograph a visible enactment of the Company's collective loyalty to the Protestant faith. On dinner days, the Company corporately processed through City streets to hear a sermon at St. Michael's Cornhill – but this was not the only expression of spiritual worthiness, for

149 Merchant Taylors, Court Minutes 1562–1574 (GL, MS34010/1, f.80).
150 DCA, MB11, f.209.
151 Clode, *Early History of the Guild of Merchant Taylors*, i. 8.
152 DCA, MB13, f.297v.
153 Ibid. ff.300r–300v.
154 M. Braddick, 'Administrative Performance: The Representation of Political Authority in Early Modern England' in M. Braddick and J. Walter (ed.) *Negotiating Power in Early Modern Society: Order, Hierarchy and Subordination in Britain and Ireland* (Cambridge: Cambridge University Press, 2001), 171.
155 Rosser, 'Going to the Fraternity Feast', 444.

ideals of honour, hospitality and morality were all bound together and entrenched in corporate dining culture.[156] Felicity Heal has argued convincingly that an honourable reputation in the early modern period was still intertwined with 'good lordship, generosity and the *appearance* of an open household'. The Drapers knowingly ensured that they incorporated displays of charity into their Hall at the time of the Election Dinner.[157]

The dispensation of charity at the time of the Election Day Dinner was by no means unique to the Drapers' Company. All companies incorporated attendance at church into their election proceedings, and generally required an offering to the poor box, although Machyn noted of the Merchant Taylors that after their 1557 attendance at church 'offered every man a penny'.[158] Clode observed of the same Company that a seat was offered to 'almsmen of the Livery' at a Quarter Dinner in 1607 'as in ancient time hath been accustomed'.[159] The Drapers' Company's Throgmorton Hall had long been associated with acts of charity even before its purchase by the Company. Recalling the Hall in the 1530s, Stow told of huge numbers of daily poor that had graced Thomas Cromwell's gate, receiving food from the great statesman. Somewhat nostalgically, Stow praised Cromwell for continuing the 'ancient and charitable custom as all prelates, noble men, or men of honour and worship his predecessors had done before him' in 'that declining time of charity'.[160] This memory perhaps had a bearing on the Drapers' commitment to continue to distribute alms to the poor from their Hall, a practice that appears to have been unusual in the context of the City companies.

Overlooked by the parlour and hall, the courtyard and great gate of Drapers' Hall were used as sites for the charitable distribution of money and food by the Wardens at election time. The Dinner Book shows that quality food items were purchased and cooked specifically for this purpose, usually given out the day after the dinner. 'Poor folks' received onion porridge in 1564, 'the neighbours afore our gate' and 'within and roundabout our great court of our hall' were given a venison pasty as well as 'all manner of ... venison, swans, goose, capon' in 1565, and beef was served in 1566.[161] In 1569, a year of plague, potage was distributed on the Tuesday following the dinner, and a large sum (38s.) was spent in the purchase of 28st. of beef,

156 L. Branch, *Faith and Fraternity: London Livery Companies and The Reformation, 1510–1603* (Leiden: Brill, 2017); J. Ward, *Culture, Faith and Philanthropy: Londoners and Provincial Reform in Early Modern England* (Basingstoke: Palgrave Macmillan, 2013).
157 F. Heal, *Hospitality in Early Modern England* (Oxford: Clarendon Press, 1990), 13. Emphasis added.
158 Machyn, *A London Provisioner's Chronicle, 1550–1563*, f.78r.
159 Clode, *Early History of the Guild of Merchant Taylors*, i. 3.
160 Stow, *Survey* (1603), i. 89.
161 DCA, DB1, f.8v, f.24r, f.45r. Other notes on charitable food gifts can be found in f.58v, f.61r, f.69v, f.94v, f.105r.

enough for over four hundred individual portions and three times the amount purchased in 1566.[162] In contrast, in 1572, instead of receiving food, 40*s.* in cash was divided among the poor 'about the hall' and sent to 'poor prisoners' throughout London.[163] Indicating that perhaps the practice of food distribution was waning, in 1604–5, money was again given out, this time by Mr Moore, the Clerk, who distributed 4*s.* to 'certain poor women at the gate' who had gathered around the time of the election.[164] Organising the people gathered at the gate of the Hall could not have been a minor undertaking. In 1630–1, upon the City-wide cancellation of all company dinners, the Wardens remained at the Hall for two hours distributing £50 to the poor.[165]

The Dinner Book concludes with a mysteriously untitled list of names. This list might identify recipients of a cash dole, though the date of the record and its connection to the Election Dinner is unclear. The sum of £7 12*s.* 2*d.* was distributed to fifty-four men and women.[166] A fair proportion of men who appear in the list appear to have been members of the Company in the late sixteenth century, and it is likely that the widows mentioned were residents of the Drapers' almshouses.[167] It is also possible that the list refers to payments made to poorer or younger members of the Company who contributed to the service of the dinner by running errands, serving in the hall, or washing up in the scullery.

CONCLUSION

Though only a small proportion of early modern Londoners would have been eligible to attend the Election Dinners of the Great Twelve companies, it is clear that all sorts of people were well aware of the character of these events, and tales of their opulence circulated. According to Stow, the scale of particular City dinners could become embedded within the civic memory to the extent that they became immortalised as fables – the division between the real and the fictitious indecipherable. Writing at the end of the sixteenth century, he regarded the Election Dinner of Goldsmith Lord Mayor Bartholomew Read in 1502 as 'far incredible and altogether impossible' owing to the alleged number of people in attendance, one hundred of 'great estate', and wealth of food.[168] The dramatic potential of such civic dinners was widely recognised by playwrights of the day. Among

---

162   Ibid. f.80r, f.88v.
163   Ibid. f.114r.
164   DCA, RA6, 1604–5, f.10.
165   DCA, WA8, 1630–1, f.50.
166   DCA, DB1, f.135r.
167   Boyd, *Roll*, unpaginated.
168   Stow, *Survey* (1603), i. 305.

others, Heywood and Dekker utilised dinners hosted by Lord Mayors drawn from the livery companies as vehicles to explore the tensions between the City mercantile elite and the monarchy.[169] Early modern urban communities understood that hospitality was still a key means of negotiating social relations in a rapidly changing world, and the extension of familiar ritual choreographies emphasised a mythical continuity the past. At this turning point in the history of the Drapers' Company, documentation concerning the Election Dinner appears to have snowballed. The Dinner Book shows that livery companies such as the Drapers' recognised the potential of their Election Dinners to reinforce the 'ancientness' of corporate authority, utilising the past as a means of legitimising their stake in the future. New record-keeping practices were established, aiming to ensure that corporate honour and the personal reputations of individual Wardens were upheld, though, as in the case of the Dinner Book, such administrative gestures could be short-lived, serving a particular purpose for a time and then falling out of use. In the late seventeenth century, Samuel Rolle indicated that many of his contemporaries were disparaging about the 'pomp' of livery company dinners, while historian Perry Gauci held that the companies' ritual ceremonies were tolerated rather than enjoyed by those who wanted to get ahead in the City.[170] As the influence of the companies waned in the seventeenth century, the Election Dinner was emptied of its political potency, though its social and cultural value remained, as it does to this day.

---

[169] In Thomas Heywood's *Edward IV* Grocer John Crosby entertains the King to dinner as Lord Mayor, and in Thomas Dekker's *The Shoemaker's Holiday* Shoemaker Simon Eyre again entertained the King as Lord Mayor. For discussion of these scenes, see L. Stevenson, *Praise and Paradox: Merchants and Craftsmen in Elizabethan Popular Literature* (Cambridge: Cambridge University Press, 1984), 115–19.

[170] S. Rolle, *The Burning of London, Vol. 3* (1667), 55, as quoted in J. B. Heath, *Some Account of the Worshipful Company of Grocers* (London: privately printed, 1869), 1; P. Gauci, *The Politics of Trade: The Overseas Merchant in State and Society, 1660–1720* (New York: Oxford University Press, 2001), 143.

EDITORIAL METHOD

For the most part, spelling has been modernised and standardised, as has the use of capitals. Punctuation has been added where necessary. Spellings of items or foods that are particularly fluid, or depart significantly from modern English, have been retained in their original form within the text. The original spelling of first names, surnames, and place names has also been retained. Variants of food, drink, people, and place names, alongside their standard versions, are listed in the index. Biographical and other explanatory notes have been entered as footnotes throughout the text. Descriptions of commodities and foods have been drafted with primary reference to the *Oxford English Dictionary* and the *Dictionary of Traded Goods and Commodities, 1550–1820*.[1]

All the dates have been preserved in their original form according to the Julian calendar. Roman numerals have been converted to Arabic numerals, and incorrect accounting, which is frequent, has been left as is. Weights have been expressed in figures (i.e. hundredweight is cwt.). A glossary explains these figures and some lesser-known measurements. Contractions commonly used in such in early modern manuscripts, for example 'wth', 'y^e' and 'Itm', have been expanded without note. Latin phrases still broadly understood have been retained, but abbreviated Latin headings have been translated into modern English.

The original layout has been tidied to improve coherence, for instance, where there is a duplicate heading, one has been deleted (see Frontispiece for a sample of the original layout of the document). Emboldened words in this edition denote underlined or larger text in the original document. I have underlined totals and sub-totals for ease of identification. Incorrect accounting, which is frequent, has been left as is.

---

1   N. Cox and K. Dannehl (ed.) *Dictionary of Traded Goods and Commodities 1550–1820* (Wolverhampton: University of Wolverhampton, 2007), [online text], http://www.british-history.ac.uk/no-series/traded-goods-dictionary/1550-1820 [accessed online 9 Jun. 2018].

THE DINNER BOOK OF
THE LONDON DRAPERS' COMPANY
1564–1602

A° . 1564 .

The Booke of the generall and
ordenarie chardge expended by the m͛r & the
wardens in and concernynge the affaires & dymers
of this House for A° .1563. by͛

Sͬ william
Chester knight

M͛r.

Mͬ. Mynors
Mͬ. Knowles
Mͬ. Skynn͛
Mͬ. Lawrence

} m͛r. wardens

First Quarter
Dynner .

in anno dñi
Januarij 1563

The proportion of the same
dynners wt the prises thereof in due
order

for the first course

{ viz. vj. messes
of meate }

First Course

Brawne . 2 . candels ————— iij d

Boyled Capons . 7 .
Rost Capons . 8 . ———

} all — xxxvj s iiij d

Turkye Cocke — 1 . ————— ij s

Roste Geese — vj . ————— xxiiij s iiij d

mynched Pyes . ij . in a ————

Disshes . vij . at . viij d . ij per . vij s iiij s

Custarde . vj . at . vj d . viij d . ————— vij d

{ m̄ . xiiij s vij d }

The Second Course

Second Course

Lambes Hole . iij . ————— viij s iiij d

Marche paynes . vj . whereof
j . rest — my the rest ——— viij s iiij d iij s viij d
the pece ——————

} { xxviij s iiij d
}

THE DINNER BOOK

ANNO 1564

The book of the general and particular charges expended by the four Master Wardens in and concerning the Feast Dinner of the house this year viz. by:

Sir Willyam Chestar,[1] Knight } Master

Mr Mynors[2]
Mr Quarles[3]
Mr Skerne[4] } our Master Wardens
Mr Lawrence[5]

First Quarter Dinner

The final day of January 1563	**The proportion of the same dinner with the service thereof in due order**		
First course viz. six messes of meat	Brawn two rounds	3*s.*	
	Boiled capons seven and roast capons eight	32*s.*	6*d.*

---

1 (Sir) William Chester served as Warden of the Drapers' Company in the years 1546–7 and 1549–50. He then served as Master seven times, in the years 1553–4, 1556–7, 1559–60, 1563–4, 1566–7, 1567–8, and 1568–9. Chester became an Alderman in 1553, Sheriff in 1554–5, Lord Mayor in 1560–1 and MP for the City in 1563. See Johnson, *History*, ii. 470–1; Beaven, *Aldermen*, ii. 34; *HP Commons, 1509–1558*, i. 598–9.
2 John Mynors served as Warden of the Drapers' Company in the years 1553–4, 1559–60, and 1563–4. See Johnson, *History*, ii. 470.
3 John Quarles served as Warden of the Drapers' Company in the years 1555–6, 1563–4, 1565–6, and 1568–9. He was twice Master of the Company, in 1570–1 and 1575–6. See Johnson, *History*, ii. 470–1.
4 Bartholomew Skerne served as Warden of the Drapers' Company only once, in 1563–4. He likely left London for Essex in the late 1560s. See Johnson, *History*, ii. 470; TNA, E115/382/36, AC/S/3/1.
5 Thomas Lawrence served as Warden of the Drapers' Company only once, in 1563–4. See Johnson, *History*, ii. 470.

Turkey cock one[6]	5s.	
Roast geese five	8s.	4d.
Minced pies two in a dish – twelve at 16d. the piece	16s.	
Custard – six at 2s. 6d.	15s.	

	£3 14s.	10d.

Second course Lambs whole three — 8s. 4d.

Marchpanes[7] six whereof one cost – 3s, the rest – 2s. 8d. the piece — 16s. 4d.

f.1v. Item for beef to boil and roast for the Cook and two servitors[8] – one whole sirloin — 4s. 8d.

Item marrowbones for boiled capons — 15d.

Item eggs for white broth for the boiled capons — 8d.

Item barberries[9] for the white broth – one pint — 6d.

Item muscadel and white wine for the white broth — 8d.

Item dates — 2s. 3d.

Item prunes 2lb. — 4d.

Item currants 2lb. — 4d.

Item large mace 1oz. — 6d.

Item sugar coarse and fine 3lb. — 2s. 9d.

Item pepper 2oz. — 5d.

Item cinnamon 1oz. — 20d.

Item ginger 1oz. — 4d.

24s. 8d.

Bisquytes[10] and caraways for marchpanes and other fruits — 20d.

Item butter for basting 8lb. 3oz. — 3s. 5d.

---

[6] Turkey cock: it is unclear whether this is a reference to a male turkey or a male guinea-fowl as both birds were known as turkeys at this time, although it is more likely to be the male turkey in this instance. The turkey was introduced into Europe from North America in the early sixteenth century, and was quickly adopted as a status item. The more prevalent and much smaller guinea-fowl was of West African origin and had been reared in England since at least the fifteenth century.

[7] Marchpane: a flat disc of wafer with a layer of sweet almond and sugar paste on top. Usually delicately decorated and served, especially during the banquet course towards the end of dinners.

[8] Servitors: assistants to the Cook.

[9] Barberries: red berries with a sharp flavour, often used similarly to lemon and oranges or in conserves.

[10] Biscuits: sweet, light, crispy, wafers served after the main meal and used as a base for marchpanes.

Item lard to draw the turkey with and cloves and sanders[11] for gallantyne[12]			7*d.*
Item oranges for the lambs			5*d.*
Item vinegar, vergewse,[13] salt and mustard			10*d.*
		6*s.*	11*d.*
Item for six dozen di of bread		6*s.*	6*d.*
Item for a stand of ale		4*s.*	
Item for a kilderkin of beer		4*s.*	4*d.*
		14*s.*	10*d.*
Sum total	£7	2*s.*	3*d.*

f.2r. Wine

Item for one gallon of muscadel	2*s.*	4*d.*
Item for one gallon of malmsey[14]		16*d.*
Item for seven gallons claret wine	9*s.*	4*d.*
Item for three pottles of sack[15]	2*s.*	
	15*s.*	

Pewter vessels

Item for six dozen of trenchers	2*s.*	5*d.*	
Item for four garnish of vessels hired	2*s.*	8*d.*	
Item 1lb. of candles and taps		3*d.*	*ob.*
Item six sacks of coals	2*s.*	8*d.*	
Item a pint of sweet rose water		12*d.*	
	9*s.*		*ob.*

Officers' wages

Item to the Butler for his pains	4*s.*	
Item to the Cook for his pains	6*s.*	
Item to Goodwife Holmes[16]		6*d.*
Item to the Clerk's wife for the washing of the naperies	2*s.*	
	12*s.*	6*d.*

---

[11] Sanders: a derivation of sandalwood, aromatic and frequently used as a colouring agent.
[12] Gallantine: jellied bread-crumb sauce, usually spiced.
[13] Verjuice: juice of unripe grapes or other sour fruit like crab-apples. Bitter and acidic in taste.
[14] Malmsey: sweet wine imported from the Mediterranean.
[15] Sack: sweet fortified wine imported from the Mediterranean. Similar to today's sherry.
[16] Goodwife Holmes: wife of the Company Beadle, Robert Holmes who served in this role from 1551 to 1569. See Johnson, *History*, ii. 474. Mrs Holmes consistently attended to dinners from 1563 to 1580, most often washing vessels in the kitchen and cleaning the house.

Pots necessary	Item six or eight pewter pots, pottle, and quarts to carry ale and beer in Furniture of plate for a Quarter Dinner for six or eight messes of meat		

Plate

Salts for every mess – one
Standing cups for every mess – one
Item six basins and six ewers
Item four nests of gilt goblets
Item four nests parcel gilt goblets
Item four nests of bowls parcel gilt and gilt
Item four dozen of drinking pots
Item five or six dozen of spoons

Napery ordinary

Napery of the hall always provided of ordinary

f.2v.

Provision for a Quarter Dinner kept in Drapers' Hall the third day of May, Anno 1564

With the charges thereof as follows:

Six messes of meat			
Boiled capons seven, roast capons eight	31*s.*	4*d.*
Green geese[17] fourteen	14*s.*	2*d.*
Chickens boiled five	2*s.*	6*d.*
Fresh salmon one	14*s.*	2*d.*
Custards six at 2*s.* 6*d.*	15*s.*	
Rabbits two dozen di	6*s.*	
Marchpanes one	3*s.*	4*d.*
Tarts of apples five at 2*s.* 8*d.* the piece	13*s.*	4*d.*
Boiled beef for cooks and servants		
Marrowbones		
Eggs		
Butter		
Barberries one pint		4*d.*
Wine for the broth		4*d.*
Dates 1lb.		10*d.*
Prunes 2lb.		
Currants 2lb.		
Large mace 1oz.		
Sugar coarse and fine		
Pepper 2oz.		
Cinnamon 1oz.		
Ginger 1oz.		

---

[17] Green geese: 'green' indicates the relative youth of the animal. In the case of geese, the term was most often used for birds under four months old.

Bread, drink	Item a stand of ale	3*s.*	
and wine	Item a kilderkin of beer	2*s.*	4*d.*
	Item seven dozen of bread	7*s.*	
	Item claret wine, white wine and sack	11*s.*	8*d.*
f.3r. **Wages**	To the Butler for his pains	3*s.*	4*d.*
	To the Cook for his pains		
	To Holmes' wife		6*d.*
	For washing the linen	2*s.*	
Pewter	Item for four garnish of vessels		
vessels	Item for four sacks of coals	2*s.*	4*d.*
	Item for two dozen trenchers		10*d.*
	Item for a broom		1*d.*
	Item for salts		3*d.*
	Item for vinegar and vergeus		11*d.*

A View Dinner of Fish	**Provision of a View Dinner kept in the hall Fifteenth of March, Anno 1563, on a fish day**		
Three messes	Item two old ling	4*s.*	4*d.*
of meat with	Item green fish[18] one fish di	3*s.*	
the charges	Item pikes four	5*s.*	8*d.*
	Item carps four	5*s.*	10*d.*
	Item fresh eels four		18*d.*
	Item one quartern of lamprets[19]		19*d.*
	Item four custards, four lamprey pies and four pippin pies[20]	26*s.*	
	Item 1lb. of butter	2*s.*	
		51*s.*	10*d.*
Herbs and	Item barberries and salad oil		8*d.*
sauce	Item oranges		2*d.*
	Item alexander buds[21] and parsley		6*d.*
	Item for yeast		1*d.*
	Item for a pottle of wine		8*d.*
	Item for spinach and carrots		4*d.*
	Item for wafers		2*d.*
	Item for eggs		4*d.*
	Item for an earthen pot		5*d.*
		4*s.*	10*d.*

18 Green fish: newly salted white fish, most frequently cod.
19 Lamprets: young lamprey fish (a fish with the appearance of an eel).
20 Pippin pies: pastry pies made with sweet dessert apples and spices.
21 Alexander buds: flowering plant used in salads and as an herb.

f.3v. **Bread and drink**	Item for three dozen bread	3s.	
	Item for a stand of ale	4s.	8d.
	Item for beer		10d.
	Item for four gallons of white and claret wine	5s.	4d.
	Item for a gallon of sack		20d.
		15s.	6d.
Spice	Item for prunes		1d.
	Item for 1lb. of currants		5d.
	Item for 1lb. of dates		18d.
	Item for half an oz. of cinnamon		10d.
	Item for ginger 1oz.		1d.	o
	Item for large mace half an oz.		6d.
	Item for one oz. of pepper		2d.	o
	Item for one lb. of sugar		12d.
	Item for bisquytes and caraways		8d.
		5s.	4d.
Wages	Item to the Cook for his pains	4s.	
	Item to the Butler	2s.	
	Item for washing the napery	2s.	
	Item to Homes' wife		6d.
	Item for hire of three garnish of vessels	2s.	4d.
	Item for coals		14d.

Sum £4 9s. 1d.

THE FEAST DINNER

**Proportion of the great Feast Dinner
being the first Monday in August, Anno
1564, with the furniture and charge as
follows:**

Butcher's meat	In primis for a boar		13*s.*	4*d.*
	Item for seething[22], killing & sousing[23]		6*s.*	8*d.*
	Item for 114lb. of suet for baked venison and otherwise	£1	9*s.*	6*d.*
	Item for two dozen and a half of long marrowbones with five dozen short		11*s.*	4*d.*
	Item for 47st. of beef, mutton and veal at 13*d. ob.* the st, that is to say, one quarter of beef, a sirloin and a brisket, three sheep, and one veal, and one roasting piece of beef		42*s.*	10*d.* *ob.*
	Item for a peck of pricks[24]			6*d.*

Sum	£6	14*s.*	1*d.* *ob.*
But we paid but[25]	£6	13*s.*	4*d.*

Marchpanes	Item of Bagatte's wife ten marchpanes of the greatest scantling at 3*s.* the piece, and ten of the next scantling at 2*s.* 8*d.* the piece, and eight of the third scantling at 2*s.* 6*d.*	£3	16*s.* 8*d.*
Sturgeon	Item of Blage[26] of the Kinges Heade[27] in New Fisshe Strete for two firkins of fresh sturgeon at 30s. the firkin	£3	

---

22 Seething: cooking the meat by boiling or stewing it.
23 Sousing: process of preserving or pickling meat in salted water.
24 Peck of pricks: a quarter of a bushel of small tapered pieces of wood, used for tying things together.
25 The 5*d. ob.* discount likely related to the pricks, which could be thrown in for free as a gratuity from the Butcher. See DCA, DB1, f.58r, f.111v.
26 According to the Dinner Book, it appears that Mr Blage was based at both The Castle and The King's Head taverns on New Fish Street. He frequently supplied the Drapers' Company with sturgeon.
27 The King's Head was located at the southern end of New Fish Street and was a popular tavern also utilised by companies such as the Goldsmiths' for corporate dinners. See F. C. Chalfant, *Ben Jonson's London: A Jacobean Placename Dictionary* (Athens: University of Georgia Press, 2008), 115.

f.4v. **Hippocras**[28]	Item of the same Blage one gallon of hippocras on Saturday at 5s. and three gallons on Sunday at 5s. six gallons, on Monday the feast day at 6s. the gallon, and three gallons on Tuesday at 5s. being in all fourteen gallons and a pottle	£4		
	Sum	£7		
Wine	Item paid to Mathew Colclough[29] for a puncheon of French wine	£3	3s.	4d.
	Item paid to Robert Ffryer[30] for a hogshead of Gascon wine		50s.	
	Item for portage and carriage			18d.
	Sum	£3	54s.	10d.
	Memorandum that we had our import allowed & given us by Master Smyth the Customer.[31]			
Other sorts of wines	Item for a rundlet of muscadel at Ratclyffe[32] containing eleven gallons and one pint at 2s. 4d. the gallon		26s.	
	Item there a rundlet of sack containing eight gallons at 16d. the gallon		10s.	7d.
	Item for carriage of a puncheon of French wine			8d.
	Item for three gallons of white wine for the cooks		4s.	
	Item to Mr Mynors for boat hire			6d.
	Item for a gallon of white wine on Tuesday for the Cook			16d.

[28] Hippocras: high status alcoholic spiced drink used for ceremonial purposes and taken towards the end of dinner as part of the banquet course with wafers and comfits.

[29] Matthew Colclough (or Colcloughe) served as a Warden of the Drapers' Company in the years 1568–9, 1576–7, and 1581–2. He was Alderman of Calais in the 1550s (see TNA, C1/1413/19) and also appears in the London Port books importing French wine, cloth, and other stuffs from Flanders and the Netherlands in the 1560s. See B. Dietz (ed.) *The Port and Trade of Early Elizabethan London: Documents* (London: London Record Society, viii. 1972).

[30] Probably Robert Fryar (or Frier), Draper, who imported large quantities of wine and other items in the 1560s. He was granted a licence to sell wine at his own 'adventure' in 1567. See Dietz, *Port and Trade; Calendar of the Patent Rolls: Elizabeth I, 1558–1575, 6 Vols.* (London: Her Majesty's Stationery Office, 1976), iv. 19.

[31] Thomas Smythe was a Haberdasher, serving as Master in 1583. He was collector of customs duties ('customer') at the Port of London from 1558 to 1569. He sat as MP between 1553 and 1563. See J. F. Wadmore, 'Thomas Smythe of Westenhanger, commonly called Customer Smythe', *Archaeologia Cantiana* 17 (1887), 193–208; *HP Commons, 1558–1603*, iii. 405.

[32] Ratclyffe (or Ratcliffe) was a small hamlet located on the Thames to the east of the City of London along Ratcliffe Highway.

Item to a Cooper to part and divide out our wine left in the cellar		4*d.*
Item for the quills[33] for the wine		4*d.*

Sum	[-]

f.5r. **Spice for the Feast Dinner**	Item of John Hartgown's saffron 1oz.		18*d.*
	Cloves & mace di lb.	3*s.*	8*d.*
	Large mace 5oz.	4*s.*	7*d.*
	Cloves 2oz.		14*d.*
	Cinnamon 6oz.	9*s.*	
	Ginger 6oz.		12*d.*
	Sanders 1oz.		2*d.*
	Nutmeg one quarter of lb.		17*d.*
	Great raisins 6lb.		10*d.*
	Prunes 6lb.		12*d.*

Sum	26*s.*	2*d.*

More spice confectional	To Mr Mynors' man laid out for spice:		
	For biskettes and caraways 1lb.		14*d.*
	For cinnamon comfits 1lb.	2*s.*	8*d.*
	For ginger comfits 1lb.	2*s.*	
	For orange comfits 1lb.	2*s.*	
	For coriander comfits di.lb.		7*d.*
	For more bisketes and caraways 2lb.	2*s.*	8*d.*
	For clove comfits di lb.		12*d.*
	For large prunes 10lb. at 2*d. ob.* the lb.	2*s.*	1*d.*
	For saffron		10*d.*
	For 2lb. of currants		9*d.*
	For nutmeg		2*d.*

Sum	15*s.*	11*d.*

More spice	Item of Mr Qwarles 25lb. three quarters sugar at 9*d. ob.* the lb. and 20 lb. at 11*d.* the lb, and 6 lb. at 9*d. ob.* the lb.

Sum	44*s.*	50*d.*	*ob.*

	Item for 6lb. of dates, at 10*d.* the lb.		5*s.*	
	Item for 10lb. currants at 5*d.* the lb.		4*s.*	2*d.*
f.5v.	Item for 2lb. of grains at 10*d.* the lb.			10*d.*
	Item for 10lb. of pepper at 3*s.* 6*d.* the lb.	£3	10*s.*	
	Item for blades for spice			3*d.*

Sum	£6	10*s.*	2*d.*	*ob.*

Sum total of the spice	£8	7*s.*	3*d.*

---

33 Quill: a hollow tube for channelling wine, or a tap inserted into a wine barrel.

For poultry	Proportion for the Poulterer laid out by Mr Qwarles:			
	Item for eighteen swans	£5		
	Item for earnest given			12*d.*
	Item given in reward for them		3*s.*	4*d.*
	Item for nine dozen pigeons of Mr Skerne, at 16*d.* the dozen		12*s.*	
	Item to Mason,[34] our Poulter, for 30lb. roasting capons at 2*s.* 2*d.* the piece	£3	15*s.*	10*d.*
	Item to him for 33lb. boiling at 2*s.* the piece	£3	6*s.*	
	Item for fourteen fat geese at 20*d.* the piece		23*s.*	4*d.*
	Item for two rabbits			10*d.*
	Item for four dozen quails at 8*s.* the dozen		32*s.*	10*d.*
	Item for twelve roasting capons more, at 2*s.* 2*d.* the piece		26*s.*	
	Item for twelve boiling capons more, at 2*s.* the piece		24*s.*	
f.6r.	Item three dozen di pigeons at 10*d.* the dozen		7*s.*	2*d.*
	Item for oats to feed the swans[35]			12*d.*
	Item for 6cwt. and a half of eggs at 3*s.* 4*d.* the cwt.		21*s.*	8*d.*
	Sum	£19	14*s.*	2*d.*

Pikes	Item paid to Robert Lucas,[36] Pikemonger, for twenty-four pikes at 22*d.* the piece	44*s.*	

Linen cloth	Item for half a piece of lockeram[37] for aprons containing forty-seven ells[38]	31*s.*	8*d.*
	Item for eight ells of soultage,[39] and three quarters, and two ells of canvas for the kitchen	3*s.*	2*d.*
	Item for two ells of fine Holland[40] for the sewers at 18*d.* the ell	3*s.*	
	Sum	32*s.*	10*d.*

[34] Robert Mason was a Draper and appears to have served as the Company's Poulterer from at least 1563 until c.1580. See Boyd, *Roll*.
[35] This payment suggests that swans were purchased alive then fattened up on-site at Drapers' Hall.
[36] Robert (or Richard) Lucas provided pikes for Election Dinners in the 1560s and was associated with Qwenehive in the Dinner Book's record for 1565.
[37] Lockeram: linen fabric used for apparel and household items.
[38] Ell: a standard measurement, the Drapers' 'ell' was 36 inches, the length of a silver yard stick held by the Company and retained as a symbol of their jurisdictional authority.
[39] Soultage: coarse cloth often used for sacks or packing.
[40] Holland cloth: fine linen fabric used for napery originally produced in the Netherlands.

Bread	Item paid the Baker for thirty-one dozen of white and wheaten bread	31*s.*	
The Baker	Item paid him for boulting[41] of our meal		13*d.*
	Sum	31*s.*	8*d.*
f.6v. **Spice bread**	Item paid him for boulting of our meal		8*d.*
	Sum	31*s.*	8*d.*
Not spice bread	Item paid to Goodwife Wall[42] for ten dozen of cakes and buns altogether	20*s.*	
Wafers	Item paid to Goodwife Thompson for six boxes of wafers after 2*s.* the box	13*s.*	
Beer	Item paid to Mr Mynors' Beer Brewer for two barrels of strong beer, at 8*s.* the barrel, and for three barrels of double beer, at 4*s.* the barrel	28*s.*	
Ale	Item paid to Martyn,[43] our tenant in Smithfield, for three barrels of strong ale, at 5*s.* 4*d.* the barrel, and three stands of ale, at 2*s.* the stand	22*s.*	
The Chandler	Item for twenty-one green pots[44] which were lacking of two dozen di	25*d.*	*ob.*
	Item for eight gallon pots lacking of two dozen	8*d.*	
f.7r.	Item for seven pottle pots wanting of two dozen received	7*d.*	
	Item for a chafer wanting of eight chafers	3*d.*	
	Item for a pan lacking of nine pans	2*d.*	
	Item for white salt for the salt cellars half a peck – 3*d.* and a pot lacking with it 2*d.*	5*d.*	
	Item for white salt one bushel	20*d.*	
	Item for bay salt half a bushel	6*d.*	

---

41 Boult: to sift or sieve through a bolting-cloth.
42 Mrs Joan Wall, possibly a widow, provided cakes and buns from at least 1563 until c.1580. She is associated with Abchurch Lane in the record for the 1569 Election Day Dinner, and 'her maid' served the Company in boulting grain in 1564 at the Election Day Dinner.
43 Martyn, an ale brewer, was Company tenant of 'The Bull' in East Smithfield.
44 Small green-glazed earthenware pots replaced wooden mugs at the Inns of Court around the same time. See F. A. Inderwick (ed.) *A Calendar of the Inner Temple Records, 9 Vols.* (London: privately printed, 1896), i. 204.

Item for red vinegar one quarter – 2*d.* and a
pot, and the pot it was brought in – *ob. qt.*   2*d. ob.*

Item vergious 2*d.* and a pot with it lost *ob.*
qt.   2*d. ob.*

Item mustard one quarter and a pot lost
with it   2*d. ob.*

Item vertious a gallon 6*d.* and a pot
lacking 1*d.*   12*d.*

Item red vinegar one gallon 8*d.* and a pot
lacking 1*d.*   9*d.*

Item white vinegar one gallon 12*d.* and a
pot that is lacking 1*d.*   13*d.*

Item for mustard a pottle 4*d.* and the pot 1*d.*   10*d.*

Item for four earthen pans lacking at 2*d.*
the piece   8*d.*

Item 3lb. of cotton candles   9*d.*

Item for 3lb. of white candles   7*d.*   *o*

Item for three pecks of oatmeal   18*d.*

Item for packthread   2*d.*

Item for the loan or occupying of five
dozen pots and pans at 4*d.* the dozen, one
with another, lacking two pans   19*d.*

                 Sum   14*s.*   4*d.*   *o*

f.7v. The Pewterer Item for the hire of fifteen garnish of
vessel of Mrs Catcher[45] at 10*d.* the garnish   12*s.*   6*d.*

Item for the loss of three platters, one
plate, and three saucers which weighed
13lb. di at 7*d.* the lb.   7*s.*   10*d.*

                 Sum   21*s.*   4*d.*

Ashen cups[46] Item for one dozen of ashen cups   20*d.*

Item for four Danisk trays[47]   2*s.*   8*d.*

Item for ten taps   2*d.*

Item for a porter to carry them   2*d.*

                 Sum   4*s.*   8*d.*

---

45   John Catcher and his wife, Ellen, of Broad Street, provided hire of pewter from 1567 to
c.1580. Master of the Pewterers' Company in 1585, John served as an Alderman from
1588 to 1596 as well as Sheriff in 1587–8. See Beaven, *Aldermen,* ii. 43; *HP Commons,
1604–1629,* iii. 461.

46   Ashen cups: cups made of the wood of an ash-tree. In 1522 these were used to serve ale
and claret wine to the second and third tables, while the high table was served red wine
and hippocras in silver cups. See W. Herbert, *The History of the Twelve Great Livery
Companies of London, 2 Vols.* (London: privately printed, 1837), i. 442.

47   Danisk trays: wooden trays, possibly of spruce fir, from either Denmark or Gdansk.

Fruit, as pears, plums and filberts	Item for 12cwt. plums at 2*d.* the cwt.	2*s.*	4*d.*
	Item for 6lb. pears	3*s.*	6*d.*
	Item the filberts were our own growing in our own garden		[-] *d.*
Trenchers	Item for 24lb. dozen trenchers	10*s.*	
Meal and oatmeal	Item for twelve bushels of meal at 2*s.* 3*d.* the bushel	32*s.*	
	Item paid to Goodwife Walls' maid for boulting out of the bran		12*d.*
	Item for six bushels of flour at 2*s.* 8*d.* the bushel	16*s.*	
	Item for a peck of oatmeal		4*d.*
	Item more for oatmeal		2*d.*

f.8r. **Butter**

	Item for a lb. of butter		3*d.*
	Item for 13lb. of butter	3*s.*	4*d.*
	Item for two dishes of sothery butter[48]		11*d.*
	Item for 70lb. of butter at 3*d.* the lb, and 2*d.* for carriage	17*s.*	8*d.*
	Sum	22*s.*	2*d.*

Cream and milk	Item for twelve gallons of cream at 14*d.* the gallon	14*s.*	
	Item for one gallon of milk		4*d.*
	Sum	14*s.*	4*d.*

Wood and coal	Item for 20lb. sacks of coals at 5*d.* the sack	8*s.*	4*d.*
	Item to Goodwife Homes for three sacks of coals		16*d.*
	Item for cwt. di of fagots	5*s.*	
	Item for one quarter of billets	2*s.*	6*d.*
	Sum	17*s.*	2*d.*

Officers' fees and wages	Item to Christopher Fulkes our Sewer[49] for two days service to saw and carve	6*s.*	8*d.*
	Item to four porters 3*s.* a piece, and to one other porter, 16*d.*	13*s.*	4*d.*

---

48 Sothery butter: likely sweet butter.
49 The Sewer was in charge of carving the meat in the great hall though sewers also typ-ically oversaw the arrangement of guests, food, and the tables. Christopher Fulkes (or Foulkes) served in this position from 1564 to 1571 and was Common Crier and Serjeant-at-Arms to the Lord Mayor from at least 1559. See P. E. Jones, 'Common Crier and Serjeant-at-Arms', *Guildhall Historical Association* (1958), 81.

Item to Stephen Triakill[50] our Cook for his wages	40*s.*	
Item to him more for all his fees, the dripping only excepted	15*s.*	
Item paid for the baking of 26lb. pasties of venison out of doors	4*s.*	4*d.*
Item to William Fowler our Butler for his wage, he finding four butlers under him	26*s.*	8*d.*
Item to Currans[51] our Musician for two days service with his whole noise	13*s.*	4*d.*
Item to one Small our Steward who took the charge and receipt of all the things into the house		

f.8v. Not wages

Item paid to the Sexton for ringing of bells and all other service at St. Michael's[52] for Sunday and Monday	4*s.*	
Item paid to Goodwife Holmes for three days labour, in the house and to a woman with her two days, at 6*d.* the day	2*s.*	6*d.*

Sum   £7   15*s.*   10*d.*

Rewards for bucks

Item given to my Lord John Grey's[53] man for three bucks given to this house unto the Wardens	20*s.*

---

50 Stephen Treacle served as the Cook of the Drapers' Company for several decades. A member of the Company of Cooks, he lived close to the Company Hall in 1582 and may have served in the household of Draper Lord Giles Paulet as one of Paulet's apprentices was set over to Treacle in 1569, entering the Company of Cooks a few years later. See R. G. Lang (ed.) *Two Tudor Subsidy Rolls for the City of London: 1541 and 1582* (London: London Record Society, xxix, 1993), 172; DCA, MB8, f.97v.

51 Currans (or Corrans) was a musician who was hired for playing at Election Dinners by the Drapers' Company along with his band (noise) in 1564 and 1568. He also performed at the Grocers' Company Election Dinner in 1554. See C. Sisson, 'Thomas Lodge and his Family' in C. Sisson (ed.) *Thomas Lodge and Other Elizabethans* (Cambridge, MA: Harvard University Press, 1933), 14.

52 St. Michael's Cornhill was the patronal church of the Drapers' Company from 1503. See Johnson, *History*, i. 164–5.

53 Lord John Grey suffered from gout for at least a decade before his death in November 1564 at his home in Pyrgo, Essex. During 1563 and 1564 he was implicated in negotiations with Queen Elizabeth on behalf of his niece Lady Katherine Grey, who was seen as a threat owing to a proclamation issued by her elder sister Lady Jane Grey in 1553, which placed Katherine in line of succession (see *Oxford DNB*). After the Drapers' Election Dinner, Lord John received one pasty and a parcel food, which was sent to his house. His wife, Lady Mary Grey, sister to Viscount Montagu, continued to send bucks to the Drapers, gifting one in 1565 and two in 1569.

Item to the Lord Mayor's[54] man for bringing of one buck		3*s.*	4*d.*
	Sum	23*s.*	4*d.*

Extra-ordinary charges	Item for six padlocks and keys	4*s.*	
	Item for one gallon of barberries	4*s.*	8*d.*
	Item for one quire of large paper for the cooks for pies bottoms		11*d.*
	Item for writing paper for the Steward		2*d.*
	Item for a quire of paper more for the cooks		3*d.*
	Item for a staff torch for the cooks to look in to the ovens		12*d.*
	Item for oranges		13*d.*
	Item for lemons		4*d.*
	Item for brooms		6*d.*
	Item for a strainer		4*d.*
	Item for carrying the sturgeon to the hall		4*d.*
	Item for onions to make porridge[55] for poor folks		12*d.*
	Item for nails		1*d.*
	Item for a pottle of gooseberries		8*d.*
	Item for lathes		1*d.*
	Item for a bushel and a peck of white salt		15*d.*
	Item for a candlestick		1*d.*
	Item for candles beside the Chandlers' bill 2lb.		10*d.*
	Item for four per tankard of water our house then lacking		23*d.*
f.9r.	Item for a link and packthread		6*d.*
	Item for two men to carry a cowl of porridge to the Counters[56] with meat therein		2*d.*
	Sum	[-]	

---

54 Sir John Whyte, a Grocer, was Lord Mayor in 1563–4. See Beaven, *Aldermen*, i. 123.
55 Porridge or pottage: a thick soup made of vegetables, pulses and/or meat. Oatmeal porridge was less usual at this date.
56 Counters: debtors' prisons in London.

Perfumes,	Item for perfumes and pans for it[57]	11*d.*
flowers and	Item for flowers for the sturgeon	2*d.*
sweet waters	Item for flowers for the Ladies' Chamber[58]	8*d.*
	Item for one quart of rose water	14*d.*
	Item for damask water and roses to Mrs	
	Lawrens[59]	3*s.*

Sum   <u>5*s.*</u>   <u>11*d.*</u>

The total sums of all particulars as follows:

The Butcher's bill came to in the whole	£6	13*s.*	4*d.*
Marchpanes	£3	16*s.*	8*d.*
Sturgeon two firkins	£3		
Hippocras fourteen gallons and one pottle	£4		
Wine of all sorts	£12	18*s.*	8*d.*
Spice with sugar	£8	6*s.*	9*d.*
The Poulterer's bill	£19	14*s.*	6*d.*
Pikes 24lb.		44*s.*	
Linen cloth		57*s.*	10*d.*
Bread of all sorts		31*s.*	8*d.*
Spice bread		20*s.*	
Wafers		13*s.*	
Beer		28*s.*	
Ale		22*s.*	
Chandler's bill		14*s.*	4*d.*
Pewterer's bill		20*s.*	4*d.*
Ashen cups, trays and taps		4*s.*	8*d.*
Fruit of all sorts		6*s.*	
Trenchers		10*s.*	
Meal and flour		49*s.*	6*d.*
Butter		22*s.*	2*d.*
Cream		14*s.*	4*d.*
Wood and coal		17*s.*	2*d.*
Officer's wages	£7	15*s.*	10*d.*
Rewards for bucks		23*s.*	4*d.*

f.9v.

---

57 Perfume was used around the hall at the time of the Election, placed in window sills in pans. The practice of perfuming the homes of the upper-middling sort in urban areas was attended to by women of the same status. See T. Hamling and C. Richardson, *A Day at Home in Early Modern England: Material Culture and Domestic Life, 1500–1700* (London and New Haven: Yale University Press, 2017), 92–3. The Dinner Book demonstrates that women associated with the Company were often involved in the scenting of the Drapers' Hall (see DCA, DB1, f.28r, f.48r, f.107r, f.126r, f.132r).

58 For a discussion of the Ladies' Chamber, see Orlin, *Locating Privacy*, 132; Milne, 'Merchants of the City', 274–9.

59 Jane Lawrence, wife of Thomas Lawrence, Fourth Warden. Her first husband was John Carden of Lewes in Sussex. See TNA, PROB 11/49/52, C 1/1338/1–6.

Extraordinary charges		9s.	3d.
Perfumes, pans, and flowers		5s.	11d.

Sum total of all totals	£82	9s.	4d.

Whereof

Received   Received towards the said charges against as follows:

First the ordinary allowance of the house towards this dinner	£10		
Item more granted the assistance by act of Court towards the augmentation thereof upon considerations	£6	13s.	4d.
Item received of Thomas Bury[60] transmuted from this house towards a hogshead of Gascon wine		40s.	
Item of Peter Smyth towards two swans, one by him		13s.	4d.
Item more received of [-] Clyff[61] for two swans		10s.	
Item for quarterage received among the Assistants		18s.	8d.
Item for quarterage received of the Livery		32s.	

Sum	£22	7s.	4d.

f.10r.	**Receipts**	Sum received as appears	£33	7s.	4d.
	Charges	And we have paid as at appears against it	£32	9s.	4d.
	Remaining	So the clear charges of our said dinner net stands in	£60	2s.	

Whereof

Division or dividend	Be equal division every man's part amounts to severally and by poll to	£15	6d.

---

60   Thomas Bury, Merchant of the Staple of Calais, transferred out of the Drapers' Company. It is not clear which Company he transferred into. See W. B. Turnbull (ed.) *Calendar of State Papers Foreign: Edward VI 1547–1553* (London: Her Majesty's Stationery Office, 1861), 338.
61   Possibly Thomas Clyff (or Cliff), a Draper, whose apprentice George Cliff became a freeman in 1565. See Boyd, *Roll.*

Memorandum we sold to Messenger
our Clerk[62] for 10*s.* by him paid all the
several quarterage which was left by him
to be levied and gathered, and also to
Mr Mynors' wait money for 4*s.* and two
hogsheads 16*d.* and two received *7d.*   16*s.*

Which was equally divided among us

f.10v.   Venison and bucks provided and given us to the said dinner
By Mr Mynors – eight bucks
By Mr Quarles – five bucks three quarters
By Mr Skerne – two bucks
By Mr Lawrence – four bucks

Nineteen bucks three quarters

Other bucks given in general
Item by the Lord Mayor, Sir John White – one buck
Item by Mr Vaghan[63] – one buck
Item by George Braythwaite[64] – one buck
Item by Mr Alderman Chestar – one buck
Whereof one half was sent by Mr Champion[65]
Item by the Lord John Graye – one buck

Five bucks di

Sum altogether - bucks – 25lb. one quarter

Whereof

Pasties baked of eighteen bucks and one quarter of the same
were made in pasties the number of – 134 pasties

And of the others seven bucks baked for Tuesday were also
made of pasties great, the number of – twenty-eight pasties

So the twenty-five bucks and one quarter made in all pasties
to the number of – 162 pasties

---

62 Edward Messenger served as Clerk from 1557 to 1569. See Johnson, *History*, ii. 474.
63 William Vaghan served as Warden of the Drapers' Company in the year 1571–2. See
    Johnson, *History*, ii. 471.
64 George Braythwaite served as Warden of the Drapers' Company in the years 1565–6,
    1572–3, and 1576–7. See Johnson, *History*, ii. 471.
65 (Sir) Richard Champion served as Warden of the Drapers' Company in the years 1550–1
    and 1556–7. He then served as Master six times, in the years 1557–8, 1560–1, 1562–3,
    1564–5, 1565–6, and 1568–9. Champion became Alderman in 1556, Sheriff in 1558–9,
    and Lord Mayor in 1565–6. See Johnson, *History*, ii. 470–1; Beaven, *Aldermen*, ii. 35.

For the which

Twenty-five bucks was provided in pepper and for the other
furniture of the dinner – 20lb.

Whereof

Spent – 13lb.
And so rest and left – 7lb. which was divided among the
Wardens, and the pepper spent to every buck was about – di lb.

f.11r.   **All which pasties of venison were bestowed as follows:**

The bestowing of the pasties

In primis on Sunday at dinner to take a taste and make a
proof – one pasty
Item for Monday at dinner – fourteen pasties
Item for the Wardens' dinner that day – one pasty
Item for the cooks' dinner that day – one pasty
Item for the Wardens of the Bachelors' dinner – two pasties
Item for Monday at supper to the Wardens – one pasty
Item for the Wardens of the Bachelors' breakfast on Tuesday
morning – two pasties
Item on Tuesday at dinner – thirteen pasties
Item to the cooks' dinner on Tuesday – one pasty

First Warden   Mr Mynors gave first to his house on Sunday, one pasty
to Mrs Hart, one pasty to Smythe the Hunt,[66] one pasty to
Martyn at the waterside, one pasty to Apton, one pasty to Mrs
Mynors[67] for her neighbours, two pasties to Wall, two pasties
to the Bishop's Head,[68] and two pasties to Mrs Asshelyn[69]
Sum – eleven pasties

**Second
Warden**   Mr Quarles allowed and gave to himself on Sunday one pasty,
to Master Calthorpp[70] one pasty, to Robert Bisshopp one pasty,
to Randoll one, to Lamberd one, divided him at twice three, to
Crofton one, to his cousin George one, to his brother's servant
one, to Mr Clifford one and to Thomas Eliot one pasty
Sum – thirteen pasties

---

66   The Common Hunt was an official position in the Lord Mayor's household. He was responsible for keeping the Lord Mayor's kennels and acting as huntsman for the Corporation.
67   Ellen Mynors (née Nicholson), wife of John Mynors, First Warden. See TNA, PROB
11/49/114.
68   The Bishop's Head was a tavern on Lombard Street. It was used occasionally by the
Drapers for small dinners, for example, a View Dinner was held there in March 1570. See
DCA, MB8, f.97v.
69   Mrs Asshelyn was the mother of John Mynors, First Warden. See TNA, PROB 11/49/114.
70   Martin Calthorp served as Warden of the Drapers' Company in 1562–3, 1569–70, and
1572–3. He then served as Master three times, in the years 1580–1, 1584–5, and 1587–8.
Calthorp became Alderman in 1579, Sheriff in 1579–80, and Lord Mayor in 1588–9. See
Johnson, *History*, ii. 470–2; Beaven, *Aldermen*, ii. 40.

Third Warden	Mr Skerne gave to Mrs Hern one pasty, to Mistress Clyff one, to Mrs Morley one pasty

Sum – three pasties

Fourth Warden	Mr Lawrence gave to Mr Best one pasty, to Mrs Lawrence two pasties

Sum – three pasties

f.11v.
Item more the Wardens gave generally to the Searchers one pasty, to the Poulterer one pasty, to the Lord Treasurer's[71] gardener one pasty, to the Porter of Blackwell Hall[72] one pasty, to my Lord Grey one pasty, to Stokes and his man two pasties, to our four porters four pasties, the channel raker[73] one pasty, to Messynger the Clerk one pasty, to Warner[74] our Renter one pasty, to Robert Holmes the Beadle one pasty, to Henry Starr our Labourer one pasty, to the Chandler one pasty, to John Chambers two pasties, to Smalle our Steward two pasties, to the Clerk of St. Michael's two, to the Parson thereof one, to the Ale Brewer one, to the Water Bailey[75] one, to the Master of the Bachelors two, to a serjeant one, to the neighbours afore our gate

Sum – fifty-four pasties

Item to the Wardens the remainder being eleven pasties a piece – forty-four pasties

Divided besides among them – four pasties

---

[71] Sir William Paulet, First Marquess of Winchester, served as Lord Treasurer from 1550 to 1572. He became a member of the Drapers' Company in 1519 and built his London residence Winchester House in Austin Friars, adjacent to the Company Hall, after the Dissolution of the Monasteries. See N. Holder, 'The Medieval Friaries of London' (Unpublished PhD thesis, University of London, 2011), 170–3; *HP Commons, 1509–1558*, iii. 189–90.

[72] Blackwell Hall: London's central cloth market, in operation since the fourteenth century. The Drapers' Company were responsible for the inspection of cloth at the market and held the right to appoint the market's Master.

[73] Raker (or Scavenger): a street and street gutter (channel) cleaner.

[74] Bartholomew Warner first served as the Drapers' Renter, taking up the position of Clerk's Assistant in October 1559. He became Company Clerk in July 1569 and served until May 1587. See Johnson, *History*, ii. 474.

[75] The Water Bailiff of London superintended fishing on London's rivers.

The expending and bestowing of the foresaid meat and provision as follows:

Saturday Item on Saturday at the potation was spent two dozen cakes, two dozen buns being all spice bread, two gallons of hippocras, pears, plums, filberts, biskettes and caraways, French wine, ale, beer, and sack

Sunday Item on Sunday at potation was spent four dozen cakes, four dozen buns, spice bread, two gallons hippocras, pears, plum, filberts, biskettes, caraways, French wine, Gascon wine, ale, beer and sack

f.12r. Item the Wardens dined at the Hall on Sunday with a boiled capon, a roast capon, a sirloin of beef, a venison pasty, mutton and porridge

Item the same night they supped in the Hall with roast capon, rabbits, pigeons and baked venison

The order of the service for the said Feast Dinner on Monday foresaid

Monday Item the hall was that day set with three tables throughout furnished

Wheroef

Four messes of meat	**The number of persons sitting at the high table**	
	First the Lord Mayor	Mr Symthe, Customer
	Sir Richard Sackfield[76]	Mr Holstock[77]
	Sir Hugh Pawlett[78] and my Lady his wife[79]	Mrs Mynors

---

[76] A member of Queen Elizabeth's Privy Council, Sir Richard Sackville was married to Winifred, daughter of Sir John Brugges, Lord Mayor of London in 1520–1. Brugges was also Master of the Drapers' Company in 1514, 1521, and 1527. Sackville sat as MP between 1547 and 1563. See *HP Commons, 1558–1603*, iii. 314; Beaven, *Aldermen*, i. 168; Johnson, *History*, ii. 468–9.

[77] William Holstock served as Warden of the Grocers' Company in 1562–3 and 1569–70. He was Deputy Treasurer of the Admiralty by 1547 and Comptroller of the Navy in 1561. Holstock was MP for Rochester from 1571. See *HP Commons, 1558–1603*, ii. 330–1.

[78] Soldier and administrator, Sir Hugh Pawlett (or Paulet) served as MP for Somerset between 1529 and 1572. He was Governor of Jersey 1550–73 and Custos Rotulorum of Somerset 1562–73. See *HP Commons, 1558–1603*, iii. 189.

[79] Lady Elizabeth Pawlett (née Blount) was the wife of Sir Hugh Pawlett and widow of Sir Thomas Pope.

Sir John Ratclyff[80]	Mrs Quarles[81]
The Lieutenant of the Tower[82]	Mrs Skerne[83]
Sir William Harper[84]	Master Alderman William
and my Lady his wife[85]	Chester our Master
Master Alderman Champion	Mr Stanley[86]
Mistress Champion[88]	and my Lady his wife[87]
Alderman Jackman[90]	Mr Chevall[89]
and his wife[91]	Mr Richards[92]
Sir Thomas Offeley[93]	Mrs Lawrence
My Lady Granado[94]	

Sum of the persons sat at that board – twenty-five

[80] Sir John Ratclyff (or Radcliffe) was MP for Castle Rising in 1558 and Grampound in 1559. He was the son of Robert Radcliffe, 1st earl of Sussex, and Mary Arundell. See *HP Commons, 1509–1558*, iii. 170–1.

[81] Agnes Quarles (née Greenaway), wife of John Quarles, Second Warden. See TNA, PROB11/72/483. Her first husband was a Grocer, John Howland. See *Oxford DNB*.

[82] Sir Richard Blount served as Lieutenant of the Tower from 1561 to 1564 and as MP for Steyning in 1553 and Oxfordshire in 1563. He died on 11 August 1564, just a few days after the Drapers' Election Dinner. See *HP Commons, 1509–1558*, i. 449–50.

[83] Jane Skerne (née Tewther), wife of Bartholomew Skerne, Third Warden. After Skerne's death she married Matthew Smyth, barrister at the Middle Temple then gentleman of Long Ashton, Somerset. See J. H. Bettley (ed.) *Calendar of the Correspondence of the Smyth Family of Ashton Court, 1548–1642* (Bristol: Bristol Record Society, 1982), xv.

[84] Sir William Harper served as Master of the Merchant Taylors' Company in 1553–4. He became Alderman in 1553, served as Sheriff in 1556–7, and as Lord Mayor in 1561–2. See *Oxford DNB*; Beaven, *Aldermen*, ii. 34.

[85] Dame Alice Harper, wife of Sir William Harper.

[86] Thomas Stanley, Goldsmith and Under-Treasurer of the Royal Mint 1561–71. See *HP Commons, 1509–1558*, iii. 370–2.

[87] Lady Joyce Stanley (née Barrett), wife of Thomas Stanley and widow of Sir James Wilford.

[88] Barbara, Lady Champion likely ran her own business as a silkwoman, sharing in the trade privileges of her husband Richard. See Orlin, *Locating Privacy*, 224, 289.

[89] William Chevall served as Warden of the Drapers' Company in 1545–6, 1549–50, 1553–4, and 1560–1. See Johnson, *History*, ii. 469–70.

[90] Edward Jakman (or Jackman) was a Grocer. He was an Alderman from 1561 and Sheriff in 1564–5. See Beaven, *Aldermen*, ii. 37.

[91] Anne Jakman, wife of Edward Jakman. See TNA, PROB 11/52/55.

[92] Henry Richards served as Warden of the Drapers' Company in 1546–7, 1552–3, and 1555–6. See Johnson, *History*, ii. 470.

[93] Sir Thomas Offley served as Master of the Merchant Taylors' Company in 1547–8. He became Alderman in 1550, and served as Sheriff in 1553–4 and Lord Mayor in 1556–7. Offley was Mayor of the Staple in 1560, 1564, and 1569 as well as a charter member of the Muscovy Company. See *Oxford DNB*.

[94] Magdalen, Lady Granado was the widow of Sir Jacques (or James) Granado, former Equerry of the Stable to Edward VI, who died in 1557. She married Sir Robert Chester as her second husband in November 1564. See R. Chester, *Robert Chester's Love Martyr, or Rosalin's Complaint*, 1601, A. Grosart (ed.) (London: The New Shakespere Society, 1878), vii–viii.

12v. Five messes of meat	**Persons at the second table**

Persons at the second table

Master Ambrose Nicolas[95] and his wife[96]
Mr Yonge and his wife[97]
Mistress Cockeram
Mr Eaton Chamberleyn[98]
Mrs Trott[99]
Mr Hall[100] and his wife
Mrs Chevall[101]
Mrs Barnam[102]
Mrs Calthroppe[103]
Mr Wilbram[104]
Mr Blont[105]
Mrs Poynter[106]
Mrs Beswick[107]
Mrs Goslyng[108]
And more to the number of twenty guests and the table filled up with ladies, gentlemen with five or six of the youngest Livery
Sum at that table sitting – thirty-two persons

---

[95] (Sir) Ambrose Nicholas was Master of the Salters' Company, possibly in this year. He became Alderman in 1566, and served as Sheriff in 1566–7, and Lord Mayor in 1575–6. See Beaven, *Aldermen*, ii. 37.

[96] Dame Elizabeth Nicholas, wife of Sir Ambrose Nicholas. See TNA, C 2/Eliz/M12/39, PROB 11/60/296.

[97] Possibly Richard Yonge who served as Warden of the Grocers' Company in 1571–2 and 1581–2. See Johnson, *History*, ii. 471.

[98] George Eaton (or Heton) was Chamberlain of the City of London 1563–77. Eaton was a Merchant Taylor and served as Master of his Company in 1556–7. He was one of the 'principal sustainers of London Protestants under Mary'. See *Oxford DNB*.

[99] Rose Trott was a silkwoman, sharing in the trade privileges of her husband John Trott the elder, who served as Warden of the Drapers' Company in 1547–8 and died in 1551. See Orlin, *Locating Privacy*, 288–9, 290, 293, 295; Johnson, *History*, ii. 470.

[100] Possibly John Hall who served as Warden of the Drapers' Company in 1579–80, 1587–8, and 1590–1. See Johnson, *History*, ii. 471.

[101] Wife of William Chevall, who had previously served as Warden of the Drapers' Company.

[102] Alice Barnham (née Bradbridge) was a silkwoman. Her husband was Francis Barnham who served as Warden of the Drapers' Company in 1558–9 and 1566–7. He was Master in 1571-2. See *Oxford DNB*; Johnson, *History*, ii. 471–2; Orlin, *Locating Privacy*.

[103] Probably the wife of Martin Calthorpe, previously Warden of the Drapers' Company.

[104] Probably Thomas Wilbraham (1530–73), a 'distinguished lawyer', who was attorney of the Court of Wards, later Recorder for the City (1569–71) and Judge at the Court of Wards and Liveries. See G. Ormarod, *History of Cheshire, 2 Vols.* (London: Lackington, Hughes, Mavor and Jones, 1819), i. 65; *HP Commons, 1558–1603*, iii. 617.

[105] Probably John Blont (or Blount), who was a Clothworker and served as Warden of his Company. See Herbert, *History*, i. 651.

[106] Wife of Richard Poynter, who served as Warden of the Drapers' Company in 1548–9, 1554–5, and 1562–3. See Johnson, *History*, ii. 470

[107] Joan Beswick (née Turner), whose husband was William Beswick, who became an Alderman in 1564. William had served as Warden of the Drapers' Company in 1556–7 and 1560–1. He died during his term as Master in 1566–7. Joan then married Draper (Sir) William Chester soon after William's death. See Johnson, *History*, ii. 470–1, 477; *Oxford DNB*.

[108] Wife of Robert Goseling, who served as Warden of the Drapers' Company in 1561–2. See Johnson, *History*, ii. 470.

Five messes **Persons at the third table**

Mr Coverdale[109]

Mr Philpot[110]

And the rest of the same table furnished with the Assistants and Livery of the Company to the number of thirty-two persons

f.13r. **The order and furniture of meat served in to all the three tables**

First service **Service to the high table**

Item to that table was served four double messes of meat viz. of brawn, one shield and three rondes sliced

Boiled capons two in every dish

Swans one in every dish

Roast capons two in every dish

Venison one pasty of a side in a dish

Pike large one in a dish

Custard one in a dish

Second
service

Quails six in a dish

Sturgeon one jowl and three rondes sliced

Marchpanes one in a dish

And at last the table taken up was presented

Wafers and hippocras

First service **The second table**

The said table was served with two double messes and three single messes viz.

Brawn sliced

Boiled capons two messes double and three single

Swans two, and for three messes three geese

Roast capons two messes double and three single, venison one side in every dish

Pike one in every dish

Custards one in every dish

---

[109] Marian exile and leading puritan preacher, Doctor Miles Coverdale moved to a tenement owned by the Drapers' Company in Dowgate sometime in 1563–4. He served at St. Magnus the Martyr from January 1564. His tenancy ended around 1566 after the death of his wife Elizabeth. Coverdale also had strong ties with the Merchant Taylors' Company and made a sermon at one of their Dinners in 1546. His son became a member of that Company. See *Oxford DNB*; DCA, RA 1563–4, f.20v, RA 1565–6, f.16v, AIII 151, Misc. Letter, 22 Jan 1564; Merchant Taylors, Wardens' Accounts (GL, MS34048/4, f.28v); Sleigh-Johnson, 'The Merchant Taylors' Company of London, 1580–1645', 157.

[110] Possibly Henry Philpot, the father of John Philpot, herald and Draper. Henry was mayor of Folkestone three times. See *Oxford DNB*.

f.13v. **Second service**	Quails six for one mess, and four messes Pigeons Sturgeon sliced five messes Marchpanes one in a dish, and the table taken up then Wafers and hippocras

The third service at the third table
Then the said third table was served throughout with all sorts of dishes both in first and second courses and in all points with wafers also and hippocras as the second table was and as many dishes

Meat sent out abroad in to the town
Memorandum there was sent out to the Lord John Graye, brawn sliced, a boiled capon, a roast capon, a pasty of venison of a side, a swan, a pie of goose giblets, a custard, a tart, French wine and claret of each a gallon

Seven messes of meat left in store on Monday	Memorandum also there was provided on Monday seven messes of meat more than was served in, which was setup, and the most part reserved to serve for Tuesday

f.14r.   **Order of service for Tuesday at dinner**

Four messes of meat	**The high table** Item that table was furnished first with Master Alderman Champion and his wife, the four new Wardens and their wives, the four old Wardens and their wives, two of the Assistants and their wives, and other guests as Alderman Lodge[111] and his wife with diverse others Worshipful to the number of nine more so as the table was set with the number of twenty-five persons
Two messes of meat	**The second table** Item that table was set all most half throughout with guests bidden and some unbidden to the number of sixteen persons

---

[111]   Sir Thomas Lodge served as Master of the Grocers' Company in 1554–5 and 1559–60. He became Alderman in 1553, and served as Sheriff in 1559–60 and Lord Mayor in 1562–3. He was a Governor of the Russia Company. See *Oxford DNB*.

The furniture of meat served into the hall on Tuesday foresaid unto the said three tables

First course **The high table**
The high table was then served with four messes of meat viz. one shield of brawn at the high mess, and three messes sliced. Item two messes double served, and two messes single served with boiled capons, two swans, and two geese, roast capons venison pasties, pike, and custard

Second course Item six quails in a dish two messes and six pigeons in a dish, other two messes one jowl of sturgeon and three messes of sliced sturgeon, and a marchpane in every dish, and after the table taken up served in with wafers and hippocras

f.14v. **First and second course** **The service of the second table**
Item that table was served with the like meat in all sorts and every dish as the high table was with two double messes and three single messes. And likewise the second service in all sorts saving there was no quails but pigeons only in there instead

Service of the third table
Item the third table was served in all sorts with as many dishes as the second table was, saving two messes which was both single service

Hippocras spent on Monday and Tuesday
Memorandum that on that day being Monday was spent – six gallons
Item on Tuesday spent – four gallons and one pottle
Item there was also one gallon left and divided among the Wardens, so that Saturday, Sunday, Monday and Tuesday was spent in hippocras – fourteen gallons and one pottle

The order of the officers of the house during the feast aforesaid

In the larder, Steward and Clerk of the Kitchen First there was a Steward whose name was Smalle who took the charge upon him to see that all the provision provided ready into the house and also did see it pointed unto every office, and had under his charge all the spice which divided into the Cook's hands and other officers that which they should occupy. Also he kept reckoning with Butcher, Poulterer, Pikemonger, Grocer, Chandler and did set out the service of meat, and did set up that which remained and gave the Wardens account of the rest when the feast was done – one

f.15r.	**Larder**	Item he had under him John Chambers[112] who kept a book of all the venison that came into the house to what Warden it was sent, and what number of pasties were made, and where they were distributed, and also kept the larder, spice and other things while the Steward was abroad, and noted up the service how it was served at and from the dresser and took in the meat that did remain above the server out of the kitchen into the larder – one
		Item the said Steward had another man of Mr Mynors' Ralph Kyng which man was always attending at his hand to fetch him spice, butter, suet, salt or any other things that the cooks lacked while the Steward was looking unto the cooks, and also to carry it from the Steward's hand anything that he called for out of any other offices, or out of doors at all times when the Steward called for it – one
	Kitchen	Item in the kitchen was the Master Cook Stephen Triacle who did furnish the kitchen and pastio[113] with all such cooks, scullions and turn-brochers[114] as did appertain there as at his own charge & had his wages as aforesaid for the same, being eight persons besides himself – eight
f.15v.	**The cellar and buttery**	Item one Dredgewede Mr. Skern's man did keep the bar, and stood there still continually to call for wine, ale, and beer to them that filled it and to deliver it from the bar to them that called to him for it. And George Daye Mr Skerne's man filled beer, George Smithurst Mr Lawrence's man filled ale. And John Dowd Mr Mynor's man filled wine. And two men kept continually without the bar to carry such drink for the butlers as they did call for that is to say Simon Stocke to carry drink for the second table, and Richard Tomson Mr Lawrence's man to carry drink to the third table – six
	The pantry	Item Hassoppe Mr Skerne's man did keep the bar of the pantry and did stand continually there to deliver such bread as was called for, and Robert Epton Mr Lawrence's man kept within the pantry to deliver bread to the bar, and two men kept always without to carry bread to the butlers when they called for it. That is to say Humphrey Humble Mr Mynor's servant who served the high table and Thomas Knight Mr Quarles' man who served the second and third tables – four

[112] Servant of John Quarles, Second Warden. See TNA, PROB 11/60/37.
[113] Pastio: the servery connected to the kitchen.
[114] Turnebrochers: those who were responsible for turning the spit to roast meat, usually boys.

Porters four   Item there were four porters, one to keep the gate, two to keep the stairs feet, and one to keep the hall door which was Cartewright,[115] who had with him John Ffetypace Mr Skerne's man who kept a book of all the meat and vessels that was spent out of the house by whom it was sent, and to whom it went – four

f.16r. **The hippocras house**   Item to the hippocras house were pointed three persons, viz. Francis Quarles Mr Quarles' man, John Hilton Mr Mynor's man, and Anne Baxter Mr Mynor's maid which three did keep the muscatel, sack, spice bread, pears, plums, filberts and wafers. And also kept full within that house who delivered out all those foresaid things as they were called for, and also took in all the meat that was brought them and also did set them upon the shelf there safe, and sorted out all the whole messes of meat from the broken meat etc – four

Butlers four   Item there was William Ffowler who was our Chief Butler, who had under him three other butlers, whereof one kept still the cupboard of plate, and had there wine and ale and beer to serve for the high table, and another butler to stand in the midst of the second table, and had his wine, ale and beer by him and brought to him when he commanded it that tended upon him and likewise bread, who did fill the cups that the waiters brought over unto him. And likewise another butler did stand and serve the third table in the same sort. And William Ffowler the Head Butler went out from table to table to see all things in order and too look to his plate and to deliver spoons and to gather them up – four

---

[115] Thomas Cartewright (or Cartwright) was a Draper. See Boyd, *Roll.*

f.16v. **The Yeomanry Waiters**

Item there were pointed the four Master Bachelors of the Yeomanry to wait with twenty more of the Bachelors of the Yeomanry the best and comeliest that could be found and best apparelled, and the four Master Bachelors were appointed to be overseers to the residue to keep their order appointed who after they had broken their fast were sent to bring six guests that were bidden and to serve them with water and towels and after to bring up the whole service from the dresser with them, serve before them to the tables, and when all the first service was done, then the Chief Master Bachelor choseth, out of all those five persons with him to attend upon the high table, over whom he took the view to see them wait on that table and no other to see the meat and they carry in the meat from the said table unto the hippocras house and none to be carried elsewhere.

And so the likeorder was kept at the second table with the second Master Bachelor and so likewise of the third Master Bachelor and the fourth Master Bachelor was appointed for the parlour and also to carry out such service as was sent out of the house in to the city unto my Lord Graye etc.

ANNO 1565

Hereafter follows the general and
particular charges and expenses disbursed
by the four Master Wardens of this year as
it did fall out in order:

Mr Richard Champion Alderman   } our Master

Mr Parker[116]
Mr Nasshe[117]
Mr Reynolds[118]   } our Master Wardens
Mr Hopton[119]

Seven messes **The proportion of the first Quarter
Dinner in gross kept the Thirteenth of
January 1564 as follows delivered to the
Clerk in form as he received it:**

In primis ten capons at 20*d.*	16*s.*	8*d.*
Item five geese at 20*d.*	8*s.*	4*d.*
Item a turkey cock	4*s.*	
Item four capons at 3*s.*		12*d.*
Item for bacon	3*s.*	2*d.*
Item six dozen of larks	8*s.*	
Item di cwt. of eggs		20*d.*
Sum	53*s.*	10*d.*

Item more a sirloin of beef	3*s.*	6*d.*
Item six marrowbones	2*s.*	6*d.*
Item three lambs		9*d.*
Item in oranges		4*d.*
Item for six dozen trenchers	3*s.*	
Item for three horse loads of great coal	5*s.*	

---

[116] William Parker served as Warden of the Drapers' Company in 1554–5, 1562–3, and 1564–5. See Johnson, *History*, ii. 470.

[117] John Nash served as Warden of the Drapers' Company in 1553–4 and 1564–5. See Johnson, *History*, ii. 470.

[118] Richard Reynolds served as Warden of the Drapers' Company in 1564–5, 1571–2, and 1574–5. See Johnson, *History*, ii. 470–1.

[119] George Hopton served as Warden of the Drapers' Company in 1564–5. See Johnson, *History*, ii. 470.

Item for a kilderkin of beer		2s.	
Item for a stand of ale		2s.	
Item for borrowing a garnish of pewter vessels		3s.	4d.
Item for five dozen of bread		5s.	
	Sum	35s.	8d.
Item 2lb. of butter		2s.	
Item for a peck of salt			5d.
Item for a pottle of vertioys with a pot			3d.
Item vinegar with a pot			2d.
Item in brooms			2d.
Item taps and thread			1d.
Item a pan to melt butter			2d.
Item in mustard with a pot			1d.
	Sum	4s.	4d.
Item claret wine five gallons		6s.	8d.
Item in white wine two gallons and a quart		3s.	
Item in sack one gallon and one pottle		2s.	
Item for a quart of muscadel			8d.
	Sum	12s.	4d.

f.21r.

Item to the Butler for his pains		4s.	
Item to Goodwife Holmes			12d.
Item to the porter of the gate			4d.
Item to the Cook for his wages		6s.	
Item for twelve pies		16s.	
Item for six custards		15s.	
	Sum	42s.	4d.
Item for 2oz. of pepper			6d.
Item for di oz. of large mace			6d.
Item for 2lb. of prunes			4d.
Item for 2lb. of currants			8d.
Item for 1lb. of dates			10d.
Item for 1lb. of fine sugar			11d.
Item for 2lb. of coarse sugar			20d.
Item for a quarter of a lb. of bisktes			4d.
Item for sanders			1d.
Item for washing the napery		2s.	
Item to the Clerk's maid for washing and making clean the whole house			4d.
	Sum	8s.	2d.

Sum total of this dinner	£7	15s.	8d.	ob.

33

f.22r. **Quarter Dinner**		**Proportion of the second Quarter Dinner kept in Drapers' Hall the Fourteenth of May, Anno 1565, as it was delivered by the Renter Warden to the Clerk**		
Seven messes	In primis sixteen capons, whereof eight to roast, and the other to boil	34s.		
	Item fifteen geese at 12d. the piece	15s.		
	Item two dozen of rabbits	6s.		
	Item six chicken pies	15s.		
	Item six custards	15s.		
	Item six marchpanes	16s.		
	Item a sirloin of beef	5s.	4d.	
	Item six marrowbones	2s.	6d.	
	Item four dozen di of bread	4s.	6d.	
	Item a kilderkin of beer	2s.		
	Item in ale		12d.	
	Item six gallons of claret wine	6s.		
	Item a gallon of sack		20d.	
	Item for white wine		20d.	
	Item to the Butler	4s.		
	Item to the Cook	6s.		
	Item to the Chandler		18d.	
	Item for washing the linen	2s.		
	Item to Goodwife Holmes		8d.	

Sum £6 9s. 10d.

f.22v. **Spice**	Item dates 1lb.	10d.
	Item prunes 2lb.	3d.
	Item currants 2lb.	8d.
	Item large mace 1oz.	12d.
	Item sugar fine 1lb.	12d.
	Item sugar coarse 2lb.	20d.
	Item pepper 2oz.	5d.
	Item ginger 1oz.	3d.
	Item biskettes 3oz.	7d.
	Item for the hire of four garnish of pewter vessel	3s. 4d.

Sum 10s.

Sum total of the Quarter Dinner £7 9s. 10d.

THE FEAST DINNER } ANNO 1565

**Proportion of the said Feast Dinner
kept the first Monday in August 1565,
with all the whole furniture and charges
thereof as follows:**

A.1.	In primis a boar bought and fed at			
Meat from	St. Katherin's at Arnold's called the			
the	Hermitage[120]		50s.	
Butcher	Item for killing and dressing of it		2s.	8d.
	Item for seething of it		6s.	8d.
	Item for carrying it from St. Katherin's			6d.
	Item given in reward to a fellow to ply him			
	with feeding to brawn			12d.

	Sum	£3		10d.

	Item paid to John Wolfstone for 18lb. of			
	suet at 3d. the lb.		39s.	6d.
	Item to him for beef 134lb. at 1d. ob. the lb.		16s.	9d.

Whereof

Within and	5st. was distributed to the poor, besides all			
roundabout	manner of fees of venison, swans, goose,			
	capon etc.			
Our great	Item for three muttons and one quarter at			
court	6s. 8d.		21s.	8d.
of our Hall	Item for long marrowbones two dozen and			
	eight at 4d.		10s.	8d.
	Item veal three quarters		8s.	
	Item middling guts three			7d.
	Item a peck of pricks			2d.

	Sum	£4	7s.	3d.

	Sum of both together	£8	8s.	1d.

---

[120] Likely purchased from a tenant living adjacent to the Hermitage of St. Katherine, Charing, London. See *Survey of London*, xvi. 225–31.

f.24v.	**B.2.** **Marchpanes and comfits**	Item paid to Balthezar Sancheshe[121] for eight marchpanes of the greatest scantling at 3*s.* 4*d.*		26*s.*	8*d.*
		Item for eight marchpanes of the second scantling at 3*s.*		24*s.*	
		Item for ten marchpanes of the least size or scantling at 2*s.* 8*d.*		26*s.*	8*d.*
	Comfits	Item cinnamon comfits 1lb.		3*s.*	
		Item ginger comfits 1lb.		2*s.*	4*d.*
		Item orange comfits 1lb.		2*s.*	4*d.*
		Item coriander comfits 2lb. 6oz.		3*s.*	2*d.*
		Item clove comfits di lb.			14*d.*
		Item caraways and biskettes 1lb. 2oz.			16*d.*
		Sum	£4	10*s.*	8*d.*
	C.3. **Sturgeon**	Item paid to Blage at the Castell in New Fysshestrete for two firkins of sturgeon at 33*s.* 4*d.* the firkin	£3	6*s.*	8*d.*
		Item more for carriage thereof and other charges			8*d.*
		Sum	£3	7*s.*	4*d.*
	D.4. **Hippocras**	Item paid to William Ffowlar our Butler for fourteen gallons of hippocras at 10*s.* 4*d.*	£3	14*s.*	8*d.*
	To the Butler for his fee	Item to him for his ordinary fees and his five men		26*s.*	8*d.*
		Sum	£5		16*d.*
	E.5. **Wine**	Item paid to Mr Reynolds for one hogshead of Gascony wine		50*s.*	
		Item to Thomas Gardynar for thirty-five gallons French wine		35*s.*	
		Item for a rundlet of muscadel containing thirteen gallons at 2*s.* 6*d.* and one pottle		21*s.*	3*d.*
		Item thirteen gallons di of sack at 20*d.*		22*s.*	6*d.*
		Item white wine three gallons		3*s.*	6*d.*
		Item more white wine one gallon			12*d.*
		Sum	£6	13*s.*	

[121] Balthesar Sanchez was a London-based comfit maker of Spanish origin. See Introduction, xxix.

f.25r.	**F.6.**	Item paid to William Smyth[122] our tenant		
	Grocer	for 1oz. saffron		20*d.*
		Item for cloves and mace one quartern	2*s.*	4*d.*
		Item for cloves 2oz.		14*d.*
		Item for mace large 4oz.	3*s.*	
		Item for cinnamon 2oz.	3*s.*	9*d.*
		Item for ginger 2oz.		4*d.*
		Item nutmeg one quartern		16*d.*
		Item damask prunes 22lb.	2*s.*	
		Item currants 12lb.	4*s.*	6*d.*
		Item dates 6lb.	4*s.*	6*d.*
		Item pepper 2lb.	5*s.*	8*d.*
		Item cinnamon di lb.	14*s.*	
		Item ginger 6oz.		12*d.*
		Item nutmeg 6oz.	2*s.*	
		Item coriander seeds di lb.		3*d.*
		Item ysanglasse[123] 1lb.	2*s.*	
		Item tormesall[124] 1lb.		20*d.*
		Item two quires of paper		6*d.*
		Item sanders 1oz.		2*d.*
		Item pepper 2lb.	5*s.*	8*d.*
		Item nutmeg 3oz.		12*d.*
		Item ginger 2oz.		4*d.*
		Item cloves and mace di oz.		4*d.*
		Item mace large 1oz.		11*d.*
		Item dates 1lb.		9*d.*
		Item pepper 1lb.	2*s.*	10*d.*
		Item sugar 10lb.		8*d.*
		Item sugar 1lb.		11*d.*
		Item currants 2lb.		9*d.*
		Item sugar 44lb. at 10*d.*	36*s.*	8*d.*
		Item pepper 10lb. at 2*s.* 10*d.*	28*s.*	4*d.*

Sum   £6   13<u>*s.*</u>   <u>4*d.*</u>

	G.7.	Item paid to Robert Mason our Poulterer		
	The Poulterer	for seventy-five capons at 2*s.* 1*d.*	£7	16*s.*	4*d.*
		Item for twenty-six geese at 20*d.*	43*s.*	4*d.*
		Item for five cygnets at 8*s.* 4*d.*	56*s.*	
f.25v.		Item for nine dozen pigeons at 20*d.*	15*s.*	
		Item for two heronshaws[125] at 3*s.* 6*d.*	8*s.*	
		Item for 6cwt. of eggs at 2*s.* 10*d.* the cwt.	17*s.*	

[122] William Smyth was a Grocer and tenant of the Drapers' Company on Cheapside. See DB, DCA, f.95r.

[123] Isinglass, a derivative of sturgeon, was used in the making of jellies.

[124] Tornesol was likely the English corruption of the Italian 'girasole', or sunflower. It may be an early reference to a Jerusalem artichoke. Its yellow flowers may have been used in the making of jelly: see DCA, DB1, f.58v.

[125] Heronshaw: a young or small heron.

	Item for ten dozen of quails at 7*s.* the dozen provided by Mr Warden Renolds	£3	10*s.*	
	Item for meat[126] for the said quails		3*s.*	1*d.*
	Item for three cygnets bought of our bull[127]		24*s.*	
	Item for meat for the said cygnets		3*s.*	
	Item for fifteen capons at 22*d.* provided by Mr Warden Reynolds		27*s.*	6*d.*

Sum	£20	14*s.*	6*d.*

Whereof

Rebated for fourteen quails		7*s.*
And so paid the whole remain	£20	7*s.*	6*d.*

H.8. **Pikemonger**	Item paid to Richard Lucas at Qwenehive[128] for twenty-seven pikes at 22*d.* the piece	49*s.*

Whereof

Four to be of twenty-four inches long and all the rest, the one half to contain twenty inches long, and the other half eighteen inches long, all perfect, sweet and good

Sum	49*s.*

J.9. **Linen cloth**	Item bought of Thomas Fyssher, Draper, half a piece of lockeram	51*s.*	
	Item two ells of white cloth which was provided by Mr Warden Reynolds	3*s.*	
	Item for two ells of canvas		16*d.*
	Item for four ells of soultage	2*s.*	

Sum	57*s.*	4*d.*

Memorandum

Two ells of fine Holland for the servers at 18*d.* the ell	3*s.*	
Item eight ells of soultage foresaid and three quarters beside two ells of canvas allowed for the kitchen	3*s.*	2*d.*

---

[126] Meat: food in general, animal fodder.
[127] Bull: the official licence issued for the cygnets.
[128] Qwenehive: Queenhithe Quay was primarily a fish market.

f.26r. **K.10.**
The Baker
for bread

Saturday	Item paid to Homfrey Veron in St. Clement's Lane for Saturday of half penny bread, and penny bread being something stale – one dozen Item for rolls three at 1*d.* being all new baked – one dozen Item for halfpenny bread new baked – one dozen		
Sunday	Item for penny bread and half penny bread being stale – five dozen Item for penny bread and half penny bread new – two dozen Item for wheaten bread – two dozen Item for rolls new – one dozen		
Monday	Item for new half bread – ten dozen Item for penny bread new – two dozen Item for rolls three at 1*d.* new – three dozen Item for wheaten bread stale and new – two dozen		
Tuesday	Item for penny loaves white bread – four dozen Item for half penny loaves white bread – one dozen		
	Sum – thirty-one dozen		
Meal and oatmeal	Item more for wheat meal two quarters	40*s.*	
	Item for received meal two bushels	4*s.*	
	Item for flour four bushels	10*s.*	8*d.*
	Item more for halfpenny white bread four dozen	4*s.*	
	Item for penny white bread one dozen		12*d.*
	Sum in all	£4 10*s.*	

f.26v. **L.11.**
Spice bread

Item paid to Joan Wall for five dozen buns, and five dozen cakes	20*s.*	

M.12. **Wafers**	Item paid to James Wharton minister[129] for eleven boxes of wafers viz. white, green, yellow, red & crimson	*22s.*
N.13. **Beer Brewer**	Item paid to the Beer Brewer for five barrels of beer at 4*s.* the barrel	*20s.*
O.14. **Ale Brewer**	Item paid to Martyn our tenant at the Bull in Smythfeld four barrels and one stand at 4*s.* the barrel	*18s.*

P.15. **Chandler**	Item for the Cook and others white salt two bushels	*3s.*	
	Item bay salt one bushel		*15d.*
	Item red vinegar two gallons		*12d.*
	Item white vinegar one gallon di		*21d.*
	Item vertious two gallons		*10d.*
	Item mustard one pottle and 2*d.* besides		*8d.*
	Item cotton candles 3lb.		*9d.*
	Item weak candles 8lb.	*2s.*	
	Item packthread		*4d.*
	Item six earthen pans	*12s.*	
	Item great boiling pots six at 2*d. ob.*		*15d.*
	Item great pots eight		*5d.*
	Item pottle pots four		*4d.*
	Item oatmeal three pecks		*20d.*
	Item oatmeal groats for puddings for the butlers		*4d.*
	Item twelve green pots		*8d.*
	Item eight gallon pots		*12d.*
	Item twelve pottle pots		*12d.*
	Item ten chafers		*20d.*
	Item two earthen pans		*3d.*
	Item for the lending of four dozen di of pots and pitchers		*11d.*

f.27r.

	Sum	*22s.*

Q.16. **Pewterer**	Item paid to Mrs Catcher[130] for nineteen garnish of vessels	*15s.*	*10d.*
R.17. **Ashen cups**	Item for two dozen of ashen cups and twelve taps	*2s.*	*2d.*

---

[129] James Wharton was a Draper. His wife provided wafers to the Company for several years. See Boyd, *Roll*.

[130] Ellen Catcher (née Suthwicke). Her husband was John Catcher, Pewterer. See *HP Commons, 1604–1629*, iii. 461.

S.18. **Fruits**	Item for 11cwt. of plum at 8*d.* the cwt.	7*s.*	4*d.*
	Item 5lb. of cherries at 3*d.* the lb.		15*d.*
	Item 2cwt. di of pears, at 10*d.* the cwt.	2*s.*	1*d.*
	Item 5cwt. of pears at 12*d.*	10*s.*	
	Item 2cwt. plum at 5*d.*		12*d.*
	Item 1cwt. pears at 8*d.*		8*d.*
	Item 1cwt. codlings		20*d.*
	Item one peck di of filberts	4*s.*	8*d.*
	Item one quart of olives		8*d.*
	Item onions		7*d.*
	Sum	26*s.*	3*d.*

T.19. **Trenchers**	Item in trenchers twenty-four dozen	7*s.*	4*d.*
Trays	Item for four Dansk trays	2*s.*	4*d.*
Bolts	Item for two bolts		4*d.*
Brooms	Item for two brooms		2*d.*
A staff torch	Item for a staff torch		11*d.*
	Sum	11*s.*	1*d.*

f.27v.
V.20. **Butter**	Item paid for 84lb. of sweet butter	22*s.*	9*d.*	*ob.*

X.21. **The Cook** **and** **his fees**	Item paid to Stephan Triacle for baking of one buck being sent before the feast	10*s.*	
	Item for two legs and a knuckle of veal	2*s.*	
	Item for 22lb. di of lard	10*s.*	
Cream	Item for thirteen gallons di of cream	13*s.*	6*d.*
	Item for his ordinary wages the feast time	40*s.*	
	Item for buying all the fees of him	10*s.*	
	Sum £4	5*s.*	6*d.*

Y.22. **Wood and** **Coal**	Item paid for 2cwt. fagots	8*s.*	
	Item paid for one quarter of billets	2*s.*	6*d.*
	Item paid for one load of coals twenty-four sacks	12*s.*	
	Sum	22*s.*	6*d.*

Z.23. **Officers' fees and wages**	Item paid to Chrispofer Ffulks our Sewer and Carver	6s.	8d.
	Item paid to Small our Steward	30s.	
	Item to the Waites	13s.	4d.
	Item to the Clerk and Sexton of St. Michael's	4s.	
Gilding of brawn and jelly	Item to Semper for the gilding of our brawn and our jelly	13s.	4d.
	Item to four porters keeping the gates and stairs	13s.	

Whereof

Four porters	To Richard Seyntpere, Chief Porter, 4s. and to the other three porters 3s. a piece

Women in the kitchen	Item the Beadle's wife Goodwife Holmes for four days labour in the kitchen and the whole house	3s.	4d.
	Item to Eeles' wife[131] for three days		18d.
	Item to two women for scraping of trenchers at 6d. the piece for two days	2s.	
	Item to Robert Beaumont[132] to help the Steward		
	Item to Henry Starr our Labourer for his pains	2s.	
	Item to our Gardener		

f.28r.

	Sum	£4	9s.	2d.

24. **Rewards for bucks**	Item to Sir Hugh Pawlett's man for bringing one buck	5s.	
	Item to the Lady Graye's[133] man for two bucks	10s.	
	Item to the Lady Wentworth's[134] man for two bucks	8s.	4d.
	Item to Sir William Chestar's man for a buck		20d.
	Item to the Lord Treasurer's man for a buck	3s.	4d.

---

[131] Denys Eles (or Denise Ellis) worked with other women in the kitchen between 1568 and 1571.

[132] Robert Beaumond was a Draper. He served as Under-Steward in 1565 and Steward in 1566, 1567, 1569, 1570, and 1571. See Boyd, *Roll*.

[133] Lady Mary Grey, widow of Lord John Grey. See *Oxford DNB*.

[134] Anne, Lady Wentworth (née Wentworth) was the wife of Thomas Wentworth, Second Baron Wentworth. See *Oxford DNB*.

Item to Mr Thompson's man the auditor
for a buck brought to our Master Mr
Alderman Champion which he paid for

	Sum	28s.	4d.

25. Perfumes, flowers and sweet waters	Item for two quarts of rosewater provided and bought by Mrs Reynolds[135]		18d.
	Item for strewing herbs and flowers		12d.

	Sum	2s.	6d.

26. Extra-ordinary charges	Item for three little padlocks and keys	16d.
	Item for a glass of rosewater	2d.
	Item for two yards of bolt-cloth	8d.
	Item for a small line	1d.
	Item for a coal basket	8d.
	Item for wine tap	2d.
	Item for guts to the Cook	3d.
	Item for carnal white for the strainers	12d.
	Item for a quire of paper for the Steward	2d.

	Sum	4s.	4d.

f.28v.

Here following the total sums in general of all the particulars:

	£	s.	d.
The Butcher's bill amounts in all to	£7	8s.	1d.
Marchpanes and comfits	£4	10s.	8d.
Sturgeon	£3	7s.	4d.
Hippocras	£3	14s.	8d.
Wine	£6	13s.	
The Grocer's bill	£6	18s.	4d.
The Poulterer's bill	£20	7s.	6d.
The Pikemonger's bill		49s.	
Linen cloth		57s.	4d.
The Baker's bill	£4	10s.	
Spice bread		20s.	
Wafers		22s.	
Beer Brewer		20s.	
Ale Brewer		18s.	
Chandler		22s.	
Pewterer		15s.	10d.
Ashen cups		2s.	2d.
Fruit		26s.	3d.
Trenchers, trays, bells, gowns and staff torches		11s.	1d.

---

135 Alice, wife of Richard Reynolds, Third Warden of the Drapers' Company in 1564–5. See Johnson, *History*, ii. 470.

Butter		22s.	9d.	ob.
The Cook, his wages and fees	£4	5s.	6d.
Wood and coal		22s.	6d.
The Butler's fee		22s.	8d.
Officers' wages	£4	9s.	2d.
Rewards for bucks		28s.	4d.
Perfumes, flowers and waters		2s.	6d.
Extraordinary charges		4s.	4d.

<u>Sum total of all the particular totals</u> £84 15s.

Whereof

Received towards the said charges per contra as follows:
First the ordinary allowance of the house towards this dinner £10
Item granted by the Assistants by act of Court towards the augmentation thereof upon certain considerations £5
Item of Rydley made free by redemption 53s. 4d.
Item for quarterage money levied by 5s. and the rest compounded with Messenger our Clerk £3 8s.

Sum <u>£21</u> <u>4d.</u>

Sum received as appears <u>£21</u> <u>4d.</u>

And we have paid as it appears per contra

So the clear charges of our said dinner net stands in £63 14s. 8d.

Whereof

By equal division every Warden's particular dividend and part severally by poll amounts unto £15 18s. 8d. net and clear £15 18s. 8d.

Venison brought in by the four Master Wardens for the said dinner
By Mr Parker – five bucks di
By Mr Nasshe – one stag and three bucks
By Mr Renolds – five bucks
By Mr Hopton – four bucks

One stag, seventeen bucks di

Other bucks in general given as follows and paid for to the bringers as before

By Sir Hugh Pawlett – one buck
By the Lady Gray – two bucks
By the Lady Wentworth – two bucks
By Sir William Chestar – one buck
By the Lord Treasurer – one buck
By Mr Tompson auditor to Mr Champion – one buck

Eight bucks

Sum in all together – bucks – twenty-five di and one stag

Whereof

Pasties baked

Pasties baked of bucks viz. [-]

ANNO 1565 AND 1566

Here after following the general and
particular charges and expenses disbursed
by the four Master Wardens for this two
years aforesaid as it did fall out in order

Sir Richard Champion
Knight and Alderman then Lord Mayor of } our Master
London yet[136]

John Quarles
John Branche[137]   } our Master
George Braithwaite   Wardens
William Throwgood[138]

First Quarter Proportion of the same dinner with the
Dinner service thereof in due order:

5th Feb. 1565 The Lord Mayor with his train almost
twelve viz. the Swordbearer, four Squires
and the rest of Serjeants

viz. eight   The two Sheriffs[139] with the two brethren
messes   George and John Barnes[140]
furnished

First course One side bacon   2s. 6d.
First collopps[141] and eggs   4s. 6d.

---

[136] Sir Richard Champion was then Lord Mayor elect. He was invested in the role in October 1565.

[137] (Sir) John Branch served as Warden of the Drapers' Company in 1557–8, 1565–6, 1569–70 and as Master in 1572–3, 1576–7, 1579–80, and 1583–4. He became Alderman in 1571, and served as Sheriff in 1571–2 and Lord Mayor in 1580–1. See Johnson, *History*, ii. 470–2; Beaven, *Aldermen*, ii. 39.

[138] William Thorowgood served as Warden of the Drapers' Company in 1565–6, 1573–4, and 1577–8. He was Master of the Company in 1585–6 and 1588–9. He was an Alderman from 1589. See Johnson, *History*, ii. 471–2; Beaven, *Aldermen*, i. 102.

[139] Edward Jakman, Grocer, and Lionel Duckett, Mercer. See Beaven, *Aldermen*, ii. 37.

[140] (Sir) George Barnes (or Barne) was Master of the Haberdashers' Company in 1586–7. He became Alderman in 1574, and served as Sheriff in 1576–7 and Lord Mayor in 1586–7. Barnes was a Governor of the Muscovy Company in 1580 and 1583, and represented the City in Parliament in 1589. His brother John was also a Haberdasher. See *HP Commons, 1558–1603*, i. 397.

Turkey cocks eight viz. four at 3*s.* and four
at 3*s.* 4*d.*
Roasted capons

Of Mr	Minced pies – sixteen at 16*d.*	21*s.*	4*d.*
Wilkockes	Custards – eight at 2*s.* 4*d.*	18*s.*	8*d.*

37v. **Second course** Item woodcocks[142] four and for
greenplovers[143] two at 4*s.*   12*s.*
Item four lambs at 3*s.*
Item larks two dozen di at 3*s.* 4*d.*
Item eight marchpanes at 3*s.* 4*d.*   26*s.*   13*d.*

Of the Item a sirloin of beef at 3*s.*
Butcher Item six marrowbones at 2*s.* 6*d.*

<u>5*s.*</u>   <u>6*d.*</u>

Wine from Item three gallons of claret wine at 4*s.*
the Bisshop's Item two gallons of sack at 3*s.* 4*d.*
Hedd Item a gallon of white wine at 16*d.*

Wine from Item four gallons of claret wine at 5*s.* 4*d.*
the Mytar[144] Item in oranges   4*d.*
Item rose water a pint   16*d.*

Of the	In primis 2lb. at 2*d.* the lb.		4*d.*	
Grocer	Item sugar 6lb. at 11*d.*	5*s.*	6*d.*	
	Item sugar 2lb. at 10*d.*		20*d.*	
	Item dates 1lb.		12*d.*	
	Item currants 1lb.		8*d.*	
	Item pepper 2oz.		4*d.*	
38r.	Item cinnamon di oz.		12*d.*	
	Item ginger di oz.		1*d.*	*ob.*
	Item sanders di oz.		2*d.*	
	Item biscaytes a quarter of lb.		4*d.*	
	Item mace 1oz.		12*d.*	

To the Baker Item of the Baker for eight dozen of white
bread and 3*d.* worth of wheaten bread   8*s.*   3*d.*

---

[141] Collops: bacon. Likely served with a fried egg on top.
[142] Woodcock: medium-sized wild fowl.
[143] Green plover: young or small plover (wild waterfowl).
[144] Likely the Mitre tavern on Broad Street, a fashionable meeting place of urban professional men. See M. O'Callaghan, 'Tavern Societies, the Inns of Court, and the Culture of Conviviality in Early 17th Century London' in A. Smyth (ed.) *A Pleasing Sinne: Drink and Conviviality in 17th Century England* (Cambridge: D. S. Brewer, 2004), 37–51 (38).

To the Brewer, Campion	Item for one kilderkin of beer at	2*s.*	6*d.*
	Item for one kilderkin of ale at	3*s.*	
The Butler	Item to the Butler for his ordinary	4*s.*	
The Cook	Item to the Cook, Stephan Treakle, for his ordinary at this time	6*s.*	8*d.*
To the Chandler	Item for a peck of salt		3*d.*
	Item for three pints of vinegar		3*d.*
	Item for three pints of vertious		3*d.*
	Item for six pounds of butter at 3*d.*		18*d.*
	Item for a birchen brown[145]		1*d.*
	Item for a pippin and packthread		1*d.*
	Item to Goodwife Holmes for washing and making clean the vessels		6*d.*
To the Pewterer, Mr Catcher	Item for the usage of five garnish of pewter vessels and a half at 10*d.*	4*s.*	6*d.*
Napery	Item to the Clerk's wife for washing the napery of the house	2*s.*	

f.38v.	**To the Collier**	Item paid for three horse loads of coals for the only and accustomed use of this dinner	3*s.*	
	Proportion of plate for this dinner	Item the just proportion of plate to serve for this dinner is written and contained by several parcels in the second leaf of the beginning of this book		
	Napery	The proportion thereof is always certain		

Sum total of all this dinner   £11   9*s.*   7*d.*

f.39r.		**Proportion of the second Quarter Dinner kept the twenty-eighth day of May 1566, my Lord Mayor, the two Sheriffs, and his train with him**
	Second Quarter Dinner	Memorandum that the order of the proportion was not here written by reason the Master Wardens brought in their bill of the charges of that dinner in particulars by gross as hereafter does follow:

[145] Birchen brown: likely a broom made of birch tree.

Eight messes	In primis for a kilderkin of beer	2s.	6d.
	Item for kilderkin of ale	3s.	
	Item for three sacks of coals		18d.
	Item for butter		18d.
	Item for a sirloin of beef	4s.	4d.
	Item for a long marrowbone		6d.
	Item for other marrowbones		18d.
	Item for oranges		6d.
	Item for lemons		2d.
	Item for a pint of rose water		10d.
	Item to the Butler	4s.	
	Item to the Chandler		22d.
	Item one gallon French wine		20d.
	Item a gallon of sack		20d.
	Item a pottle of white wine		8d.
	Item six dozen trenchers	2s.	6d.
	Item for a fresh salmon	13s.	
	Item for sturgeon	6s.	
39v.	Item to the Pewterer	4s.	2d.
	Item Mrs Wilcockes for eight chicken pies at 3s. 1d.	26s.	8d.
	Item for eight custards at 2s. 4d.	18s.	8d.
	Item for eight marchpanes at 3s. 4d.	26s.	8d.
	Item to the Cook for dressing the dinner	6s.	8d.
	Item to the Poulterer for nine capons at 2s. 2d.	19s.	6d.
	Item for sixteen geese at 12d.	16s.	
	Item two dozen di of chicken	12s.	6d.
	Item two dozen rabbits	5s.	
	Item for washing the napery	2s.	
	Item for 2lb. of prunes		4d.
	Item for sugar 3lb.	2s.	9d.
	Item for sugar 2lb.		20d.
	Item dates 1lb.		12d.
	Item currants 2lb.		8d.
	Item pepper 2oz.		5d.
	Item ginger di oz		2d.
	Item sanders di oz.		2d.
	Item biskettes quarter lb.		4d.
	Item long mace 1oz		14d.
	Item seven dozen breads	7s.	
	Item to Goodwife Holmes		6d.

<u>Sum</u>   <u>£10</u>   <u>9s.</u>   <u>8d.</u>

FEAST DINNER } ANNO 1566

The eighth year in the reign of Queen
Elizabeth etc.

Sir Richard Champion Knight then Lord Mayor of London

Preparation before the same dinner for two days as follows:

Saturday 27 July 1566 for potation
In primis four dozen spice cakes and buns
Item rolls of white bread for servants and
waiters – two dozen
Item codlings with rose water and sugar
Item biskettes and caraways
Item pears
Item plums
Item comfits of all sorts
Item hippocras

Two messes

**Sunday 28 July two messes of meat for
the Wardens and their guests viz.**
Item boiled capons – two
Item roast beef pieces – two
Item pastries of venison – two
Item bread, ale, beer and wine of the house

Potation on that day in the afternoon
Item like service in all things as on Saturday before etc.

f.41v.

At supper that Sunday at night
Item four shoulders of mutton roasted – four
Item capon roasted – two
Item pasties of venison – four

First course

Service on Monday at dinner being the Feast Day

Four messes

To the high table in the hall
In primis brawn and mustard
Item boiled capons – eight
Item swans – four
Item venison pasties – four
Item pikes – four
Item roast capons and herons – eight
Item custards – four

50

Seven messes **To the parlour for the ladies and their train**
Item brawn and mustard
Item boiled capons – thirteen
Item swans – six
Item goose – one
Item venison pasties – seven
Item pikes – seven
Item roasted capons and herons – thirteen
Item custards – seven

f.42r. Four messes **To the second table in the hall**
Item brawn and mustard
Item boiled capons – eight
Item swans – three
Item geese – one
Item venison pasties – four
Item pikes – four
Item four roasted capons and two herons – six
Item custards – four

Five messes **To the third table in the hall**
Item brawn and mustard
Item boiled capons – eight
Item swans – one
Item geese – four
Item venison pasties – five
Item six roast capons and one heron –
seven
Item custards – five

Two messes **To the table in the parlour behind the travers of arras[146]**
for the Wardens, Swordbearers and other officers
Item brawn and mustard
Item boiled capons – two
Item geese – two
Item venison pasties – two
Item pikes – two
Item roasted capons – two
Item custards – two

f.42v. **Second course To the high table in the hall**
Item jelly dishes – twenty-six
Item quails dozens – two
Item pasties of red deer – four

[146] The travers of arras was a temporary partition constructed to subdivide the parlour so
that officers could put on their garlands in private and arrange themselves to re-enter the
hall for the Election ceremony. There were so many important guests in attendance at this
particular Election Dinner in 1566 that the Wardens instead appear to have set up a table
in the parlour and positioned themselves there, with a special table for the ladies perhaps
on the other side of the travers.

Item sturgeon jowl – one
Item rondes of sturgeon – three
Item marchpanes – four

And at the last
Wafers and hippocras

Eight messes **To the parlour for the ladies' table**
Item jelly dishes – forty-two
Item quails three dozen and pigeons di dozen
Item pasties of red deer – one
And the rest being sliced dishes – six
Item one sturgeon jowl, three rondes and three sliced
sturgeon dishes
Item marchpanes – seven

And at the last
Wafers and hippocras

Four messes **To the second table in the hall**
Item jelly dishes dozens – two
Item quails dozens – two
Item red deer sliced dishes – four
Item sturgeon dishes sliced – four
Item marchpanes – four

And at last
Wafers and hippocras

f.43r. Five messes **To the third table in the hall**
Item jelly dishes dozens – two di
Item one quail and one di pigeons dozen – two di
Item red deer sliced dishes – five
Item sturgeon sliced dishes – five
Item marchpanes – five

And at last
Wafers and hippocras

Memorandum that day in the morning at seven of the
clock the twenty-four Bachelor waiters brake their fast with
mutton and porridge

One whole **Also provided for the four Master Bachelors and the
mess waiters of the Company for their dinner viz.**
Item boiled capon – one
Item roast goose – one
Item venison pasty – one
Item roast capon – one
Item custard – one

Monday at night supper for the Wardens
Item capon roasted – one
Item venison pasties – three

Finis for that day

f.43v.   Service for Tuesday

First course   **To the high table in the hall**
Four messes   In primis brawn and mustard
Item pudding both black and white
Item boiled capons – eight
Item swans – two
Item geese – two
Item venison pasties – four
Item pikes – four
Item roast capons – eight
Item custards – four

Five messes   **To the second table there**
Brawn and mustard
Item puddings black and white
Item boiled capons – eight
Item geese – five
Item venison pasties – five
Item pikes – five
Item roasted capons – eight
Item custards – five

Four messes   **To the third table there**
Item brawn and mustard
Item puddings as above
Item boiled capons – four
Item geese – four
Item venison pasties – four
Item pikes – two
Item roast capons – four
Item custards – four

f.44r. One mess   **To the table in the parlour behind the travers of arras for Master Wardens, the Clerk and the Renter**
Item brawn and mustard
Item puddings enough
Item boiled capon – one
Item goose – one
Item venison pasties – one
Item pike – one
Item roast capon – one
Item custard – one

53

	Second course	**To the high table**		
	Four messes	Item jelly dishes dozens – one		
		Item quails dozens – two		
		Item pasties of red deer – four		
		Item sturgeon one jowl and three rondes		
		Item marchpanes – four		
		And after that		
		Wafers and hippocras		

	Five messes	**To the second table**		
		Item jelly dishes dozens – two and di		
		Item pigeons dozens – two and di		
		Item red deer sliced dishes – five		
		Item marchpanes – five		
		And after that		
		Wafers and hippocras		

	Four messes	To the third table		
		Jelly dishes dozens – one and di		
		Item pigeons dozens – one and di		
f.44v.		Item red deer sliced dishes – four		
		Item sturgeon sliced dished – four		
		Item marchpanes – one		
		At the last		
		Wafers and hippocras		

f.45r.	**Feast Dinner}** **1566**	**The whole accounts with the expenses and** **whole charges by particulars as follows viz.:**		
	The Butcher	In primis for a boar	45*s.*	
		Item for three shoulders of veal	2*s.*	8*d*
		Item for four pairs of calves feet		12*d*
	Saturday	Item for twelve pounds of suet	3*s.*	
		Item for a sirloin of beef poise[147] – 4st. di	4*s.*	6*d*
	Sunday	Item for a quarter of mutton	2*s.*	
		Item for two long marrowbones		10*d*
		Item 60lb. of suet	15*s.*	
		Item twenty long marrowbones	8*s.*	4*d*
		Item two sirloins of beef poise 8st. and 2lb.	8*s.*	3*d*
		Item two muttons	16*s.*	
		Item a quarter of mutton	2*s.*	6*d*
		Item a peck of pricks		6*d*
	Monday	Item twelve long marrowbones	5*s.*	
		Item 40lb. of suet	10*s.*	

[147] Poise: weighing.

54

Item 6lb. of suet				18*d.*
Item a sirloin of beef poise 4st. and 6lb.		4*s.*		9*d.*
Item a quarter of beef for the poor				
distributed on Tuesday after dinner		20*s.*		

	Sum	£7	10*s.*

Marchpanes — Item paid to Mrs Wilcockes for thirty
marchpanes at 3*s.* 4*d.* the piece — £5

	Sum	£5

45v. **Comfits**

Item 1lb. di of almond comfits at 14*d.*		21*d*
Item 1lb. quarter of clove comfits at 2*s.*	2*s.*	6*d.*
Item 1lb. quarter of oranges comfits at 2*s.*	2*s.*	6*d.*
Item 1lb. quarter of ginger comfits at 2*s.*	2*s.*	6*d.*
Item 1lb. quarter cinnamon comfits at 2*s.* 4*d.*	2*s.*	11*d.*
Item 1lb. three quarters caraways at 14*d.*	2*s.*	
Item 2lb. quarter of biskettes at 14*d.*	2*s.*	8*d.*

	Sum	16*s.*	10*d.*

Sturgeon

Item to Mr Quarles for a firkin of sturgeon	27*s.*
Item to Blage for a firkin of sturgeon	33*s.*

	Sum	£3

Hippocras — Item to Blage for seventeen gallons of
hippocras at 5*s.* the gallon — £4 5*s.*

	Sum	£4	5*s.*

Wine of all sorts

Item Robert Ffryar for one puncheon of French wine and two hogsheads of Gascon wine	£12	16*s.*	8*d.*
Item to Cuthbert Buckell for a rundlet of sack containing twelve gallons at nineteen the gallon		19*s.*	
Item a rundlet of muscadel quart thirteen gallons at 2*s.* 2*d.* the gallon		28*s.*	2*d.*
Item for a rundlet of Rhenish wine quart eleven gallons and a pottle at 23*d.* the gallon		22*s.*	2*d.*
Item for a pottle of white wine			8*d.*
Item for four gallons of wines for jelly bought by Robert Beamond		5*s.*	4*d.*
Item for a quart of white wine by him bought to fill up sturgeon			4*d.*
Item for four gallons and a quart of wine for broths by him bought		5*s.*	8*d.*

Item for carriage of the rundlets of sack,
muscadel, and Rhenish wine by him   4*d.*

Sum   £16   18*s.*   4*d.*

f.46r. **Grocer, Brokbanck**	Item two sugar loaves that 21lb. and quarter at 10*d. ob.*		18*s.*	7*d.*
	Item three sugar loaves that 19lb. at 9*d. ob.*		15*s.*	1*d.*
	Item sugar pieced that 24lb. at 8*d. ob.*		17*s.*	
	Item nutmeg 6oz. at 6*d.*		3*s.*	
	Item ginger 8oz. at 3*s.* 4*d.*			20*d.*
	Item colyander seeds 8oz.			4*d.*
	Item turnesall 1lb. di at 16*d.*		2*s.*	
	Item ysonglas 1lb.		20*s.*	
	Item pepper 16lb. at 2*s.* 8*d.*		42*s.*	8*d.*
	Item saffron 2oz.		3*s.*	4*d.*
	Item cloves 2oz.			12*d.*
	Item mace 4oz.		2*s.*	8*d.*
	Item nutmeg 5oz.		2*s.*	6*d.*
	Item cinnamon 4oz.		2*s.*	8*d.*
	Item ginger quarter lb.			10*d.*
	Item mace long 6oz. at 12*d.*		6*s.*	
	Item sanders 1oz.			3*d.*
	Item damask prunes 14lb. and 2*d.*		2*s.*	11*d.*
	Item currants 12lb.		4*s.*	
	Item dates 10lb. at 10*d.*		8*s.*	4*d.*
	Item rose water one quart and di quart		2*s.*	1*d.*
	Item cap paper three quires			9*d.*
	Item 1oz. cloves			6*d.*
	Item 1lb. of cinnamon bought by Mr Throwgood		12*s.*	

Sum   £7   11*s.*   6*d.*

Poulterer, Mason	Item eight dozen and ten capons at 2*s.*	£10	12*s.*
	Item eight cygnets at 8*s.* the piece	£3	4*s.*
	Item a dozen of heronshaws at 3*s.* 4*d.*		40*s.*
	Item eight dozen of pigeons at 20*d.*		11*s.* 8*d.*
	Item two dozen and one goose at 20*d.*		41*s.* 8*d.*
	Item for one dozen capons bought by Master Warden Throwgood		20*s.*
	Item 7cwt. eggs and a quarter at 2*s.* 10*d.* the cwt.		19*s.* 10*d.*
	Item eight swans of Thomas Whelar[148] at 7*s.* the piece		56*s.*

[148] Thomas Whelar (or Wheeler) served as Warden in the Drapers' Company in 1569–70 and 1573–4 (he died during his second term). He was a member of the Inner Temple and MP for Ludlow between 1539 and 1553. See Johnson, *History*, ii. 471; *HP Commons, 1509–1558*, iii. 602–3.

Item eleven dozen quails at 9*s.* the dozen		£4	10*s.*
	Sum	£27	15*s.*

46v. Pikemonger, Lucas — Item to him for thirty-six pikes whereof six of twenty-four inches, twelve at twenty inches and twelves at eighteen inches, price every pike one with the other – 22*d.* £3 4*s.*

Sum £3 4*s.*

Linen cloth

Item paid to Mr Branch's man for four ells of soultage 2*s.*

Item paid for a piece of lockeram and for Holland cloth to Mr Quarles 48*s.*

Item to Mr Throwgood for four ells Holland, thirteen ells lockram and two ells soultage 22*s.* 10*d.*

Sum £3 12*s.* 10*d.*

The Baker, Storar

Item for two dozen rolls at two a penny, and one dozen halfpenny bread on Saturday at night 3*s.*

Item two dozen of halfpenny bread, two dozen of penny bread, one dozen of rolls at two a penny, and one dozen white bread on Sunday 6*s.*

Item seven dozen of penny white bread, seven dozen of halfpenny breads, six dozen of stale penny white four dozen of new rolls at three a penny, and two dozen of wheaten brea*d.* Item more that day four dozen of penny white and three dozen of penny white 33*s.*

Item on Tuesday five dozen rolls at three a penny

Item four dozen new penny white, two dozen of wheaten, two dozen of stale penny white 13*s.*

Item bushels of fine flour at 4*s.* a bushel 12*s.*

Item by Mr Throwgood twenty bushels meal and the carriage 55*s.*

Sum £6 2*s.*

Spice bread

Item paid to Goodwife Wall for six dozen buns and six dozen cakes 24*s.*

Sum 24*s.*

f.47r.	**Wafers, Wharton**	Item paid to Wharton's wife for fifteen boxes of wafers at 2*s.* the box	30*s.*	
		Sum	30*s.*	

	Beer Brewer, Mr Campion	Item to Mr Campion for four barrels of the Queen's beer at 5*s.* the barrel	20*s.*	
		Item more a barrel di of double beer of the Butler at 4*s.* the barrel	6*s.*	
		Sum	26*s.*	

	Ale Brewer, Martyn	Item for four barrels of ale	16*s.*	
		Item for a stand of penny ale		10*d.*
		Item for two pales of yeast		12*d.*
		Sum	17*s.*	10*d.*

	Chandler	Item for three dozen green pots at 12*d.* the dozen		
		Item three dozen pots at 18*d.* the dozen and for all other particulars of his two bills	32*s.*	

f.47v.	**The Pewterer, Catcher**	Item paid to him for nineteenth garnish of vessels at 10*d.* the garnish	15*s.*	10*d.*
		Item for twenty dozen jelly dishes at 6*d.* the dozen	10*s.*	
		Item paid to him for 8lb. of pewter lost at 7*d.* the lb.	4*s.*	8*d.*
		Sum	30*s.*	6*d.*

	Ashen cups	Item bought by R. Beaumonde two dozen of cups at 10*d.* the dozen		20*d.*
		Item to the Butler for two dozen	2*s.*	
		Sum	3*s.*	8*d.*

	Fruits	Item for 6cwt. pears per Beamond	5*s.*	8*d.*
		Item for 3cwt. plums	2*s.*	6*d.*
		Item for cwt. di of codlings	2*s.*	4*d.*
		Item for a gallon of barberries	5*s.*	4*d.*
		Item for radishes		4*d.*
		Sum	16*s.*	2*d.*

Trenchers	Item for twenty-four dozen trenchers	10*s.*	
and trays etc.	Item for four Danask trays	3*s.*	4*d.*
with other	Item for taps for beer and ale		2*d.*
trash	Item for strainers		8*d.*
	Item for brooms		6*d.*
	Item for two baskets and a coal shovel		12*d.*
	Item for taps of wine and broaching of the same		12*d.*
	Item for yeast for pike broths		4*d.*
	Sum	17*s.*	
Butter and	Item for 102lb. of butter	25*s.*	6*d.*
cream	Item for fifteen gallons of cream and one pottle	16*s.*	
	Sum	41*s.*	6*d.*
The Cook	Item paid to Tryacle our Cook for his wages	40*s.*	
	Item to him for baking of twenty-four pasties of venison	4*s.*	
	Item for di bushel of flour by him bought		16*d.*
	Sum	45*s.*	4*d.*
f.48r. **The Painter**	Item to Young, the painter, for gilding of brawn, jelly and sturgeon	36*s.*	8*d.*
Wood and	Item paid for cwt. di of fagots	6*s.*	6*d.*
coal	Item for di thousand of billets	5*s.*	
	Item for twenty sacks of coals at 6*d.*	10*s.*	
	Sum	21*s.*	6*d.*
Butler	Item paid to Edmond Wright our Butler and for nine men with him	36*s.*	
Musicians	Item to the Waits of London[149]	13*s.*	4*d.*
	Item to the Children of Westminster[150]	20*s.*	
	Sum	33*s.*	4*d.*

[149] See Introduction, xxvi.
[150] Ibid.

Officers fees and wages	Item to Christopher Fulkes our Sewer and Carver		6*s.*	8*d.*
	Item to Robert Beaumont our Steward		40*s.*	
	Item to five porters viz. Cartwright and Semper[151] for keeping the hall door 3*s.* a piece		6*s.*	
	Item to Robert Selby[152] for keeping the middle door		3*s.*	
	Item to Robert Yeve for keeping the same			20*d.*
	Item to George Hills[153] for keeping the gate		3*s.*	
	Item to Henry Starr our Labourer for three days		2*s.*	
	Item to Goodwife Holmes attending the kitchen		2*s.*	
	Item to two women also labouring the kitchen and the whole house		3*s.*	

		Sum £3	7*s.*	4*d.*

Perfumes, flowers and sweet waters	Item for flowers and herbs		2*s.*	2*d.*
	Item to Bass' wife for a pottle of rose damask water		2*s.*	8*d.*

	Sum	4*s.*	10*d.*

f.48v. **Extra-ordinary charges**	Item to Pigeon of the Tower for hire of three pieces of cloth of arras being the story of David and Uriah and for the carriage and re-carriage[154]	21*s.*	

---

151 Peter Semper was apprenticed to Warden John Branch in the Drapers' Company. See *Boyd, Roll.*

152 Robert Selby was a Draper. See Boyd, *Roll.*

153 George Hills (or Hill) was a Draper. See Boyd, *Roll.*

154 'Pigeon' was likely the Keeper of the Wardrobe at the Tower of London. Pieces of hanging arras were set up in the parlour on a specially made partition. Hired from the Tower of London, the arras hired depicted the biblical story of King David and Uriah the Hittite. Almost certainly, the tapestry belonged to the Crown and it seems likely it was later installed at Somerset House as part of a set of five Flemish hangings. It is probable that the hanging depicted on the left in the 'The Somerset Conference' painting of 1604 is the same that hung in the Drapers' parlour. It has been described by Campbell as 'King David giving Uriah the Hittite the sealed message that will send him to his death'. He regarded this story to be 'a well-known exemplum of deceitfulness'. It was hung in the Drapers' parlour to conceal a 'backstage' space. See S. Pegge, *Curialia: or an historical account of some branches of the royal household, Parts IV and V* (London: Nichols and Son, 1806), 103; T. Campbell (ed.) *Tapestry in the Baroque: Threads of Splendor* (New York: Metropolitan Museum of Art, 2008), 111.

Item for great hooks, fire pots, setting
up the partition and hanging up the said
clothes ... 4s. 6d.
Item for carriage and portage of a
puncheon of French wine and a hogshead
of Gascon wine ... 2s. 6d.
Item for salt to trim them ... 3d.
Item for both hire and drinking at diverse
times in bidding of guests ... 2s. 2d.
Item for carrying of sturgeon ... 2d.
Item for dinner on Saturday for the officers
in the kitchen in bread, fish and drink ... 12d.
Item for radish roots at supper on Sunday
for Master Wardens ... 4d.
Item to the water bearers for forty tankards
of water ... 12d.
Item for writing paper for the steward ... 1d.
Item for oranges and lemons ... 4s.
Item for padlocks ... 19d.

	Sum	38s.	7d.

Rewards for bucks

Item to the Lord Treasurer's man for a
buck ... 5s.
Item to Robert Friar's man for two bucks ... 3s.
Item to the Lord Wentworth's[155] man for
one buck ... 5s.
Item Morgan Richards for one buck ... 12d.

	Sum	14s.

Here follows the total sums in general of all the particulars aforesaid in brief:

The Butcher's bill amounts to	£7		
Marchpanes	£5		
Comfits		16s.	10d.
Sturgeon	£3		
Hippocras	£4	5s.	
Wine of all sorts	£16	18s.	4d.
Grocer's bill	£7	11s.	6d.
Poulterer's bill	£27	15s.	
Pikemonger	£3	4s.	
Linen cloth	£3	12s.	10d.
The Baker	£6	2s.	
Spice bread		24s.	
Wafers		30s.	

---

[155] Thomas Wentworth, Second Baron Wentworth, was a soldier and administrator who owned land in Suffolk, Yorkshire, Oxfordshire, and Lincolnshire. See *Oxford DNB*.

Beerbrewer	26s.	
Alebrewer	17s.	10d.
Chandler	32s.	9d.
Pewterer	30s.	6d.
Ashen cups	3s.	8d.
Fruits	16s.	2d.
Trenchers, trays and other trash	17s.	
Butter and cream	41s.	6d.
The Cook	45s.	4d.
The Painter for brawn and jelly	36s.	8d.
Wood and coal	21s.	6d.
Butler	36s.	
Mustard	33s.	4d.
Officers' fees and wages	£3 7s.	4d.
Perfumes, flowers and sweet waters	4s.	10d.
Extraordinary charges	38s.	7d.
Rewards for bucks	14s.	

f.49v.

Sum total of all the particulars in general £112 12s. 6d.

Whereof

Received towards the said charges per contra as follows:

First the ordinary allowance of the house towards this dinner – £10, and for the Lord Mayor's mess being of our Company – £10   £20

Item for quarterage money received among the Assistants present in the hall   21s. 4d.

Item for quarterage received of the Livery then in the hall   26s. 8d.

Item the quarterage of the rest being then absent sold to Messenger our Clerk for   10s.

Sum £22 18s.

ANNIS 1566 AND 1567

In the time of William Beswick,
Master of the Mystery, and

Francis Barnham
William Dumar[156]
Brian Calverley[157]   } Wardens
Thomas Pullyson[158]

Quarter Dinner	**Expenses of first Quarter Dinner kept the twenty-third day of November 1566**		
	First paid for six dozen of bread	6s.	
	For a kilderkin of strong beer	4s.	
	For a stand of strong ale	4s.	
To the Poulterer	For eight boiling capons at 22d.	14s.	8d.
	For one turkey cock at 4s.	4s.	
	For eight roasting capons at 2s. 2d.	17s.	4d.
	For six geese at 20d.	10s.	
	For one dozen woodcocks	7s.	
	For five dozen larks at 10d.	4s.	2d.
	For eggs		8d.
To Mrs Wilcockes	For fourteen minced pies at 16d.	18s.	8d.
	For seven custards at 2s. 6d.	17s.	6d.
	For five apple tarts at 2s. 6d.	12s.	6d.
	For two marchpanes at 3s. 4d.	6s.	8d.
For wine	Item for a gallon of muscadel	2s.	
	For one gallon of malmsey		16d.
	Item for six gallons and three pints of claret	8s.	6d.

f.52v.

[156] William Dumar (or Dummer) served as Warden of the Drapers' Company in 1566–7, 1570–1, and 1573–4. He was one of the Clerks of the Lord Mayor's Court in the 1530s and Controller of the Chamber of London from 1544. See Johnson, *History*, ii. 471; VCH, *Hants*, iii. 358–9.

[157] Brian (or Bryan) Calverley served as Warden of the Drapers' Company in 1566–7, 1574–5, and 1579–80. See Johnson, *History*, ii. 471.

[158] (Sir) Thomas Pullyson (or Pullison) served as Warden of the Drapers' Company in 1566–7 and Master in 1574–5, 1578–9, 1582–3, and 1586–7. He became Alderman in 1573 and served as Sheriff in the same year (1573–4). Pullyson was Lord Mayor in 1584–5. See Johnson, *History*, ii. 471–2; Beaven, *Aldermen*, ii. 39.

	For seven quarts of sack at 5*d*.	2*s*.	11*d*.
	Item for one pottle sack more		10*d*.
To the Grocer	Item for 2lb. of prunes		3*d*.
	For 2lb. of currants		7*d*.
	For 1oz. great mace		12*d*.
	For 1lb. fine sugar		11*d*.
	For 2lb. cast sugar		18*d*.
	For 2oz. pepper		4*d*.
	For cinnamon 1oz.		10*d*.
	For ginger 1oz.		2*d*.
	For 1lb. bisquytes and caraways		14*d*.
	For 1lb. dates		10*d*.
To the Butcher and Poulterer	For three rondes of brawn	8*s*.	
	For a sirloin of beef	4*s*.	
	For six long marrowbones	2*s*.	6*d*.
For other ordinary necessaries	For oranges		4*d*.
	For a pint of barberries		6*d*.
	For a pottle of vertgious		12*d*.
	For a pint of vinegar		2*d*.
	For mustard		1*d*.
	For salt and a birchen brown		3*d*.
	For 1lb. of candle		2*d*.
	For a pint of rose water		10*d*.
	For 8lb. of butter	2*s*.	
	For six dozen trenchers	2*s*.	
	For a quarter of small ale		
	For three loads of horse coals	3*s*.	6*d*.
	For the Butler for his pains	4*s*.	
	For the Cook his pains	6*s*.	
	For the loan of four garnish of pewter vessel to the Pewterer	3*s*.	4*d*.
	For washing the napery to the Clerk's wife	2*s*.	
	For Goodwife Holmes for her pains		6*d*.

f.53r.

Sum total of this dinner	£9	6*s*.	2*d*.

Whereof

Mr Calverley's part besides the house money being £5 bore	45*s*.	7*d*.
Mr Pullyson as much viz.	45*s*.	8*d*.

f.54r. **Second Quarter Dinner, Fish Day**	**The second Quarter Dinner charges kept the fourth day of March 1566:**		
	Item for three ling di	8*s.*	4*d.*
	Item for three green fishes at 18*d.*	4*s.*	6*d.*
	Item for seven pikes at 2*s.*	14*s.*	
	Item for seven carps at 20*d.*	11*s.*	8*d.*
	Item for four roasting eels at 16*d.*	5*s.*	4*d.*
	Item for one quarter di of lampreys		19*d.*
	Item hundred and four quarters of smelts[159]		18*d.*
	Item for sweet butter	3*s.*	
	Item for salt butter 6lb. at 3*d.*		18*d.*
	Item for salad herbs		5*d.*
	Item for alexander buds for salads		8*d.*
	Item for eggs to the salads		6*d.*
	Item for spice to the Grocer according to his bill	8*s.*	4*d.*
	Item for di cwt. oranges		3*d.*
	Item for a quarter of barberries	2*s.*	
	Item for di pecks of flour		4*d.*
f.54v.	Item for a pint of salad oil		6*d.*
	Item for salt		3*d.*
	Item for vergious, vinegar and mustard		8*d.*
	Item for a birchen brown and a pipkin		2*d.*
	Item for yeast to the pike broth		2*d.*
	Item for a pint of rose water		10*d.*
	Item for two dozen of trenchers		8*d.*
	Item for two sacks of great coals		12*d.*
	Item paid to Tracle our Cook for baking fourteen lampern[160] pies at 12*d.* the piece	14*s.*	
	Item for seven custards at 2*s.* 4*d.* the piece	16*s.*	4*d.*
	Item for seven tarts at 2*s.* 6*d.* the piece	17*s.*	6*d.*
	Item to the said Cook for dressing that dinner	6*s.*	
	Item to the Butler	4*s.*	
	Item for six dozen breads	6*s.*	
	Item for a kilderkin of beer	3*s.*	
	Item for a stand of ale	3*s.*	
	Item for two gallons of sack	3*s.*	4*d.*
	Item for eight gallons of claret and white	10*s.*	8*d.*
	Item for four garnish and two dozen pewter vessels	3*s.*	10*d.*
	Item to the Clerk's wife for washing the napery	2*s.*	
	Item to Holmes' wife		6*d.*
	Item to the Clerk's maid for watering the fish		2*d.*
	Sum total	£7 18*s.*	4*d.*

[159] Smelt: a small type of fish, mostly coastal and allied to the same species of fish as salmon.
[160] Lampern: a river lamprey.

Whereof

Mr Calverley bore over £5 allowed by the house his moitie and part viz.	29*s.*	2*d.*
And Mr Pullyson as much viz.	29*s.*	2*d.*

FEAST DINNER } ANNO 1567

The ninth year in the reign of Queen
Elizabeth etc.

Sir William Chester knight then our } Master

Mr Barnam
Mr Dumar } our Master
Mr Calverley Wardens
Mr Pullyson

Preparation before the same dinner for two days as follows
} viz.

Saturday 2 August 1567 for potation for four messes
In primis cakes and buns dozens –three
dozen
Item biskyttes and caraways
Item plums and apples
Item comfits – two dishes
Item codlings and pears
Item comfits – two dishes
Item filberts

Potation Sunday 3 August 1567 for twelve messes
Item for everything as aforesaid to the full content of twelve
messes etc.

First course	**Service on Monday at dinner being the Feast Dinner**
Four messes	**To the high table in the hall**

In primis brawn and mustard
Item boiled capons

Roasted swan
Baked venison
Pikes
Roasted capons and herons
Custards

Five messes **To the second table in the hall**
Brawn and mustard
Boiled capons
Roasted swan

Baked venison
Pikes
Roasted capons
Custards

Five messes	**To the third table in the hall**

Brawn and mustard
Boiled capons
Swan and goose
Baked venison
Pikes
Roasted capons
Custards

Two messes **To the table in the parlour**
As above brawn and mustard
Boiled capons
Swan and goose
Baked venison
Pikes
Roasted capons
Custards

f.57r. Two messes **To the women above in the gallery chamber**
Brawn and mustard
Boiled capons
Swan and goose
Baked venison
Pikes
Roasted capons
Custards

One mess **To the cooks**
Item to them one mess of all the like service as above

Four messes **To the Bachelor waiters**
Received into the larder which furnished the table for the
second dinner for the Bachelor waiters and others as required

Second course To the table in the hall
Four messes Item jelly dishes
Quails
Red deer
Sturgeon
Marchpanes

Five messes **To the second table in the hall**
Jelly dishes
Quails

Red deer
Sturgeon
Marchpanes

f.57v. Five messes **To the third table in the hall**
Jelly dishes
Quails and pigeons
Red deer
Sturgeon
Marchpanes

Two messes **To the table in the parlour**
Jelly dishes
Quails and pigeons
Red deer
Sturgeon
Marchpane

Wafers and hippocras to them all

Service on Tuesday at dinner ten messes prepared in all things as on Monday at dinner

The whole accounts with the expenses and whole charges by particulars as follows viz.:

Pikes Paid to Lucas the Pikemonger for twenty-eight pikes whereof six were scantling twenty-four inches, twelve of twenty inches and other twelve of eighteen inches at 22*d.* one with another. So paid him £51

Monday dinner – twenty
Tuesday dinner – eight

f.58r. **Poultry** Item paid to Robert Mason, Draper, occupying poultry as follows viz.

Sunday In primis for two boiling capons and two roasting capons for Sunday at dinner at 2*s.* 2*d.* one with another 4*s.* 8*d.*
Item for 1cwt. eggs at 3*s.* the cwt. 3*s.*

Monday Item forty-two boiling capons and thirty-seven roasting capons at 2*s.* 2*d.* the piece one with another £8 11*s.* 2*d.*
Item for five herons at 3*s.* 4*d.* the piece 16*s.* 8*d.*
Item ten swans at 7*s.* 6*d.* the piece £3 15*s.*
Item twelve geese at 20*d.* the piece 20*s.*
Item six dozen quails at 7*s.* 4*d.* the dozen 44*s.*

	Item five dozen pigeons at 20*d*.	8*s*.	4*d*.
	Item 4cwt. eggs at 3*s*.	12*s*.	
Tuesday	Item twenty boiling capons at 2*s*. 2*d*.	43*s*.	4*d*.
	Item twenty roasting capons at 2*s*. 2*d*.	43*s*.	4*d*.
	Item four swans	30*s*.	
	Item six geese	10*s*.	
	Item four dozen quails at 7*s*. 4*d*.	29*s*.	4*d*.
	Item three dozen pigeons at 20*d*.	5*s*.	
	Item 2cwt. eggs at 3*s*. the cwt.	6*s*.	

Sum paid £26

Sawyer the Butcher

Saturday for jelly	Item paid to the Butcher for four shoulders of veal price [-] the piece	3*s*.	4*d*.
Sunday dinner	Item sirloin of beef at 12*d*. the st. for Sunday at dinner		
	Item for a hind quarter of mutton		
	Item for a shoulder veal at 10*d*.		10*d*.
	Item for two long marrowbones at 6*d*.		12*d*.
	Item for 21lb. of suet at 3*d*. lb.	5*s*.	3*d*.
Monday	Item twenty-two long marrowbones at 6*d*.	11*s*.	
	Item two sirloins of beef at 12*d*. the st.		
	~~Item for a quarter of beef for the poor weighing___ at 12*d*. the stone~~		
	Item for di a mutton for the waiters' breakfast		
	Item for 30lb. of suet at 3*d*. the lb.	15*s*.	
	Item for a peck of pricks		
f.58v. Tuesday	Item received of the Butcher ten long marrowbones at 6*d*. the piece	5*s*.	
	Item one sirloin of beef		
	Item one quarter of beef for the poor		
	Item 52lb. of suet		
	Item guts and blood		
	Item one boar price	53*s*.	4*d*.

Sum paid £8 12*s*. 8*d*.

Grocer	Paid to Gabriel Colsell, Grocer, for 2lb. di of cinnamon at 7*s*. 6*d*. lb.
For hippocras	Item for 1lb. quarter of ginger at 3*s*. 8*d*.
	Item for 4oz. cloves
	Item for 8oz. nutmeg
	Item 3oz. corianders
	Item for 24lb. middle sugar

70

For jelly	Item 1lb. di cinnamon
	8oz. ginger
	Isenglas 1lb. at 18*d.*
	Corianders 6oz.
	Turnesall 1lb. di
	Nutmegs 6oz.
	Pepper 20lb. 2oz. at 2*s.* 7*d.*
	Cloves and maces beaten 6oz.
	Long mace 8oz.
	Ginger beaten 10oz.
	Cinnamon beaten 6oz.
	Nutmegs di lb.
	Sanders 1oz.
	Saffron 2oz.
	Cloves 2oz. whole for perfume
	Sugar fine 16lb. at 12*d.* lb.
	Sugar middle 30lb. at 10*d.* lb.
	Sugar coarse 20lb. at 10*d.*
	Dates 10lb.
	Currants 12lb.
	Damask prunes 14lb.
	Paper for custards three quires

<u>Sum paid the Grocer</u>   £10   16*s.*

f.59r. **Sturgeon**	Paid to Mr Blage dwelling in New Fyshe Streat for two firkins of sturgeon at 30*s.* the piece	£3
Marchpanes	Paid to Mrs Wilcockes for sixteen marchpanes on Monday for dinner at 3*s.* 4*d.* the piece and to her for eight marchpanes at the same price for Tuesday at dinner	£4
	Item paid to Midleton Grocer for six parchpanes for Monday at dinner whereof three of them at 3*s.* and other three at 2*s.* 8*d.* the piece	17*s.*
Baker	Paid to Storar the Baker for fifty-five dozen of bread to whit two dozen rolls seventeen dozen of three a penny, twenty-seven dozen of penny white bread, four dozen of half penny white bread and five dozen of penny wheaten bread set all as follows:	
Saturday – two dozen	One dozen rolls and one dozen of half penny bread	

71

Sunday – seven dozen	Three dozen half penny bread, two dozen penny white bread, one dozen rolls and one dozen of wheaten penny bread			
Monday – thirty-three dozen	Eight dozen penny white bread and twelve dozen penny white bread, eleven dozen at three for a penny and two dozen penny wheaten			
Tuesday – thirteen dozen	Five dozen penny white bread, six dozen at three a penny and two dozen penny wheaten		55s.	
Meal	Item paid to him for twenty bushels meal at 2s. 11d. the bushel		58s.	1d.
Flour	Item for 12oz. of flour at 3s. the bushel and to the carman for the bringing thereof to the hall 6d.		36s.	6d.
	Sum paid	£7	8s.	4d.
Wafers	Paid to Wharton's wife for fourteen boxes of wafers for the two days		28s.	
	Sum of page	£16	13s.	4d.
f.59v. **Spice bread**	Paid to Wall's wife for thirteen dozen of buns and cakes at 2s. the dozen viz. Saturday for the potation, one dozen buns and one dozen cakes and on Sunday at night for the potation five dozen buns and five dozen cakes		25s.	
Comfits	Paid for 1lb. di of almond comfits at 14d. the lb. – 21d. For 1lb. of clove comfits – 2s. For 2lb. of orange comfits at 2s. the lb. – 4s. For 1lb. quarter of ginger comfits at 2s. lb. – 2s. 6d. For a lb. di cinnamon comfits – 3s. For all of caraways – 14d. For 2lb. di of biskettes at 14d. – 2s. 11d. And for a lb. of corianders – 14d.		18s.	6d.
Fruit	Paid for six pears – 4s. For 7cwt. plums – 2s. 8d. For 1cwt. di codlings – 18d. And to a porter carrying the same fruit at two times – 3d.		8s.	5d.

72

Butter	Paid for 1cwt. 1lb. of butter in the market at 3*d. ob.* the lb.		29*s.*	2*d.*
Wine	Paid for one hogshead, one tiers[161] of Gascon wine and for one tiers of French wine	£5	8*s.*	4*d.*
Sack	Item for rundlet of sack at eighteen gallons at 16*d.* the gallon		24*s.*	
Muscadel	Item for a rundlet of muscadel at ten gallons at 2*s.* 4*d.* the gallon		23*s.*	4*d.*
Rundlets	Item paid for the two rundlets for the same sack and muscadel		2*s.*	4*d.*
Portage and cartage	Item paid for carriage and portage of the Gascon wine and French wine into the cellar			14*d.*
Ale	Paid to Mathew Marten, Ale Brewer, our tenant, for four barrels of ale whereof three at 5*s.* and one at 4*s.*		19*s.*	
Beer	Paid to Campion, Beer Brewer, for five barrels beer whereof two at 5*s.* the barrel, two at 4*s.* the barrel and one at 3*s.*		21*s.*	

<u>Sum of page</u> £14 <u>3*d.*</u>

f.60r. **Pewter**	Paid to Catcher the Pewterer for the hire of pewter vessels viz. two dozen di of great chargers, three dozen di of small chargers, five dozen of three platters, five dozen of great French platters, five dozen small French platters, five dozen pie platters, two dozen barrels platters, four dozen dishes, twenty dozen saucers all that accounted for seventeen garnishes di at 10*d.* the garnish – 14*s.* 7*d*, and more eighteen dozen dishes for jelly and fruit at 6*d.* the dozen – 9*s.*	23*s.*	
Chandler	Paid to the Chandler for diverse things set of him as salt, mustard, vinegar, vergious and pots	41*s.*	

---

[161] Tiers: third.

73

Coals	Paid for twenty sacks of charcoal at 6*d.* the sack	10*s.*	
Billets and fagots	Paid for billets and fagots	13*s.*	4*d.*
	Paid for half a piece and ten ells of lockeram for aprons	£3	15*d.*
	Item for four ells Holland for the Sewer and Carver	6*s.*	
	Item for eight ells of canvas at 6*d.* ell	4*s.*	
Musicians	Paid to the musicians for the two days	13*s.*	4*d.*
Lard	Paid for 12lb. of lard for the red deer	10*s.*	
Seething the boar	Paid for seething the boar	10*s.*	
Coal baskets	Paid for two coal baskets – 8*d.*		
Coal shovel	Item for a coal shovel – 4*d.*		
Taps	Item for taps for beer and ale – 2*d.*		
Ashen cups	Item for three dozen ashen cups – 2*s.* 6*d.*		
Trenchers	Item for twenty-six dozen trenchers – 8*s.* 8*d.*		
Dansick trays	Item for four Dansick trays – 4*s.*		
Brooms	Item for brooms – 4*d.*	16*s.*	8*d.*
Sweetwater	Paid for a gallon of rose water and a gallon of damask water	12*s.*	8*d.*
Barberries	Paid for barberries	2*s.*	
Cream and milk	Paid for fourteen gallons cream and one gallon milk	16*s.*	8*d.*
Wine extra-ordinary	Paid for wine red, white and claret in all nine gallons for jelly, hippocras and broths at 16*d.* the gallon	12*s.*	

	Sum of page	£12	11*s.*	11*d.*

f.60v. **Painter**	Paid to Bullock painter for gilding the brawn and jelly	13*s.*	4*d.*
Porters	Paid to Cartwright,[162] Porter – 3*s.*		

---

[162] Thomas Cartwright, a Draper. See Boyd, *Roll*.

	Item to Robert Yeve, Porter – 2*s*.		
	Item to George Hills, Porter – 3*s*.		
	Item to Robert Selby, Porter – 3*s*.		
	Item to Richard Thompson,[163] Porter – 3*s*.	14*s*.	
Butler	Paid to Edmond [-] Butler for his fee and his men waiting here	36*s*.	
Cook	Paid to Tryegle our Cook for his fee for the three days – 40*s*., and for his bran as he had the year last past – 2*s*. 6*d*.	42*s*.	6*d*.
Steward	Paid to Robert Beaumond, Steward, for his pains in reward	40*s*.	
Labourers	Paid to Henry Starr our Labourer for his pains for two days at 8*d*. per day		16*d*.
Women in the kitchen	Paid to Goodwife Holmes being in the kitchen for three days – 2*s*., and to two other women serving there also – 3*s*. in all	5*s*.	
Sewer	Paid to Mr Ffulx the Sewer for his fee for the two days	6*s*.	8*d*.
Clerks and Ringers	Paid to the Clerks and Ringers of St. Michael's	5*s*.	
The Waiters	Paid to the Master Bachelors towards the baking of their venison for the waiters	5*s*.	
Calves feet for jelly	Paid for four pairs or calves feet for the jelly at 3*d*. the pair		12*d*.
Pepper	Paid for 2lb. of pepper as such time as hast required and could not sent to the Grocers that served as	5*s*.	
Jelly bags and strainers	Paid for bags for jelly and strainers	2*s*.	2*d*.
Scavenger	Paid to the Scavenger for carrying away the garbage and offal out of the street		4*d*.
Wine taps	Paid for wine, spigots and taps for the drawing of wine		8*d*.

Sum of page   £8   18*s*.

163 Richard Thompson was a Draper. See Boyd, *Roll*.

f.61r. **Carriage of wine and sturgeon**	Paid for the carriage by porters of two firkins of sturgeon and two rundlets of wine viz. sack and muscadel	4*d.*
Meal	Paid for a bushel di of wheaten meal	4*s.*
Venison baked abroad	Paid for baking of fifty-two abroad out of this house	8*s.* 8*d.*
Spices for hippocras	Paid for 3lb. of sugar, 4oz. cinnamon, 2oz. ginger for hippocras	5*s.*
Bread for the poor	Paid for bread for the poor	2*s.*

Extra-ordinary charges

Paid for fish, bread and drink for the Steward on Saturday for his dinners and others with him attending in the hall about their business — 8*d.*

Item for drink on Saturday for him that boulted the meal – 1*d*, for writing paper – 2*d*, to the carpenter for setting up the partition in the parlour – 6*d*, for a quarter of mutton on Sunday at night for supper – 2*s.* 4*d.* and for radishes – 4*d.* — 3*s.* 5*d.*

Rewards for bucks

Paid for Lord Treasurer's man for bringing of a buck	5*s.*
Item to Doctor Gibbon's[164] servant	3*s.* 4*d.*
Item to him that brought the person's buck in reward	2*s.* 4*d.*
Item paid to him that brought a buck from John Prestwicke	3*s.* 4*d.*
Item to Robert Fryar's man	2*s.*
Item to Sir Hugh Pawlett's man	5*s.*
Item to him that Richard Kellett's[165] buck	2*s.*
Item from Hall and Dawes[166] a buck	12*d.*
Item from Thomas Herdson[167] a buck	2*s.*

[164] John Gibbon was a member of the Doctors' Common. He acted as Principal of New Inn Hall between 1548 and 1550, and was Master in the Chancery Court by 1570. He also sat as MP for Hindon in 1558. Gibbon's second wife was Elizabeth, daughter of Sir William Roche, Draper, previous Master of the Company and Lord Mayor 1540–1. See *HP Commons, 1509–1558,* iii. 206; Johnson, *History,* ii. 469–70, 481.

[165] Richard Kellett was a Draper. See Boyd, *Roll.*

[166] Possibly Thomas Dawes, a Liveryman in the Drapers' Company. See Johnson, *History,* ii. 263.

[167] Thomas Herdson served as Warden of the Drapers' Company in 1576–7. He became a Freeman of the Company in 1565, having served his apprenticeship under Francis Barnham, First Warden in 1566–7. See Johnson, *History,* ii. 471; Boyd, *Roll.*

Item from Richard Champion[168] a buck	2s.		
Item from Sir Robert Chestar[169] a buck	5s.		
Item from Thomas Wicken[170] and ~~Jeffrey~~ Lewes a buck	2s.		
Item from Jeffrey Lewes[171]		12d.	
Item from Yeward[172] a buck	2s.		
Item from Sir William Chestar	2s.	4d.	
Item to Mr Quarles servant at the receipt of a buck	2s.		

Sum of all given in reward	42s.	4d.	
Sum of page	£3	6s.	5d.

f.61v.

Sum total of all the whole charges of the dinner in general amounts to £103 9s.

Whereof

Received of the Masters and Livery for their quarterage and Livery money	£8	7s.	6d.
Received more of the new Livery last coming in according to the order	£9	9s.	
More the allowance of the house ordinary towards the great dinner	£10		
Sum received and allowed is	£27	16s.	6d.

So the clear charges of the said dinner stands us in £75 12s. 6d.

Which being divided in to four parts every man's part amounts to £18 18s. 1d. *ob.*

Bucks given to the Master Wardens in general
From the Lord Treasurer – one
Item from Doctor Gibbons – one
Item from the Parson of St. Michael's – one
Item from John Prestwick – one

---

168 Richard Champion the younger was the son of Sir Richard Champion. He became Free of the Company in 1560 after serving an apprenticeship under his father. See Boyd, *Roll*.

169 Sir Robert Chester was the eldest son of Sir William Chester, five times Master of the Drapers' Company. Sir Robert became a Freeman of the Company in 1566 by redemption. See Boyd, *Roll*.

170 Thomas Wicken served as Warden of the Drapers' Company in 1578–9. See Johnson, *History*, ii. 471.

171 Jeffrey (or Geffrey) Lewes was a Draper. See Boyd, *Roll*.

172 Possibly Thomas Howard, a Draper. See Boyd, *Roll*.

Item from Robert Fryar – one
Item from Sir Hugh Pawlet – one
Item from Richard Kelletts – one
Item from Hall and Dawes – one
Item from Thomas Herdson and Richard
Champion – two
Item from Sir Robert Chester – one
Item from Thomas Wigen and Low – one
Item from Jeffray Lewes – one
Item from Sir William Chester – one
Item from Thomas Yoward – one

Sum – sixteen bucks

f.62r.

Bucks and stags sent to Mr Barnam
From the Dean of Salisbury[173] – one stag
From John Chester[174] – di buck
From Harding – one
From Sir John Sellynger[175] – one
From William Carowe[176] – one
From Mr John Brooke[177] – one
From Mr Quarles – one
From Thomas Barnham[178] – one
From Humphrey Chafen[179] – one
From William Garway[180] – one
From Doctor Smyth – one

Sum – nine bucks di and one stag

Bucks sent to Mr Dumer
From Thomas Wheler – one buck di
From Mr Tossyer of Kent – two

---

[173] William Bradbridge, later Bishop of Exeter. Bradbridge was the brother of Alice Barnham, wife of Warden Francis Barnham. See *Oxford DNB*.
[174] John Chester was a younger son of Sir William Chester, five times Master of the Drapers' Company. He was admitted to the Company by patrimony in 1560. See Boyd, *Roll*.
[175] Sir John St. Leger, landowner. He was an MP from 1555. See *HP Commons, 1558–1603*, iii. 327.
[176] William Carowe (or Carew) served as Warden of the Drapers' Company in 1580–1. See Johnson, *History*, ii. 471.
[177] John Brooke served as Warden of the Drapers' Company in 1558–9. See Johnson, *History*, ii. 470.
[178] Thomas Barnham, Draper, was the brother of Warden Francis Barnham. See Orlin, *Locating Privacy*, 25.
[179] Humphrey Chaffyne was a Draper who had served his apprenticeship under Warden Francis Barnham. See Boyd, *Roll*.
[180] Sir William Garway (or Garraway) served as Warden of the Drapers' Company in 1583–4 and 1592–3. He was Master of the Company in 1599–1600 and held the position of Chief Farmer of Customs. See Johnson, *History*, ii. 471–2; *Oxford DNB*.

From Mr Alford[181] – two
From the Lord of Buckhurst[182] – two

<u>Sum – seven bucks di</u>

Bucks sent to Mr Calverley
From Mr Keme – two bucks
From Forrand[183] – one

<u>Sum – three bucks</u>

Bucks sent to Mr Pullyson
From Spenser[184] – one buck
From Mr Kempe[185] – one
From Mr Ffyshe[186] – one

<u>Sum – three bucks</u>

<u>Sum total of stags and bucks – forty</u>

All which stags and bucks made in pasties
– 184 pasties
Besides five bucks di that were delivered
again to the masters, di a buck to the Cook,
one buck not sweet and one buck given to
the Master Bachelors being waiters – eight
bucks

---

181 Possibly MP Roger Alford, son of Robert Alford who was Warden of the Drapers' Company in 1541–2. See *HP Commons, 1509–1558*, i. 306.
182 Sir Thomas Sackville, First Baron Buckhurst and later First Earl of Dorset, succeeded his father in 1566 and was knighted in 1567. His mother was Winifred Brydges, daughter of Sir John Brydges (or Brugges), former Master of the Drapers' Company and Lord Mayor in 1520–1. See *Oxford DNB*.
183 Probably Richard Forrand, a Draper. See Boyd, *Roll*.
184 Probably Nicholas Spenser, a Draper. See Boyd, *Roll*.
185 John Kempe served as Warden of the Drapers' Company in 1567–8. See Johnson, *History*, ii. 471.
186 Possibly Thomas Fysher, a Draper. See Boyd, *Roll*.

f.64r.

In the time of the Masters:

William Parker[187]
Roger Sadler[188]   } Wardens, Anno
William Chestar[189]   1567–1568
John Kempe

Sir William Chestar knight and Alderman then } Master

Proportion of the first Quarter Dinner,
Anno 1567, kept the 9th day of December
for the eight messes of meat as follows:

First three rondes of brawn
Item a sirloin of beef
Item six long marrowbones
Item sixteen minced pies
Item eight custards
Item six apple tarts
Item two marchpanes
Item eighteen capons
Item eight geese
Item six woodcocks
Item eight dozen of larks
Item one turkey cock

f.64v.

Proportion of the second Quarter Dinner
kept in our hall the 7th day of April, **Anno
1568,** for eight messes of meat

First for four green fishes
Item for four dried lings
Item for eight pikes
Item for eight carps
Item for 2cwt. of smelt
Item for five roasting eels
Item for a quarter di of lamperns
Item for sixteen lampern pies
Item for eight custards
Item for six tarts

---

[187] William Parker senior served as Warden of the Drapers' Company in 1567–8. See Johnson, *History*, ii. 471.

[188] Roger Sadler served as Warden of the Drapers' Company in 1560–1 and 1567–8, although it appears that he did not see out his second term, having temporarily relocated to Edmonton in controversial circumstances. See Orlin, *Locating Privacy*, 132.

[189] Younger son of Sir William Chester, William Chester junior served as Warden of the Drapers' Company in 1567–8, 1575–6, and 1580–1. He was Master of the Company in 1589–90. See Johnson, *History*, ii. 471–2.

Item for di a fresh salmon
Item for two marchpanes

f.65r.

Proportion of the third Quarter Dinner kept
the first day of July, **Anno 1568,** for eight
messes of meat

First for one dozen and three chickens
Item for nine geese
Item for nine capons
Item for sixteen rabbits
Item for eight custards
Item for eight chicken pies
Item for a sirloin of beef
Item for long marrowbones
Item for a skeg[190] of sturgeon
Item for seven tarts
Item for one marchpane

---

[190] Skeg (or keg): a quantity of sturgeon to fill a small barrel or cask.

FEAST DINNER} ANNO 1568

The tenth year in the reign of Queen Elizabeth

Sir William Chester knight then our   } Master

Mr Parker
Mr Hewar[191]   } our Master
Mr William Chestar   Wardens
Mr Kempe

Provision for the same Feast Dinner and for the potations on Saturday and Sunday as also for the day after the said Great Dinner

Comfits	Paid to Ballthaser the Comfit-Maker for all and di of almond comfits at 14*d.* the lb. – 21*d.* For 2lb. of orange comfits at 2*s.* the lb. – 4*s.* For a lb. of ginger comfits at – 2*s.* For all di of cinnamon comfits at 2*s.* the lb. – 3*s.* Item for a lb. of pyneaple comfits[192] – 2*s.* For a lb. of corianders – 14*d.* For a lb. of caraways and 2lb. of byskettes at 13*d.* the lb. – 3*s.* 3d.	17*s.*	2*d.*
Fruits	Paid for fruits of diverse sorts bought for the potations viz. first for 4cwt. pears – 2*s.* 8*d.* Item for 2cwt. of plums – 2*s.* Item for 3cwt. codlings – 3*s.*	7*s.*	8*d.*
f.69v. **Poulterer**	Paid to Robert Mason our Poulterer paid for these parcels of poultry-ware bought of him as follows:		

---

[191] Edward Hewar served as Warden of the Drapers' Company in 1567–8, stepping in to fill the void left by Roger Sadler's untimely departure. See Johnson, *History*, ii. 471.

[192] Pineapple comfits: an early example of the incorporation of this 'New World' fruit into English dining, likely on account of Balthesar Sanchez' Spanish origins.

Sunday	First for capon on Sunday at dinner price – 2*s*. 1*d*.
	Item for six pigeons the same day at dinner – 10*d*.
Monday	Item for five dozen of pigeons for Monday at 20*d*. the dozen – 8*s*. 4*d*.
	For four dozen of quails at 7*s*. the dozen – 28*s*.
	For four dozen di of capons at 2*s*. 1*d*. the piece – £5 13*s*.
	For 5cwt. of eggs at 2*s*. 10*d*. the cwt. – 14*s*. 2*d*.
	For twelve geese at 22*d*. the piece – 22*s*.
	For six swans at 8*s*. 4*d*. the piece – £2 10*s*.
Tuesday	Item paid for seventeen capons for Tuesday at 2*s*. 1*d*. – 35*s*. 5*d*.
	For seven geese at 22*d*. – 12*s*. 10*d*.
	For two swans at 8*s*. 4*d*. for the piece – 16*s*. 8*d*.
	For two dozen of pigeons – 3*s*. 4*d*.
	For a dozen of quails – 7*s*.
	For a cwt. di of eggs – 2*s*. 10*d*. the cwt. £15 17*s*.

Butcher   Paid to Sawyer the Butcher:

Saturday	First for four shoulders of veal for jelly on Saturday
Sunday	Item for a sirloin of beef
	Item for a hind quarter of mutton
	Item for a dozen di of marrowbones
	Item for 50lb. of suet
	Item for two muttons
Monday	Item for six sirloins of beef
	Item for a boar received on Monday
	Item for a mutton
	Item for blood and guts for puddings
	Item for 30lb. of suet
Tuesday	Item for a sirloin of beef
	Item for six marrowbones
	Item for 12lb. of suet
	Item for 6st. of beef for the poor £4 11*s*. 8*d*.

Item paid to him for above 56*s*. 8*d*.
Item paid for four pairs of calves feet for jelly bought abroad 15*d*.

f.70r. **Grocer**   Paid to William Smyth, Grocer, our tenant in Cheapside, as follows:

For hippocras	First 2lb. of cinnamon
	Item 1lb. of ginger
	Item 24lb. of middle sugar
	Item 3oz. of cloves
	Item 3oz. of corianders
	Item 4oz. of nutmeg

Item for two loaves of sugar quart 21lb.
three quarters
Item for two loaves of sugar quart 22lb.
Item 24lb. of broken sugar
Item for 16lb. of pepper
Item for 2oz. of saffron
Item for 6oz. of cloves and mace
Item for 5oz. of nutmeg
Item for 4oz. of cinnamon
Item for 4oz. of ginger
Item for 3oz. of large mace
Item for 1oz. of sanders
Item for 14lb. of damask prunes
Item for 12lb. of currants
Item for 10lb. of dates
Item for three quires of cap papers
Item for an oz. of cloves

For jelly	Item for di lb. of cinnamon			
	Item for 6oz. of ginger			
	Item for nutmegs 3oz.			
	Item for 4oz. coriander			
	Item for an oz. di of cloves			
	Item for di lb. of isenglas			
	Item for 12oz. of turnesall			
	Item for 6lb. of middle sugar	£6	17*s.*	8*d.*

Pikemonger	Paid to Lucas Pikemonger for twenty-seven pikes according to the old scantling of our book at 22*d.* the piece lacking 6*d.* in the whole	49*s.*	

f.70v. **Baker**	Paid to Storar, Baker, for bread set of him as follows viz.:	
Saturday	First for a dozen of cakes and a dozen of buns spice bread	
	Item for two dozen of white bread of three for a penny	

Sunday	Item for four dozen and four cakes and four dozen and four buns spice bread for the potation on Sunday at night	
	Item for three dozen of white bread of three a penny for the dinner and potation the same day	
	Item for a dozen of wheaten bread	
Monday	Item sixteen dozen of white bread of three for a penny, four dozen stale white bread and two dozen wheaten bread	
Tuesday	Item one dozen of white bread of three for a penny, one dozen of penny white, one dozen of stale white bread, two dozen of half penny white bread, one dozen of wheaten bread	55s.
Beer and ale	Paid to Platt, Beer Brewer, for three barrels of double beer and one of stronger beer	18s.
	Item paid to Mathew Marten at the Bull in Smithfield for eight stands of ale	20s.
Wine	Paid to Robert Ffryar for our hogshead of Gascon wine – 50s.	
	Item to Mr Colclough for three gallons of French wine on Sunday at night for potation and fifteen gallons on Monday in all eighteen gallons at 12d. the gallon – 18s.	
f.71r.	Item paid to Lowe of the Myter for wine sett from his house viz.: First for two gallons for red wine for hippocras Item for a gallon and di of white wine for jelly Item two gallons of white wine for white broth Item for one pottle of sack Item for a pottle of white wine Item for a gallon of sack Item for eight gallons three quarters of sack in a rundlet at 18d. the gallon – 13s. 1d. Item for eight gallons three pints muscadel at 2s. the gallon – 16s. 9d. Item for two gallons of red wine	44s. 9d.

85

Marchpanes	Paid to Balthazar for sixteen marchpanes whereof eight at 3*s.* 4*d.* the piece four of 3*s.* and four of 2*s.* 8*d.* the piece	49*s.*	4*d.*
	Item paid to Triacle the Cook for twelve marchpanes whereof six at 3*s.* and six at 2*s.* 8*d.* the piece	34*s.*	
Wafers	Paid to Mrs Wharton for fifteen boxes of wafers at 2*s.* the box	30*s.*	
Pewterer	Paid to Catcher, Pewterer, for the loan of one dozen 7lb. chargers, one dozen of 5lb. chargers, three dozen of 4lb. trenchers, two dozen of 3lb. platters, five dozen of great French platters, five dozen of 3lb. platters, five dozen of small French platter, fourteen dozen of saucers, five dozen of small jelly dishes three dozen of large jelly dishes, three dozen of large jelly dishes, six dozen of plates	16*s.*	
Sturgeon	Paid for one firkin received from Thomas Chester[193] price	33*s.*	
	Item for a jowl and ronde of sturgeon bought of Mr Blagge in Fish Street	10*s.*	7*d.*
	Item paid for bringing of the sturgeon to the hall		2*d.*
f.71v. **Meal**	Paid to Mrs Rookes for two quarters of wheat meal price	37*s.*	4*d.*
	Item for one bushel of rye meal		20*d.*
Linen cloth	Paid for fifty-three ells three quarters of lockeram at 13*d.* the ell	58*s.*	2*d.*
	Item for four ells of Holland cloth at 16*d.* the ell	5*s.*	4*d.*
	Item for eight ells of canvas at 6*d. ob.*	4*s.*	4*d.*
Butter	Paid for 80lb. butter at 3*d.* the lb. and for bringing thereof to the Hall in all	20*s.*	2*d.*
Cream	Paid for twelve gallons three quarters of cream for both days at 12*d.* the gallon	12*s.*	9*d.*
Lard	Paid for 7lb. three quarters of lard for the red deer at 10*d.* the lb.	6*s.*	5*d.*

[193] Thomas Chester was a younger son of Sir William Chester, five times Master of the Drapers' Company. Thomas was admitted as a Freeman of the Company by patrimony in 1560. See Boyd, *Roll.*

Sweetwater	Paid for a pottle of washing water[194] and a pottle of rosewater – 5s. 4d. Item for two glasses for the same waters – 6d. Item for a pint of rosewater more – 12d.	6s.	10d.
Chandler	Paid to the Chandler Richard Nelson for stuff set from as mustard, vinegar, vergious, onions, salt, oatmeal, packthread, staff torches, candles etc. in all	18s.	
Painter	Paid to Thomas Lambe[195] for gilding the jelly and brawn	6s.	8d.
Wood and coal	Paid for a quarter of billets after 11s. the quarter – 2s. 9d. Item for 1cwt. of faggots – 4s. 8d. Item for eighteen sacks with coals – 7s. 6d.	14s.	11d.
Trays, ashen cups and trenchers	Paid for four trays – 2s. 2d. For three dozen of ashen cups – 2s. 9d. For twenty-four dozen of trenchers – 8s.	12s.	11d.
f.72r. **Barberries**	Paid for a gallon of barberries	4s.	
Flower and herbs	Paid for flowers for the Ladies' Chamber – 12d. Item for herbs for the hall and flowers – 8d.	20d.	
Taps	Paid for taps for wine and beer	4d.	
Earthen pots	Paid for three steynes[196] – 9d. For seven gallon pots and six pottle pots – 16d. And for two dozen of green pots – 12d.	3s.	1d.
Bowlters and jelly bags	Paid for two yards of boulter at 7d. the yard – 14d. And for two yards of boulter at 4d. the yard – 8d. And for two yards di of [cartnall?][197] white for jelly bags – 14d.	3s.	

---

[194] 'Sweet' water or washing water for guests to wash their hands at dinner.

[195] Possibly Thomas Lambe, a painter active in York in the 1560s. See R. Tittler, *Portraits, Painters, and Publics in Provincial England, 1540–1640* (Oxford: Oxford University Press, 2012), 80.

[196] Steyne: a 'stein', an earthenware beer mug.

[197] Illegible.

Extra-ordinary charges	Paid to Mr Lovell my Lord Treasurer's man for his reward for my Lord's warrant for impost of a tun of wine – 5s.		

Item for a quire of writing paper – 4d.

For three padlocks – 16d.

Item for the servant's dinner on Friday going about provision of things – 3d.

Item for bread for the officers on Saturday – 4d.

Item for salt for butter – 1d.

Item for eggs – 2d.

Item for tenterhooks[198] – 1d.

Item for bread for the cooks on Sunday at night – 2d.

Item paid for carriage of plate from Sir Richard Champion's – 7d.

Item paid for carriage of a pot of porridge to the White Lion in Southwark[199] – 6d.

Item the wine cellar for two days – 20d.

Item to four labourers for carrying the meal in to the pastry – 4d.

Item for three rundlets for wine – 3s.

Item for carriage of the rubbish and offal off the kitchen away out of the street by the raker – 2d.

Item for two birchen brooms – 3d.   14s.   3d.

Item paid to the Cook for baking of venison at home at his own house   2s.

f.72v. **Rewards for bucks**

Paid to Crockson's[200] man our tenant for his pains in reward bringing a buck – 6s.

Item to my Lord Giles'[201] servant for bringing a buck – 5s. both brought in generally   7s.

Item paid by Master Warden Hewar a reward for a buck brought him   5s.

---

[198] Tenterhooks were used to stretch cloth by holding it taut and under strain. The modern-day phrase 'to be on tenterhooks' derives from this practice and refers to being in a state of anxious suspense.

[199] It is not clear whether the White Lion, Southwark, was operating as an inn or prison at this time. See *Survey of London*, xxv. 16–19.

[200] Simon Crockson (or Croxon) was tenant of the Drapers' Company on Cheapside. Also see DCA, DB1, f.73r.

[201] Lord Giles Paulet, son of Lord Treasurer, Sir William Paulet. Giles was admitted to the Livery of the Drapers' Company in 1559. See Johnson, *History*, ii. 191.

Item for charges and in rewards for bucks
brought to Master Warden Parker viz. to
Sir Richard Knightly's keeper[202] – 6*s.* 8*d.*
For carriage of the same buck up to
London – 8*s.*
Item paid to Barton's servant to ride to
Brigstock Park[203] for a buck – 3*s.* 4*d.*
To the keeper of the same park – 6*s.*
For carriage of the same buck to London
– 10*s.*
Item paid in reward to him that brought Mr
Mydleton's buck of Colchester[204] – 5*s.*

Sum 39*s.* paid to Mr Parker	39*s.*
Item paid by Mr Chester in reward for a buck brought him and repaid	5*s.*
Item paid to Master Warden Kemp for summage[205] by him disbursed in reward for bucks brought him to the hall	35*s.*

		Sum	£4	11*s.*

Ffulke the Sewer	Paid to Fulke, the Common Crier, our officer and Sewer, for his pains for two days serving – 6*s.* 8*d.*		
Musicians	Paid to Corran's noise[206] for two days serving here	13*s.*	4*d.*
Porters	Paid to George Hill – 3*s.* To Thomas Cartwright – 3*s.* To Robert Selby – 3*s.* To Richard Thompson – 3*s.* To Robert Brushwood[207] – 3*s.* All porters waiting the three days viz. Sunday at night, Monday and Tuesday	15*s.*	

---

202 Sir Richard Knightley (1533–1615) was a politician and landowner in Northampton-shire. *HP Commons, 1558–1603*, ii. 405–6.

203 i.e. Brigstock Park in Northamptonshire.

204 Robert Middleton the elder, Alderman and Bailiff of Colchester, or his son Robert Mid-dleton the younger, a barrister who was educated at Inner Temple. See *HP Commons, 1558–1603*, iii. 48.

205 Summage: a toll paid for loads carried on horseback.

206 Noise: a company or band of musicians.

207 Robert Brushwood was a Draper. See Boyd, *Roll.*

Women in the kitchen	Paid to Goodwife Holmes for four days labour in the kitchen and house – 3*s*. 4*d*. Item to Goodwife Eles for four days labour in the kitchen also – 2*s*. And to her sister for three days – 18*d*.	6*s*.	10*d*.

Labourer Paid to Henry Star our Labourer for three
days sweeping and carrying of necessaries 2*s*.

f.73r. **Clerk and** Paid to the Clerk and Sexton of St.
Sexton at St. Michael's for the singing and ringing
Michael's 5*s*.

Butler Paid to Edmond Wright our Butler for his
wages and his man the three days 26*s*. 8*d*.
and in reward – 16*d*. 28*s*.

Cooks Paid to Treegle our Cook for his wages 40*s*.
And for his fees 10*s*.

<u>Sum total of the whole charges</u>

Bucks brought in viz.:

For the generality
From the Lord Giles Pawlet – one
Item from Croxon in Cheap – one

Two bucks

For Master Warden Parker
From Mr Kempe – one
Item from Mr Parker – one
Item from Brigstock Park – one
Item from Sir Richard Knightley – one
Item from Mr Mydleton – one

Five bucks

For Mr Hewar
Received for him – one buck

For Mr Chester
Received from him – one buck

f.73v. **From Master Warden Kempe**
Received from Mr Kempe – one

Item from my Lord Cobham[208] – two
Item from Mr Henry Haward[209] – one
Item from Mr Colt – one

Five bucks

Sum of the bucks – thirteen

Whereof

Delivered to the cooks nine bucks and
thereof baked in the house of large pasties
for the table – thirty
Item in Livery pasties – twenty-three
More delivered to the Cook three bucks
and thereof baked in the house in large
pasties for the table – nine
Item in Livery pasties – ten

Sum of the pasties baked in the house –
seventy-two

Pasties of venison spent and given

First on Sunday at dinner – two pasties
Item to Mr Parker and Mr Kempe – one
pasty
Item to Mr Hewar and Mr Chester – one
pasty
Item from Mr Kempe to Mr Dimocke[210] –
one pasty
Item on Monday at dinner spent – eighteen
pasties
Item in red deer the same day spent – four
pasties
Item to Mr Coverdale from Mr Kempe –
one pasty
Item for the latter dinner on Monday – two
pasties
Item from Mr Parker to Goodwife Powell
– one pasty
Item from Mr Kempe to Morris – one pasty

---

[208] William Brooke, Tenth Baron Cobham, Lord Warden of the Cinque Ports and Constable of Dover Castle. He was JP for Kent and MP in 1547 and 1555. See *HP Commons, 1509–1558*, i. 512–13.

[209] Possibly Henry Howard who was made earl of Northampton in 1603. See *Oxford DNB*.

[210] John Dimocke (or Dymocke) was Warden of the Drapers' Company in 1557–8. See Johnson, *History*, ii. 470.

Item in generality to him that kepeth the
conduit – one pasty
Item to Mr Hewar's – one pasty
Item to Mr Parker's – one pasty
Item from Mr Parker and Mr Kempe to
Walter – one pasty
Item from Mr Parker to Mr Starkey[211] –
one pasty

f.74r.
Item from generality to Mr Calverley –
one pasty
Item from Mr Parker to himself – three
pasties
Item from generality to Parker, Clerk of
the Market – one pasty
Item for dinner for Tuesday into the hall –
nine pasties
Item into the parlour by the Master's
appointment – two pasties
Item from Master Parker to the Furner[212] –
one pasty
Item from generality to Mason the
Poulterer – one pasty
To Plomtun of the Chamber[213] – one pasty
To the Cook – one pasty
To the Clerk – one pasty
To the Renter – one pasty
To Thomas Rombe – one pasty
Divided amongst the four Master Wardens
– twelve pasties

Four messes
**Potation on Saturday to the Masters in
the parlour at the secret nomination**
Spiced cakes and buns
Codlings and pears
Biskettes and caraways
Comfits two dishes
Filberts and plums
Comfits two dishes

Twelve
messes
**Potation Sunday at night to the Masters
and Livery**
In like manner as before

---

[211] Probably Thomas Starkey, a Draper. See Boyd, *Roll*.
[212] Furner: a baker or cook in charge of oven.
[213] Possibly Thomas Plumpton, who acted as an official at the Port of London in the 1590s
and died a gentleman of London in 1610. See TNA, PROB 11/116/374.

Four messes	**Service for Monday at dinner at the high table**
	In primis brawn and mustard
	Boiled capons two
	Swan
	A pasty of venison
	Pike
	Roasted capons two
	Custard
Second course	Jelly, quails, red deer
	Sturgeon and marchpanes
	Wafers and hippocras

f.74v. Five messes **The second table**
The first mess of all double the rest single the fare in all like unto the high table

Eight messes **The third table**
The first mess double the rest as at the second table saving that in place of quails they were served with pigeons

Four messes viz. two double **Service on Tuesday at dinner at the high table**

The first course
Brawn and mustard
Boiled capons
Puddings
Swan and goose
Venison pasty
Pike
Roast capon
Custard

The second course
Jelly
Quails and pigeons
Red deer
Sturgeon
Marchpane

Five messes single **The side table**

The first course	Brawn and mustard
	Puddings
	Boiled capons
	Goose
	Venison pasty
	Pike
	Roast capon
	Custard

Second course	Jelly
	Pigeons
	Sturgeon
	Marchpane

f.80r. **Feast Dinner** In the eleventh year in the reign of Queen Elizabeth, by the grace of God, eighth day August

Sir William Chester, knight and Alderman – our Master

Mr Quarles
Mr Whelar
Mr Maye[214]   } our Master Wardens
Mr Colclough

Provision for the same Feast Dinner and for the potations on Saturday and Sunday as also for the next day after the said Great Dinner

Butcher Paid to the Butcher for these parcels following viz.:

Sunday at dinner

First a rib of beef and a sirloin poise 7st. at 12*d.* the st.	7*s.*	
Item a hindquarter of mutton price	2*s.*	
Item a shoulder of veal price	12*s.*	
Item two long marrowbones at 6*d.* the piece		12*d.*
Item for 50lb. of suet at 3*d.* the lb.	12*s.*	6*d.*

For Monday

Item twenty-four long marrowbones at 6*d.* the piece	12*s.*	
Item two sirloins of beef weighing 12st. di at 12*d.* the st.	7*s.*	6*d.*
Item 32lb. of suet at 3*d.* the lb.	8*s.*	

[214] Henry Maye (or May) served as Warden of the Drapers' Company in 1568–9. See Johnson, *History*, ii. 471.

	Item two muttons for breakfast at 8*s*. the piece	16*s*.	
	Item for one peck of pricks		4*d*.
For Tuesday	Item for 36lb. of suet at 3*d*. the lb.	10*s*.	
	Item for twelve long marrowbones at 6*d*.	6*s*.	
	Item for twenty-eight stone of beef for the poor	38*s*.	
	Item for half a mutton for breakfast	4*s*.	
	Item for guts and blood for puddings	3*s*.	
	Item for a boar ready sodden	53*s*.	4*d*.
	Item for twenty-four gallons of saucing drink	4*s*.	

Sum   £8   14*s*.   8*d*.

f.80v. **Poulterer**	Paid to Robert Mason, Draper, for these parcels following:			
Sunday at dinner	First boiling capons and two roasting capons at 2*s*. the piece one with another		8*s*.	
	Item six quails of Mr Colclough at 7*s*. dozen		3*s*.	6*d*.
Monday	Item forty-one boiling capons and forty-one roasting capons at 2*s*. the piece one with another	£8	4*s*.	
	Item eleven cygnets provided by Master Maye at 7*s*. 6*d*. the piece	£4	2*s*.	6*d*.
	Item twelve geese at 20*d*. the piece		20*s*.	
	Item six dozen of quails at 7*s*. the dozen provided by Mr Colclough		42*s*.	
	Item five dozen pigeons at 20*d*. the dozen		8*s*.	4*d*.
	Item 4cwt. eggs at 2*s*. 8*d*. the cwt.		10*s*.	8*d*.
Tuesday	Item twenty boiling capons and twenty roasting capons at 2*s*. the piece one with another	£4		
	Item six cygnets at 8*s*. the piece provided by Mr Whelar of the Chamber		43*s*.	
	Item six geese at 20*d*. the piece		10*s*.	
	Item three dozen di of quails at 8*s*. the dozen provided by Mr Colclough		24*s*.	6*d*.
	Item three dozen pigeons at 20*d*. the dozen		5*s*.	
	Item from Mr Whelar Warden five capons at 2*s*. the piece		10*s*.	
	Item for 1cwt. and di of eggs at 2*s*. 8d the cwt.		4*s*.	

Sum   £26   6*d*.

Spicebread	Paid to Mrs Wall in Abchurch Lane			

Saturday – three dozen	For one dozen di or buns and one dozen and di of cakes, for the potation on Saturday after the secret nomination of the Master and Wardens at 2*s*. the dozen		6*s*.	
Sunday – ten dozen	Item for five dozen buns and five dozen cakes at 2*s*. the dozen for the potation on Sunday at night in the hall at their coming from St. Michael's		20*s*.	

	Sum	26*s*.

f.81r. **Baker**   Paid to Sarcefeeld, Baker, in Bishopsgate Street:

Saturday – one dozen	First for one dozen rolls at three for a penny for the potation			12*d*.
Sunday – seven dozen	Item two dozen penny white whereof one dozen stale Item two dozen halfpenny white whereof one dozen stale Item one dozen penny wheaten Item two dozen white at three for a penny		7*s*.	
Monday – thirty-three dozen	Item eight dozen penny white stale Item eleven dozen white of three for a penny Item twelve dozen penny white new Item two dozen penny wheaten bread		33*s*.	
Tuesday – thirteen dozen	Item two dozen penny white stale Item three dozen penny white new Item two dozen penny wheaten Item six dozen white three for a penny		13*s*.	
Meal	Item for twenty-one bushels meal at 20*s*. the quarter		52*s*.	6*d*.

	Sum	£5	6*s*.	6*d*.

Grocer   Paid to Mr Hart, Grocer, for these parcels of spice following:

For hippocras	Item for 2lb. di of cinnamon at 6*s*. 8*d*.		16*s*.	8*d*.
	Item for 1lb. a quarter of ginger at 4*s*. 8*d*.		5*s*.	10*d*.
	Item for 4oz. of cloves		2*s*.	
	Item for 8oz. of nutmeg		4*s*.	
	Item 16lb. of pepper at 4*s*. the lb.	3li.	4*s*.	

96

Item for cloves and mace 6oz.			
Item for mace fifty di all		8*s*.	
Item for 10oz. of ginger			
Item for 6oz. of cinnamon			
Item for 7oz. of nutmeg		4*s*.	
Item for 1oz. of sanders			
Item for 2oz. of saffron			
Item for 10lb. of dates at 8*d*. the lb.		6*s*.	8*d*.
Item for 12lb. of corinthes[215] at 4*d*.		4*s*.	
Item for 14lb. of prunes at			
Item for an oz. of cloves for perfume			
Item for large paper for custards three quires at [-] the quire			
Item for 19lb. quarters of fine sugar at 11*d*.		17*s*.	7*d*.
Item for 80lb. middle sugar at 9*d*. the lb.	£3		

Sum £10 9*s*. 9*d*.

f.81v. **Wafers –** Paid to Mrs Wharton for ten boxes of
fifteen boxes wafers on Monday and five boxes on
Tuesday at 2*s*. the box 30*s*.

Marchpanes Paid for thirty parchpanes[216] whereof six
large and twenty-four middle at 3*s*. 8*d*. the
piece one with another £5 10*s*.

Pikemonger – Paid to Lucas Pikemonger twenty pikes for
Monday Monday whereof four were of twenty-four
inches, eight of twenty inches and eight of
eighteen inches long at 22*d*. the piece one
with another 36*s*. 8*d*.

Tuesday Item for ten pikes on Tuesday whereof two
were of twenty-four inches four of twenty
inches and four of eighteen inches long at
22*d*. the piece 18*s*. 4*d*.

Sum 55*s*.

Beer Brewer Paid for four barrels of beer of 5*s*. the
barrel and one barrels at 4*s*. 24*s*.

Ale Brewer Paid to Mathew Marten our tenant in
Smithfield for three barrels ale at 6*s*. the
barrel and one barrel at 4*s*. 22*s*.
Item three pales of yeast for pikebroth 12*d*.

Sum 23*s*.

215 Corinthes: raisins of Corinth, currants.
216 Misspelling, i.e. marchpanes.

Sturgeon	Paid for two firkins of sturgeon at 30*s*. the firkin	£3		
Fruit	Paid for hundred di of codlings – 18*d*. For 4cwt. of plums white at 2*d*. the cwt. – 8*d*. For di cwt. old pippins – 2*s*. 6*d*. Pears and plums from Mr Colclough		4*s*.	8*d*.
Butter	Paid for 100lb. butter at 3*d*. the lb.		25*s*.	
f.82r. **Comfits**	Paid for 1lb. di of almond comfits at 14*d*.			21*d*.
	Item for a lb. of clove comfits at 2*s*.		2*s*.	
	Item for 2lb. of orange comfits at 2*s*.		4*s*.	
	Item for 1lb. quarter of ginger comfits at 2*s*.		2*s*.	6*d*.
	Item for 1lb. di of cinnamon comfits at 2*s*.		3*s*.	
	Item for 1lb. of caraways at 14*d*. the lb.			14*d*.
	Item for 2lb. of bisketts at 14*d*.		2*s*.	11*d*.
	Item for 1lb. of coriander comfits at 14*d*.			14*d*.
	Sum		18*s*.	6*d*.
Wine	Paid for a puncheon of French wine	£4		
	Item one hogshead of Gascon wine of John Carter being turned from this Company to the Company of Vintners and therefore – gratis			
	Item for white wine for broths		2*s*.	4*d*.
	Item for wine to fill the said wines lying in the cellar at diverse times and to the porters for laying the same two pieces in to the cellar and carts in all		6*s*.	6*d*.
	Item for seventeen gallons one pottle of sack drawn into a rundlet at 20*d*. the gallon		29*s*.	2*d*.
	Item for ten gallons one pottle of muscadel at 2*s*. 4*d*.		24*s*.	6*d*.
	Sum	£7	2*s*.	6*d*.
Cooper	Paid to Godd the Cooper for one rundlet of eighteen gallons for sack at			18*d*.
	Item for another of ten gallons for muscadel at			12*d*.
	Item for two taps of canes and one quill for the broaching of the same wine			6*d*.
	Item for his pains drawing the wine		3*s*.	
	Sum		6*s*.	

98

Linen cloth	Paid for fifty-three ells di of lockeram	55s.	
	Item more for four aprons lockeram	3s.	10d.
	Item for two ells Holland cloth at 20d. the ell for the Sewer and Carver	3s.	4d.
	Item for eight ells of soultage for the kitchen women etc. at 7d. the ell	4s.	8d.

Sum   £3   6s.   10d.

| **Cream** | Paid for ten gallons of cream for custards on Monday and for four gallons of cream on Tuesday at 14d. the gallon and more for a gallon of milk on Tuesday for pudding at 4d. the gallon in all | 16s. | 8d. |

f.82v. **Pewterer**	Paid to the Pewterer for nineteen garnish pewter at 10d. the garnish	15s.	10d.
	Item for seven dozen fruit dishes at 6d. the dozen hire	3s.	6d.
	Item for loss of pewter		20d.

Sum   21s.

| **Chandler** | Paid to the Chandler for pots, pans, oatmeal, salt, onions, mustard, vinegar, veriuce etc. in all with loss of earthen pots and for the hire of the other delivered | 28s. | 8d. |
| | Item for two bushels of flour | 6s. | |

Sum   34s.   8d.

Wood and coal	Paid for a quarter of billets	3s.	
	Item for cwt. and di of fagots at 4s. 8d. the cwt.	7s.	
	Item for twenty-eight sacks of coals at 6d.	14s.	

Sum   24s.

Trenchers, trays, taps, ashen cups and strainers	Paid for forty-three dozen trenchers price	12s.	1d.
	Item four Dansick trays at 16d. the piece	5s.	4d.
	Item taps for beer and ale		2d.
	Item three dozen ashen cups at 10d. dozen	2s.	6d.
	Item for strainers		10d..

Sum   20s.   11d.

| **Barberries** | Paid for one gallon and a quarter of barberries | 2s. | 6d. |

Coal baskets,	Paid for two coal baskets	8*d*.
brooms and	Item for birchen brooms and green	4*d*.
coal shovel	Item for a coal shovel	4*d*.

Sum	16*d*.

Rosewater for the kitchen and washing Paid for a gallon of washing water
Item given by Goodwife Basse three pints
of red rose water for meat – gratis

f.83r. **Flowers and herbs** Paid to Mr Maye's servant for flowers and herbs to strew — 3*s*.

Lard for red deer Paid for 9lb. of lard for the baking of the red deer at 8*d*. the lb. — 6*s*.

Porters at the gate and doors Paid to six porters for their pains viz. Robert Whitefield and Thomas Carter[217] at the hall door, Richard Thomson and Robert Selby at the stair foot, George Hall and Robert Brushwood at the great gate to every of them – 3*s*. — 18*s*.

Sewer Paid to Mr Ffulke the Common Crier for his pains sewing the two days viz. Monday and Tuesday according to the common custom of this house — 6*s*. 8*d*.

Preacher Paid to Mr Crowley[218] in reward he taking pains to preach before the Company on Monday at St. Michael's — 10*s*.

Musicians Paid to Ffrythe's wife attending the two days playing upon the voills[219] — 13*s*. 4*d*.

Clerks and Sexton of St. Michael's Paid to the Clerks and Sexton of St. Michael's church in Cornhill for their pains Sunday and Monday — 5*s*.

---

[217] Thomas Carter was a Draper. See Boyd, *Roll*.

[218] A Marian exile, Robert Crowley was a popular preacher during the reign of Edward VI and became increasingly Puritan in his preaching and writing during the reign of Elizabeth I. In 1568–9 he resigned his office at St. Giles Cripplegate, refusing to wear clerical vestments. He was a friend of John Foxe. See *Oxford DNB*.

[219] Viol: a five-, six- or seven- stringed instrument played with a bow.

Butler	Paid to Edmond Wright, Butler, for himself with five men serving the four days viz. Saturday at night, Sunday at noon, and potation at night Monday and Tuesday	26s.	8d.
f.83v. **Cook**	Paid to Stephen Triegle our Cook for his pains with his men dressing the dinners on Monday and Tuesday and also on Sunday for the Master Wardens and their wives etc.	40s.	
Women serving in the kitchen	Paid to Goodwife Holmes for three days Item to two women for three days either of them at 8d. per day	2s. 4s.	
Steward	Paid to Robert Beaumond for his pains of the Master's liberality serving as steward	40s.	
Scavenger	Paid to the Scavenger for the carriage away of the rubbish and carriage out of the kitchen		8d.
Extra-ordinary charges	Paid for writing paper a quire		3d.
	Item for six locks	3s.	
	Item for a basket to keep spice in		18d.
	Item for wine for the sturgeon		18d.
	Item for carriage of the sturgeon		4d.
	Item for carriage of butter		3d.
	Item for carriage of sack and muscadel		3d.
	Item for nails		1d.
	Item to waterbearers for water	2s.	6d.
	Item to a woman that boulted meal	2s.	
	Item to Master Wardens for boat hire by them paid going to bid guests		12d.
	Item for bread on Tuesday at night		4d.
	Item paid to the drums and flutes in reward	2s.	6d.
	Item paid for bringing the buck from Arrowsmith's[220]		6d.
	Item to the Cook for venison baked at his own house	8s.	4d.
	Item to Henry Starr our Labourer for three days	2s.	
	Item for carriage of fruits		1d.
	Item paid to Francis Tull in reward supplied the room of the Beadle	10s.	

[220] Possibly William Arrowsmith, Draper. See Boyd, *Roll.*

Item paid to a woman to whom the
Masters spake to provide quails and had
none of her   5*s.*

| | Sum | 41*s.* | 5*d.* |

<table>
<tr><td rowspan="4">f.84r. Rewards
for bucks
given to the
generality</td><td>Paid to the Lord Treasurer's servant</td><td>6s.</td><td></td></tr>
</table>

f.84r. **Rewards**   Paid to the Lord Treasurer's servant   6*s.*
for bucks   Item to Doctor Gibbon's servant   6*s.*
given to the   Item to Mr Candeler's servant   3*s.*   4*d.*
generality   Item to Mr Renold's man   3*s.*   3*d.*
  Item to Mr Candeler's man   3*s.*   4*d.*

| | Sum | 22*s.* | |

| | Sum total | £98 | 9*s.* | 5*d.* |

Deductions   Allowance of the house   £20
Item for the impost of a tun of wine given
by the Lord Treasurer   50*s.*
Item for quarterage money   £3   13*s.*   4*d.*
Item for a hogshead of beer   6*s.*

Sum of the deductions is   £26   9*s.*   4*d.*

So the whole to be divided into four parts
amounts to   £92   1*d.*
And so every Master Wardens part comes to   £18   q

f.84v.   **Bucks by generality**
From Burdocke[221] – one
From Mr Candeler[222] – two
From my Lord Treasurer – one
From Mr Fryar – one
From Doctor Gibbons – one
From Mr Renoldes – one

Sum is – seven bucks

Bucks by Mr Quarles
From my Lady Grey – two
From Spirling – one
From Mr Dorrell[223] – one

---

[221] Following his father Thomas Burdocke the elder, Thomas Burdocke (or Burdock) the younger was admitted as a Freeman to the Drapers' Company by patrimony in 1568. See Boyd, *Roll.*
[222] Possibly Richard Candler, Mercer, a factor of Thomas Gresham and teller of the Exchequer in 1568. See G. Rossi, *Insurance in Elizabethan England: The London Code*, Cambridge Studies in English Legal History (Cambridge: Cambridge University Press, 2016), 89.
[223] Possibly Thomas Darrell, Draper. See Boyd, *Roll.*

From Mr Roffe[224] – one

Sum is – five bucks

Bucks by Mr Whelar
From his house – three
From his son-in-law – one

Sum is – four bucks

Bucks by Mr Maye
From Asshedowne[225] – one
From Chandeler – one
From Sir Henry Jarningham[226] – one
From Bedington park[227] – one
From Oxffordshere – one

Sum is – five bucks

Bucks by Mr Colclough
From Alderman Becher[228] – one
From Mr Ffanchow – one
From Lady Harrington[229] – one
From Wyndsor – one
From Churchehill – one
From Mr Hare in Cheape[230] – one

Sum is – six bucks

f.85r.   <u>Sum of all the bucks received as –
            twenty-seven bucks</u>

Two bucks   Whereof two were given away whole unbaked to which one
given away   to Mr Wilbram and one to the Mr Bachelors and Waiters –
            two bucks

---

[224] Possibly Thomas Roff, Draper. See Boyd, *Roll.*

[225] Likely Ashdown Forest in Kent, East Sussex, or the Forest of Assheton on Ashbury Manor in Berkshire.

[226] Sir Henry Jerningham, courtier of Queen Mary and MP for Suffolk and later Gloucester, retired to the Manor of Costessey in Norfolk on the accession of Queen Elizabeth. See *Oxford DNB.*

[227] Beddington Park, Sutton, owned by the Carew family.

[228] Henry Becher, a Haberdasher, served as Alderman from 1567 and as Sheriff in 1569–70. See Beaven, *Aldermen*, i. 63; ii. 38.

[229] Possibly either Lady Elizabeth Harington (née Moton), widow of Sir John Harington senior (see *HP Commons, 1509–1558*, ii. 256–7), or Lady Lucy Harington (née Sydney), wife of Sir James Harington (see *HP Commons, 1558–1603*, ii. 255–6).

[230] Possibly Nicholas Hare, son of John Hare, a wealthy Mercer who lived on Cheapside. See J. Strype, *A Survey of London* (London: 1720), iii. 38.

Fifteen bucks baked The rest being twenty-five bucks were spent in the house and given away in pasties at the discretion of the Master Wardens – twenty-five bucks

Which twenty-five bucks made one hundred and thirty pasties whereof four pasties were baked for red deer – one hundred and thirty pasties

Pasties of venison baked in the house spent and given away by the Master Wardens to their friends to officers of the house and others as appears by the particulars following:

First by generality to Mr Randall the Common Serjeant[231] – one pasty
For Mr Whelar to John Turner[232] – one pasty
For Mr Colclough to Hamond[233] – one pasty
For Mr Maye to his brother Maye – one pasty
For Mr Maye to Giles[234] – one pasty
For Mr Whelar to Woodcock[235] – one pasty
For Mr Colclough to Robert Sadler[236] – one pasty
For Mr Quarles to Altham[237] – one pasty
For Mr Quarles to Dawson[238] – one pasty
For Mr Whelar to Lane[239] – one pasty
For Mr Whelar to Mistress Heath[240] – one pasty
For the Master's dinner on Sunday – two pasties
For the Cook's dinner on Sunday – one pasty
For Mr Maye to Chandler – one pasty
For the Masters to supper on Sunday – one pasty
For generality to the Cook – one pasty
For generality to the Porter's supper – one pasty
From generality to the Steward's supper – one pasty
From generality to the [perker][241] officer – one pasty
From Mr May to Rydley[242] – one pasty

231 Bernard Randolph (or Randall), Common Serjeant of London (1563–83). See W. H. Overall and H. C. Overall (ed.) *Analytical Index to the Series of Records Known as the Remembrancia 1579–1664* (London: privately printed, 1878), 278, 553.
232 Likely John Turner, Draper. See Boyd, *Roll*.
233 Possibly William Hamond, Draper. See Boyd, *Roll*.
234 Possibly Raffe (or Raph) Giles, Draper. See Boyd, *Roll*.
235 Possibly John Woodcock, Apprentice of the Drapers' Company.
236 Robert Sadler was a founder of the Venice Company. See Brenner, *Merchants and Revolution*, 21, 64n.
237 Possibly James Altham, London merchant. See Boyd, *Roll*.
238 Possibly Thomas Dawson, Draper. See Boyd, *Roll*.
239 Possibly Henry Lane, Draper. See Boyd, *Roll*.
240 Possibly wife of Thomas Heath, Baker. Mrs Heath supplied bread for the Election Dinner in 1575. Her husband is noted as a supplier in 1570 and 1574. See DCA, DB1, f.94v, f.122v.
241 Illegible.

f.85v.

From generality to the Lord Treasurer – one pasty
From Mr Colclough to a gent at Mr Brooke's – one pasty
From Mr Colclough to Mr Calthorppe – one pasty
From Mr Colclough to Williamson[243] – one pasty
From Mr Quarles to Heron – one pasty
From Mr Maye to Hewes[244] – one pasty
From generality to the Searchers[245] – one pasty
From Mr Whelar to Mr Crowley – one pasty
From generality to Mr Friar – one pasty
From generality to Mr Gough[246] – one pasty
From generality to the waiters at waterside – one pasty
From generality to the Bishoppes Head – one pasty
From Mr Maye to Bap. Fortini[247] – one pasty
From generality to my Lady Chester – one pasty
From generality to my Lady Champion – one pasty
From generality to Mr Smith's clerks – one pasty
From Mr Colclough to Mr Howlett[248] and Harker – one pasty
From generality to the Furner – one pasty
From generality to the Porters of Blackwell Hall – one pasty
From generality to Shorter[249] – one pasty
From generality to Mrs Quarles and Mrs Whelar[250] – one pasty
From generality spent in the house Monday dinner – twenty-four pasties
From generality to the Cook's dinner – one pasty
From generality to the Porter's dinner – one pasty
From generality to the Ale Brewer – one pasty
From generality to him that kepeth the conduit – one pasty
From generality to Mr Rennoldes – one pasty
From Mr Whelar – three pasties
From Mr Quarles – one pasty
From Mr Maye to Lamkin – one pasty
From Mr Quarles to Tatton[251] – one pasty
From Mr Maye – two pasties
From generality spent in the house Tuesday – nine pasties
From generality for the Cook's dinner – one pasty
From generality for the Furner – one pasty
From generality spent in red deer – four pasties

[242] Possibly Thomas Rydley, Draper. See Boyd, *Roll*.
[243] Possibly William Williamson, Draper. See Boyd, *Roll*.
[244] Possibly David Hughes, Draper. See Boyd, *Roll*.
[245] The Searchers were members of the Company Livery who assessed whether retail Drapers were adhering to the set standards lengths (ells) for the sale of their cloths.
[246] Possibly Thomas Goughe, Draper (see Boyd, *Roll*) or John Gough, preacher (see DCA, DB1, f.97r).
[247] Baptiste (or Baptista) Fortini, Florentine merchant, resident in London. See M. A. S. Hume (ed.) *Calendar of State Papers, Spain (Simancas), 4 Vols.* (London: 1894), ii. 156.
[248] Possibly Richarde Howlett, Grocer. See TNA, PROB 11/57/479.
[249] Possibly William Shorter, Draper. See Boyd, *Roll*.
[250] Warden Thomas Wheeler married Kathryn (née Andesby) in 1554 until her death a few years later. His second wife was Kinborowe Evans. It is not clear whom he was married to in 1569. See TNA, PROB 11/60/593.

From Mr Whelar to Turner[252] – one pasty
From generality to Mr Yeve of the Crown Office[253] – one pasty
From generality to Mr Pelter – one pasty
From Mr Colclough to his house – one pasty
From Mr Quarles and Mr Whelar's ring – one pasty
From generality to Mr Hayward[254] – one pasty
From generality to the waiters' dinner – one pasty
From generality to the four cooks – three pasties
From generality to the Poulterer – one pasty
From generality to John Elliot – one pasty
From generality to Lennard and Prestwicke – one pasty
From generality to Thomas Elyott – one pasty

From generality to Mrs Wharton – one pasty
From generality to Mr Ffulkes – one pasty
From generality to Cotton[255] – one pasty
From generality to the Clerks of St. Michael's – one pasty
From generality to the porters – four pasties
From generality to the Clerk Bartholomew Warner – one pasty
From generality to Mrs Messinger[256] – one pasty
From generality to Robert Richards[257] – one pasty
From generality to Robert Holmes[258] – one pasty
From generality to Hallye[259] – one pasty
From generality to Thomas Whelye – one pasty
From generality to the butlers – one pasty
From generality to the Glasier – one pasty
From generality to Dorrell and Agar's son[260] – one pasty
From generality to Henry Starr and the Butcher – one pasty
From generality to one of the Inns of Court – one pasty
From generality to the Steward which were stolen from him that said – one pasty

Sum total – one hundred and thirty pasties

Pasties of venison spent in the house and given by generality – ninety-eight pasties

[251] Possibly John Tatton, Draper. See Boyd, *Roll*.
[252] Possibly William Turner, Draper. See Boyd, *Roll*.
[253] John Yeve (or Eve), deputy attorney in the Crown Office. See B. R. Masters (ed.) *Chamber Accounts of the Sixteenth Century* (London: London Record Society xx, 1984), 30–1.
[254] Possibly Edward Hewar who served as Warden of the Drapers in 1559–60 and 1567–8. See Johnson, *History*, ii. 470–1.
[255] Possibly John Cotton, Matthew Cotton, Roger Cotton or William Cotton, all Drapers. See Boyd, *Roll*.
[256] Mrs Messenger (or Messinger) was the widow of Edward Messenger, former Clerk of the Drapers' Company who died in June 1569. See Johnson, *History*, ii. 474.
[257] Robert Richards was elected to the position of Renter of the Drapers' Company in July 1569, taking over from Bartholomew Warner. See Johnson, *History*, ii. 474.
[258] Robert Holmes was Beadle of the Drapers' Company from October 1551 until December 1569. See Johnson, *History*, ii. 474.
[259] Possibly John or William Hallye (or Halley), both Drapers. See Boyd, *Roll*.
[260] Likely Thomas Awgar, the son of Nicholas Awgar. Both were Drapers who practised as chandlers. See Boyd, *Roll*.

Given by Mr Quarles as above – six pasties
Given by Mr Whelar as above – nine pasties
Given by Mr Maye as above – nine pasties
Given by Mr Colclough – eight pasties

So was spent and given away as appears – one hundred and thirty pasties

Four messes   **Potation for the Masters on Saturday**
Cakes and buns
Byskettes and caraways
Plums and codlings
Comfits two dishes
Pears and pippins
Comfits two dishes
Gascon wine and French
Sack and hippocras
Ale and beer

f.86v. Twelve messes   **Potation for the whole Livery on Sunday at afternoon**
Cakes and buns
Bisketts and caraways
Plums and codlings
Comfits two dishes
Pears and pippins
Comfits two dishes
Gascon wine and French wine
Sack and hippocras
Ale and beer

Two messes   **For the Wardens' wives and Bachelor Wardens**
As above

For servants
Manchets
Pears
Plums
Codlings

Two messes single   **Sunday at dinner for the four Masters the Wardens their wives, officers of the house etc.**
Brawn and mustard
Boiled capon
Roasted beef
Baked venison
Roasted capon
Quails – six

For servants and cooks
Boiled mutton and pottage
Roasted beef
Roasted veal

Monday for breakfast for waiters, officers, servants, cooks etc.
Boiled mutton and potage

f.87r. **Monday for dinner prepared twenty messes full furnished as follows:**

First course   **For the high table**
Four messes   Brawn and mustard
double   Boiled capon
                    Roasted swan
                    Baked venison
                    Pikes
                    Roasted capon
                    Custard

First course   **For the second table**
Five double
messes   Brawn and mustard
                    Boiled capon
                    Roasted swan or goose
                    Baked venison
                    Pikes
                    Roasted capons
                    Custards

First course   **For the third table**
Five messes
double   As above

First course   For the parlour
Three messes
single   As above

First course   For the Master Wardens
One mess
single   As above

First course   For the Lady Chester
One mess
single   As above

First course   For the Lady Champion
One mess
single   As above

108

First course   For gentlewomen and friends in the gallery

One mess

single   As above

First course   **To Mr Colclough's house for that he was sick**

One mess   Boiled capon

single   Baked venison

Roasted capon

Custard

f.87v. One mess   **For the cooks at their dinner**

single   Boiled capon

Roasted goose

Baked venison

Roasted capon

Custard

Two messes   **Received into the larder**

double   As above

Monday at dinner to the high table and other tables for the second course

Second course   **For the high table in the hall**

Four messes   Quails

Red deer

Sturgeon

Marchpane

Second course   **For the second table in the hall**

Five messes   Quails or pigeons

Red deer

Sturgeon

Marchpanes

Second course   **For the third table in the hall**

Five messes   Quails or pigeons

Red deer

Sturgeon

Marchpane

Second course   **Into the parlour**

Two messes   As above

Item after dinner wafers and hippocras
throughout the whole house

f.88r.   **Tuesday for dinner ten messes full
                          furnished as follows:**

**The first
course**   **For the high table in the hall**
Four messes   Brawn and mustard
double   Boiled capon
                      A pudding white and black
                      Roasted swan
                      Baked venison
                      Pike in herblade[261]
                      Roasted capon
                      Custard

**The first
course**   **For the second table in the hall**
Four messes   Brawn and mustard
double and   Puddings white and black
two messes   Boiled capon
single   Roasted swan or goose
                      Baked venison
                      Pike in herblade
                      Roasted capon
                      Custard

**The first
course**   **For the cooks**
One mess   Puddings
single   Boiled capon
                      Roasted goose
                      Baked venison
                      Roasted capon
                      Custard

Three messes   **Received into the larder**
single   As above

                      **Tuesday for dinner at the second course
                      as follows:**

Second course   **For the high table in the hall**

---

[261] Herblade or herbage: a garnish of herbs.

110

Four messes	Quails
	Red deer
	Sturgeon
	Marchpane

Second course For the second table

Five messes	Quails or pigeons
	Red deer
	Sturgeon
	Marchpane

f.88v.

Item as on Monday after dinner wafers and hippocras throughout the house

Item all meat that was reserved in the larder was disposed at the pleasure of the Master Wardens and their wives and other things equally divided amongst them

On Tuesday for the poor   Item to the poor on Tuesday, beef and potage ordained only for that purpose

Officers in that house appointed:

In the larder – two   Robert Beaumond, Draper, Steward, and to assist him Israell Johnson,[262] son to Mistress Colclough[263]

In the buttery and cellars – seven   That is two at the buttery hatch to deliver, two to carry wine, ale and beer up to them that delivered it, two to draw ale and beer, two to draw wine whose honesty and diligence did preserve that none was lacking his name was Richard Goad, Cooper

In the pantry – three   That is one at the pantry hatch, one to fetch bread to him that kept the hatch and one without the pantry door to carry bread to the tables or to see that it was carried nowhere else

---

[262] Israell Johnson was son of Otwell Johnson, a Draper. See Boyd, *Roll*.

[263] Maria Colclough (née Warner) was first married to Otwell Johnson, who died in 1551, and then to Matthew Colclough. See B. Winchester, 'The Johnson Letters, 1542–1552', 4 Vols. (Unpublished PhD thesis, University of London, 1952), iii. 559–63; E. Freshfield (ed) *The Vestry Minute Books of the Parish of St. Bartholomew Exchange in the City of London, 1567–1676* (London: privately printed, 1890), 2.

At the stair head coming from the kitchen – one — John Chambers to see that the meat accordingly went to furnish the house and that nothing was purloined which was sent from the kitchen

In the bookhouse – six — That is to take meat at the door in the hall going into the parlour, two to receive it of them and so bring it into the bookhouse and two maids or women to mess it, dish it, and see it orderly used

Porters – six — That is two at the hall door going down the stairs where of one did write and take note of all pewter and napkins etc. as went out of the house that it might be called for again, two at the door at the stair foot and two at the great gate

f.89r. **Butlers – six** — Edmond Wright the Butler findeth five men besides himself to serve the house and taketh of the plate

Sewer — Mr Fulkes, Common Crier, is Sewer yearly and hath for his fee of the house a noble the two days

Waiters — The four Master Bachelors came on Sunday in the afternoon and gave their attendance on the Masters and Livery at their potation, and drink.
Item the said four Master Bachelors on Monday coming with twenty-four of the comeliest and handsomest men of the Yeomanry decently apparelled at nine of the clock and break their fast with mutton and potage and so two and two go for the guests as they are appointed by the Clerk which giveth several bills for whom they shall go, and after wait till dinner be done.
Item in Tuesday likewise the four Master Bachelors with twelve more of them which the day before waited coming likewise to go for guests and wait as above.
In consideration of which their pains the Master Wardens gave them this year one good fat and sweet buck unbaked.

ANNIS 1569 AND 1570

In the time of Francisii Barnam Alderman
our Master and

Johannis Branche
Martini Calthorpe
Roberti Diconson[264] and } Wardens
Gualteri Garway[265]

Quarter **Expenses of the first Quarter Dinner**
Dinner   **kept the fifteenth day of November 1569,**
            for eight messes of meat as follows:

First paid to Triegle the Cook for sixteen minced pies at 16*d.* the piece	21*s.*	4*d.*
Item for eight custards at 2*s.* 4*d.* the piece	18*s.*	8*d.*
Item for eight quince pies at 2*s.* 10*d.*	22*s.*	8*d.*
Item for six long marrowbones	2*s.*	4*d.*
Item for a sirloin piece of beef	2*s.*	4*d.*
Item to the Cook for his fee	6*s.*	
Paid to Edward Wright,[266] Butler, for a stand of ale, half of one and half of another	3*s.*	
Item for a kilderkin of beer	3*s.*	
Item for seven dozen of bread	7*s.*	
Item to him for his fee	4*s.*	
Paid to the Vintner for ten gallons and a quart of claret wine at 16*d.* gallons	13*s.*	8*d.*
Item for three pottles of white wine	2*s.*	
Item for a pottle of muscadel		14*d.*
Item for a gallon of malmsey		20*d.*
Item for three pottles of sack	2*s.*	6*d.*
Paid to the Pewterer for four garnish of pewter vessels at 10*d.* the garnish	3*s.*	4*d.*

---

[264] Robert Diconson served as Warden of the Drapers' Company in 1569–70, 1577–8, and 1583–4. He was Master in 1591–2. See Johnson, *History*, ii. 471–2.
[265] Walter Garway served as Warden of the Drapers' Company in 1569–70. See Johnson, *History*, ii. 471.
[266] Edward Wright is also referred to as Edmond in the Dinner Book.

Paid for three rondes of brawn	6s.	
Item for saucing drink to the same		2d.
Paid for six sacks of great coal	2s.	6d.
Paid for 6lb. di of butter	2s.	2d.

f.91v.

Paid to the Chandler for a pack of white salt		3d.	
Item for candles for the kitchen		1d.	
Item for vergys		3d.	
Item for mustard		3d.	
Item for vinegar		2d.	
Item for a boiling pot		1d.	
Item for a half a pack of white salt		4d.	
Item for a birchen broom		1d.	
Item for a pot		1d.	
Item for packthread and white salt		1d.	ob.
Item for a lb. of cotton and a lb. of wick candles		5d.	ob. q
Paid for a pint of rosewater		12d.	
Paid to Mason the Poulterer for twenty fat capons at 22d. the piece	36s.	8d.	
Item for eight geese at 18d. the piece	12s.		
Item for twelve suytes[267] at 3d. the piece	3s.		
Item for nine dozen larks	5s.		
Item for eggs		8d.	
Item for a pint of barberries		2d.	
Item for eight dozen trenchers	4s.		
Item for a couple of rabbits for supper		8d.	
Item for two shoulders of mutton		21d.	
Item for olives and butter		6d.	
Paid to the Grocer for 2oz. of pepper		6d.	
For 1oz. long mace		12d.	
For 1oz. of ginger		4d.	
For 1lb. of dates		8d.	
For di a lb. of bisketes		6d.	
For 1lb. of fine sugar		12d.	
For 2lb. of middle sugar		20d.	
For 2lb. of currants		6d.	
For 2lb. of prunes		4d.	
Item more for 2lb. of sugar	2s.		

Sum	£3	16s.	10d.	ob. q

Sum total of this Quarter Dinner amounts to	£10	2s.	6d.	ob. q

Whereof the house allows	£8			
Mr Diconson		21s.	3d.	qt. d
Mr Garwaye		21s.	3d.	qt. d

---

[267] Suyte or suite: possibly young geese or goslings.

114

£.92r. **Quarter Dinner**	**Expenses of the second Quarter Dinner kept the twenty-first day of February 1569, for eight messes of meat as follows:**		

First paid for three lings and a half	11*s.*	2*d.*
Item for three green fishes and a half	3*s.*	8*d.*
Item for a jowl of fresh salmon	4*s.*	
Item for a quarter and a half of roasting lamperns	3*s.*	
Item for five great roasting eels	10*s.*	
Item for 2cwt. of smelts	2*s.*	8*d.*
Item paid to Ravens,[268] Pikemonger, for eight pikes at 20*d.* the piece and eight carps at the same price	26*s.*	8*d.*
Item paid for alexander buds for salads		12*d.*
Item for eggs		9*d.*
Item for half cwt. of oranges		6*d.*
Item for sweet butter for the table		16*d.*
Item for salad oil		9*d.*
Item for parsley		6*d.*
Item for salad herbs		4*d.*
Item for half a pack of flour		4*d.*
Item for sorrel		2*d.*

Paid to the Cook for fourteen lampern pies at 14*d.* the piece	16*s.*	4*d.*
Item for eight custards at 2*s.* 4*d.* the piece	18*s.*	8*d.*
Item for [-] tarts at [-]		
Item to him for his wages dressing the dinner	6*s.*	

Paid to the Grocer for 2oz. of pepper		7*d.*
Item for an oz. of cinnamon		6*d.*
Item for an oz. of ginger		5*d.*
Item for an oz. and di of large mace		18*d.*
Item for 1lb. di of prunes		4*d.*
Item for 1lb. di of currants		6*d.*
Item for 1lb. of dates		8*d.*
Item for 2lb. of coarse sugar		20*d.*
Item for 3lb. of fine sugar	3*s.*	
Item for one quarter of byskettes		4*d.*

Paid to the Butler for his pains	4*s.*	
Item for a stand of ale and a kilderkin of beer at 3*s.* the piece	6*s.*	

---

268 William Raven, pikemonger of London, supplied the Star Chamber with pike, carp, tench, and eels from Cambridge in October 1582. See *Calendar of the Manuscripts of the Most Honourable the Marquess of Salisbury: The Cecil Papers* (London: Royal Commission on Historical Manuscripts, 1888), ii. 525.

Item for six dozen of bread	6s.	
Paid to the Pewterer for the hire of five garnish of vessel at 10d.	4s.	2d.
Paid for a pint of rosewater		10d.

f.92v.

Paid for di cwt. of fagots	2s.	2d.
Item for coals to Robert Richards		13d.

Paid for di a peck of salt	6d.
Item for vinegar, vergys and mustard	5d.
Item for 4lb. of butter to the Cook	16d.
Item for 9lb. of butter to the Chandler	
Item for fine white salt for the table	3d.
Item for onions	1d.
Item for a boiling pot	3d.
Item for vinegar more – 1d, and for a pot – 1d, and for a birchen broom – 1d.	3d.

Paid to the Vintner at the Bishopp's Hed for seven gallons and a pottle of claret wine and one quart of white wine at 16d. the gallon – 5s. 4d, and for two gallons and a pottle of sack at 2s. the gallon – 5s.	15s.	4d.
Item to the Goodwife Holmes for her pains		6d.

<u>Sum total of this Quarter Dinner amounts to</u>   [-]

Quarter Dinner

Expenses of the third Quarter Dinner kept the sixth day of June 1570, for seven messes of meat as follows:

Paid to Mason the Poulterer for sixteen capons at 22d. the piece one with another	29s.	4d.
Item for fourteen geese at 12d. the piece – 14s, and for twenty-one rabbits at 4d. the piece – 7s. 4d, and for eggs – 8d. in all paid	22s.	

Paid to the Cook for two salmons – 15s, for a sirloin of beef – 6s. 2d, for six long marrowbones at 6d. the bone – 3s, for seven chicken pies at 3s. the piece – 21s, for seven custards at 2s. 4d. the piece – 16s, for one marchpane – 3s, for his pains – 6s.	£4	5s.

f.93r.

Paid to the Butler for a stand of ale for a kilderkin of beer – 3s, for seven dozen of bread – 7s, for his fee – 4s.	17s.	1d.

Paid to the Vintner for ten gallons claret
wine – 13*s.* 4*d,* for two gallons sack – 4*s,*
for a quart of white vinegar – 4*d.* | 17*s.* | 4*d.*

Paid for water from the conduit | | 16*d.*

Paid to the Grocer for 2oz. of pepper, 1lb.
di of currants – 6*d,* 1lb. of dates – 8*d,* 1oz.
of maces – 12*d,* byskettes and caraways –
7*d,* 2lb. of prunes – 4*d,* 2lb. of fine sugar
– 2*s,* and 2lb. of middle sugar – 20*d.* | 7*s.* | 3*d.*

Paid to the Pewterer for occupying of four
garnish of vessels at 10*d.* the garnish | 3*s.* | 4*d.*

Paid to the Chandler for di a peck of white
salt – 3*d,* for a quart of vinegar – 1*d. ob,*
for vergys – 3*d,* for a quarter more of
vinegar – 1*d. ob*, for packthread – *ob*, for
fine white salt – 3*d,* for a pan – 2*d,* and for
a broom – 2*d.* | | 15*d.*

Paid for six sacks of coal | 3*s.* | 6*d.*
Item paid for 6lb. of fresh butter | | 18*d.*

Paid for two rondes of sturgeon | 7*s.*
Paid for a pint of rosewater | | 10*d.*
Paid for parsley – 1*d.* pricks – 1*d.* and
ale – 1*d.* | | 3*d.*
Paid to Goodwife Holmes for her pains | | 12*d.*

Sum | £3 | 20*d.*

Sum total of this Quarter Dinner amounts to | £9 | 18*s.*

117

FEAST DINNER } ANNO 1570

In the reign of Queen Elizabeth of
England, France and Ireland etc. seventh
day of August Monday

Mr Ffrancys Barnam Alderman then   } our Master

Mr John Branche
Mr Marten Calthorpp   } our four
Mr Robert Diconson and   Master Wardens
Mr Walter Garway

**Provision for the same Great Dinner
and for the potation on Saturday and
Sunday as also for the Tuesday the day
after the Feast Dinner:**

Poulterer   Paid to Robert Mason, our Poulterer, for
these parcels

Sunday   First for two boiling capons and two
roasting capons at 2*s.* the piece   8*s.*
Item for 2cwt. eggs   5*s.*

Monday   Item for forty-two boiling capons and
forty-two roasting capons at 2*s.* the piece   £8   8*s.*
Item for thirteen cygnets at 8*s.* the piece   £5   4*s.*
Item for nine geese at 20*d.* the piece   15*s.*
Item for three dozen and ten partridges at
10*d.*   38*s.*   4*d.*
Item for three dozen pigeon at 20*d.*   5*s.*
Item for 3cwt. of eggs at 2*s.* 6*d.* the cwt.   7*s.*   6*d.*
Item for two dozen di of quails at 10*s.*   25*s.*

Tuesday   Item for eleven boiling capons and eleven
roasting capons at 2*s.* the piece   44*s.*
Item for four cygnets at 8*s.*   32*s.*
Item for three geese at 20*d.* the piece   5*s.*
Item for two dozen and six pigeons at 20*d.*   4*s.*   2*s.*
Item for di cwt. of eggs at 2*s.* 2*d.*   15*d.*

                                      Sum paid   £23

118

94v. **Butcher**	Paid to the Butcher for one rib and one sirloin of beef weighing 4st. and di at 12*d.* the st.	4*s.*	6*d.*
Sunday	Item for a hind quarter of mutton	2*s.*	
	Item for a breast of veal		20*d.*
	Item for four long marrowbones at 6*d.*	2*s.*	
	Item for 4lb. of suet		12*d.*
Monday	Item for two sirloins of beef weighing 8st. at 12*d.* the st.	8*s.*	
	Item for two whole sheep	18*s.*	
	Item for 40lb. of suet at 3*d.* the lb.	10*s.*	
	Item for twenty-four long marrowbones at 6*d.*	12*s.*	
	Item for one peck of pricks		4*d.*
Tuesday	Item for 30lb. of suet at 3*d.*	7*s.*	6*d.*
	Item for eight long marrowbones at 6*d.*	4*s.*	
	Item for 31st. 2lb. of beef for to make porridge for the poor at 12*d.* st.	31*s.*	3*d.*
	Item for twelve long guts and a gallon of blood	2*s.*	10*d.*
	Item for 6lb. of suet at 3*d.* the lb.		18*d.*
	Item for one boar ready sodden	£3 13*s.*	5*d.*
	Item for that was given him in earnest upon the bone		12*d.*

	Sum paid	£9 12*d.*

Baker	Paid to Thomas Heath, Baker, for bread as follows:		
Saturday – one dozen	First for one dozen rolls at three for a penny		12*d.*
Sunday – seven dozen	Item for two dozen rolls three for a penny	2*s.*	
	Item two dozen penny white bread whereof one dozen stale	2*s.*	
	Item for two dozen half penny white bread whereof one dozen stale bread	2*s.*	
	Item for one dozen wheaten bread		12*d.*
Monday – thirty-three dozen	Item for eleven dozen rolls, twelve dozen penny white new, eight dozen penny white stale, and two dozen wheaten penny bread	33*s.*	
Tuesday – thirteen dozen	Item for six dozen rolls, three dozen penny white new, two dozen penny white stale and two dozen penny wheaten	13*s.*	

	Sum paid	54*s.*

119

f.95r. **Meal**	Paid for twelve bushels of meal bought at 2s. 8d. the bushel	32s.	
	Item for the carriage of the same		4d.
	Item paid to the Baker's man in reward for boulting of the same meal		4d.
	Sum paid	32s.	8d.
	Item more paid for a bushel di of rye meal	3s.	

Grocer Paid to William Smyth, our tenant in Cheap, and Grocer the parcels of spice here following viz.:

Ginger 1lb. – 5s, nutmeg di lb. – 3s, cinnamon 2lb. di – 16s, sander 1oz. – 2d, cloves 1 quarter – 2s. 2d, saffron 2oz. – 2s. 4d, nutmeg di lb. – 3s, dates 10lb. – 5s, pepper 10lb. – 33s. 4d, currants 12lb. – 4s, cloves and mace 6oz. – 4s, prunes 12lb. – 2s, cloves 1oz. – 6d, long mace di lb. – 2s. 6d, sugar fine one loaf 11lb. di at 11d. the lb. – 10s. 6d, ginger di lb. – 2s. 6d, cinnamon 6oz. – 2s. 6d, paper three quires – 8d. £5 4s.

Item paid to Thomas Cordall[269] for 25lb. quarter of sugar at 10d. ob. the lb. – 22s. and for 53lb. three quarters of sugar at 9d. ob. the pound – 42s. 8d. £3 4s. 10d.

Sum paid £8 9s.

Comfits Bisketts 2lb. – 2s. 4d, coriander 1lb. – 14d, caraways 1lb. – 14d, almond di lb – 7d, ginger 1lb. – 2s, cloves 1lb. – 2s, cinnamon 1lb. di – 3s, dredge[270] 1lb. quarter – 2s. 11d, orange 1lb. quarter – 2s. 6d. 17s. 8d.

Wafers Paid to Mrs Wharton for fifteen boxes with wafers viz. ten spent on Monday and five on Tuesday at 2s. the box 30s.

---

[269] Thomas Cordall (or Cordell) was a member of the Spanish Company, Venice Company, and the Merchant Adventurers. See R. Brenner, *Merchants and Revolution: Commercial Change, Political Conflict and London's Overseas Traders, 1550–1653* (London: Princeton University Press, 2003), 18–19, 21, 63, 64n, 72n, 86n, 206.
[270] Dredge: a spiced or seeded comfit.

95v.	**Spicebread**	Paid to Mrs Wall for thirteen dozen of cakes and buns at 2*s*. the dozen viz. one dozen and di of buns and one dozen and di of cakes for the potation in the parlour on Saturday at night for the Masters, and five dozen buns and five dozen cakes for the potation in the hall to the Masters and Livery on Sunday at night	26*s*.	

Marchpanes	Paid for twelve marchpanes bought of Treegle our Cook at 3*s*. 4*d*. the piece	40*s*.	
	Item for eight marchpanes bought of Balthazar at 3*s*. 8*d*. the piece	29*s*.	4*d*.
	Item for six marchpanes bought of one dwelling in Fleet Street	20*s*.	8*d*.
	Sum paid	£4	10*s*.

Pikemonger Monday	Paid to John Lucas,[271] Pikemonger for twenty pikes bought of him the scantlings here-to-fore accustomed at 22*d*. the piece for Monday	36*s*.	8*d*.
Tuesday	Item more for four pikes bought of him at the same time and price for Tuesday	7*s*.	4*d*.
	Sum paid	44*s*.	

Sturgeon	Paid to Blagg of the Kings Hedd and the Castel in New Fyshe Streat for two firkins of fresh sturgeon	£3	

Wine	Paid to Buckle of the Bishoppes Head in Lombard Streat for two hogsheads of wine at £3 the hogshead. Whereof John Chalonner[272] paid for the one being a fine for license to alienate his lease in Sherbourne Lane so paid	£3	
	Item more paid to him for twenty gallons of sack at 22*d*. the gallon – 36*s*. 8*d*, for eleven gallons of muscadel at 2*s*. the gallon – 22*s*. Item one gallon of white wine for broths – 16*d*. and for a gallon of red wine for hippocras – 16*d*.	£3	16*d*.
	Sum paid	£6	16*d*.

---

271 Likely John Lucas, member of the Drapers' Company. See Boyd, *Roll*.

272 Possibly John Chaloner, auditor of Calais 1547–c.1558, then Secretary of State for Ireland 1559–80. See *HP Commons, 1509–1558*, i. 610–11.

f.96r. **Beer Brewer**	Paid for five barrels of beer whereof three barrels at 5*s.* the barrel and two barrels at 4*s.* the barrel	23*s.*	
Ale Brewer	Paid to Mathew Marten our tenant in Smythfield for three barrels of ale of 6*s.* the barrel – 18*s.* and for one barrel of 4*s.* the barrel – 4*s.* Item for a stand of penny ale – 8*d.* and for two pails of yeast – 4*d.*	23*s.*	
Fruits	Paid for 4cwt. plums – 2*s.* 6*d.* for 3cwt. di of pears – 3*s.* for di cwt. of red filberts – 2*s.* and for one hundred and fifty codlings – 2*s.* more di cwt. of genetings[273] brought by Mrs Calthorppe	9*s.*	6*d.*
Butter	Paid for 100lb. weight of butter at 2*d.* quarter the lb.	23*s.*	
Cream Monday	Paid to the Goodwife Sweete of Hacqueney for nine gallons of cream at 14*d.* the gallon	10*s.*	6*d.*
Tuesday	Item for three gallons of cream on Tuesday at the same price and one gallon of milk for pudding on Tuesday at 4*d.*	3*s.*	10*d.*
	Sum paid	14*s.*	4*d.*
Barberries	Paid for a gallon of barberries	2*s.*	
Lard	Paid for 14lb. of lard bought for the larding of red deer etc. at 10*d.* the lb.	11*s.*	8*d.*
f.96v. **Chandler**	Paid for six chafers whereof three were broken at 2*d.* the piece		6*d.*
	Two dozen pots whereof twenty broken at 1*d.* the piece		20*d.*
	Four steynes received and redelivered Eight candlesticks whereof four broken at *ob.*		2*d.*
	Three dozen di green pots whereof two dozen and ten were broken	2*s.*	
	Six pans whereof four pans broken at 2*d.* Three perfuming pots redelivered		8*d.*
	Two links		8*d.*
	A pack of fine white salt		6*d.*
	1lb. of packthread		6*d.*

[273] Geneting: an apple that ripens early usually around June.

One bushel of oatmeal	2*s.*	
One bushel of white salt		20*d.*
One bushel of bay salt		7*d.*
Two gallons of red vinegar		16*d.*
Two gallons of veriuce		12*d.*
One peck of piked[274] oatmeal		7*d.*
Two gallons of white vinegar	2*s.*	
Two great boiling pots redelivered		
8lb. of candles at 3*d.* the lb.	2*s.*	
Mustard and a pot		12*d.*
Paid for loan of pots etc. redelivered		4*d.*

Sum paid   <u>19*s.*</u>   <u>2*d.*</u>

Pewterer   Paid to Hawkes, Pewterer, for the loan of this vessel hereafter mentioned viz.

One dozen of 7lb. chargers, one dozen di of 5lb. chargers, three dozen di of 4lb. chargers, five dozen of 3lb. platters, four dozen di of 4lb. chargers, five dozen of 3lb. platters, four dozen and ten great French platters, five dozen and two small French platters, five dozen plates, two dozen barrel platters, four dozen dishes, twenty dozen saucers whereof twelve dozen of one sort and eight dozen of another sort, seven dozen fruit dishes and two dozen jelly dishes. All making twenty-two garnish and one dozen at 10*d.* the garnish   18*s.*   7*d.*

Item for three rough platters for the standing dishes weighing 10lb. three quarters at 5*d. ob.* the lb.   5*s.*

Sum paid   <u>23*s.*</u>   <u>6*d.*</u>

f.97r. **Linen cloth**   Paid to Thomas Browne for two ells of Holland at 22*d.* the ell for the sewers   3*s.*   8*d.*

Item for eight ells of Handfordes[275] for the kitchen at 6*d.* the ell   4*s.*

Item for half a piece of dowlas[276] – 50*s.* 6*d,* and more nine ells and di of dowlas at 13*d.* the ell – 10*s.* all for aprons   £3   10*d.*

Sum paid   <u>£3</u>   <u>13*s.*</u>   <u>6*d.*</u>

---

[274] Piked: tapered, pointed or peaked.
[275] Harford: a linen cloth, likely of Flemish origin and principally in use during the sixteenth century.
[276] Dowlas: a coarse linen.

Sweetwater	Paid to Goodwife Basse for a quart of red rosewater for meat		20*d.*
	Item to her for three quarts of washing water musked at 20*d.* the quart	5*s.*	
	Sum paid	6*s.*	8*d.*
Wood and coal	Paid for 1cwt. of fagots – 4*s.* 8*d,* for a quarter of billets – 2*s.* 11*d,* and for twenty-eight sacks of coal at 5*d.* the sack – 11*s.* 8*d.*	19*s.*	3*d.*
	Item for six sacks of thorn coal	2*s.*	6*d.*
Trenchers, ashen cups and trays etc.	Paid for three gross[277] of trenchers	14*s.*	
	Item for ashen cups, taps for ale and beer, brooms, a coal shovel and small trays in all	6*s.*	6*d.*
	Item for four great trays at 16*d.* the piece	5*s.*	4*d.*
	Sum paid	25*s.*	10*d.*
Flowers, herbs and roots	Paid to Goodwife Basse for onions – 8*d,* for parsley – 6*d,* for herbs for the puddings – 4*d,* for radish roots, cucumbers and salad oil – 8*d.*	2*s.*	2*d.*
Preachers	Given in reward to Mr Knell[278] preaching on Sunday at afternoon and to Mr Gough[279] preaching on Monday the forenoon	20*s.*	
f.97v. **Musicians**	Paid to the Waits of the City for Monday and Tuesday playing upon diverse instruments	13*s.*	4*d.*
	Item in reward to Segar a Dutchman playing the same two days with the Waits	5*s.*	
	Sum paid	18*s.*	4*d.*
Clerks of St. Michael's	Given in reward to the Clerks and Sexton of St. Michael's	5*s.*	

---

[277] Gross: twelve dozen.

[278] Thomas Knell the elder was a religious writer who spent time in either Geneva or Frankfurt in the mid-1550s. He was Rector at Warehorne in the diocese of Canterbury, and was possibly between positions in August 1569. By 1571 he was instituted in London churches and by 1574 was chaplain to Walter Devereux, First Earl of Essex. See *Oxford DNB*.

[279] John Gough, Rector of St. Peter's Cornhill until 1566, when he was embroiled in the vestments controversy and deprived of his position. Along with Robert Crowley, he is said to have been 'an emerging leader of the London puritan movement'. See M. Morrissey, *Politics and the Paul's Cross Sermons, 1558–1642* (Oxford: Oxford University Press, 2011), 194.

Rewards for bucks in generality	Paid to the Lord Treasurer's servant for one buck brought into the hall	5*s.*	
	Item to Alderman Barnam's servant in reward for bringing of a buck	2*s.*	
	Item paid to Doctor Gibbon's servant for bringing of a buck	5*s.*	
	Sum paid	12*s.*	
Porters	Paid to William Tattam, Robert Whitfeld, Robert Brushewood, George Shawe, John Taylor and Thomas Cartwright[280] all porters attending the two days at 3*s.* every of them	18*s.*	
Sewer	Paid to Chrispofer Fulke, Sewer, for his paines the two days sewing	6*s.*	8*d.*
Steward	Paid to Robert Beaumond the Steward for his pains	40*s.*	
Cooks	Paid to Stephen Treegle Cook for his pains and others with him the two days viz. Monday and Tuesday as also for the dinner on Sunday	40*s.*	
Butlers	Paid to Edmond Wright for himself and five others with him	26*s.*	8*d.*
f.98r. **Women in the kitchen**	Paid to Goodwife Holmes for four days – 2*s,* to Denys Eles for five days – 2*s.* 6*d,* and to Margaret Smyth for three days – 18*d,* washing the dishes, scraping the trenchers and washing the house	6*s.*	
Scavenger	[-]		

[280] All these porters were Drapers. See Boyd, *Roll.*

125

Extra-ordinary and ordinary charges	Paid to the Keeper of the Wardrobe in the Tower for certain pieces of arras of the story of King Davyd[281] and others for the hanging of the parlour – 20s. and a hot venison pasty. Item to his servant in reward for bringing of the same in it again to the Tower re-carriage of it again to the Tower and to the Warders as also to Father Sharppe and Mr Keltredge's[282] man hanging up the same – 5s.	25s.	
	Item paid to Richard Rennolds the younger[283] for summage by him spent riding to Eltham for the serving of a warrant in one of the parks there the same warrant received of Simon Croxton and refused	2s.	6d.
	Item paid for the bringing to the Hall out of Fyshe Streat of two firkins sturgeon		3d.
	Item paid for two rundlets the one for muscadel the other for sack – 2s. 6d, for quills to set all the wines a broche – 6d, for carriage of the muscadel and sack to the hall – 2d. and to the Cooper's man for setting the wines a broche – 4d.	3s.	6d.
	Item paid for a boiling pot – 2d, for writing paper a quire – 4d, for two strainers – 10d, for a peck of white salt – 6d.		22d.
	Item paid to Master Alderman Becher's porter in reward for bringing of a pasty of red deer sent from his Master		12d.
	Item paid for baking of sixteen pasties of venison at the Cook's house	2s.	8d.
	Sum	36s.	9d.
f.98v.	Item paid to Richard Thompson[284] drawer of the wine in the cellar for his pains	3s.	
	Item to Stephen Malyn[285] for his pains drawing beer and ale in the cellar	2s.	6d.
	Item paid to three officers helping to carve and to sew among them	3s.	

[281] Likely drawn from the same series of tapestry as in 1566, which depicted David and Uriah. See DCA, DB1, f.48v.

[282] William Keltredge (or Keltridge) served as Warden of the Drapers' Company in 1580–1, 1588–9, and 1592–3. Johnson, *History*, ii. 471–2.

[283] Richard Rennoldes the younger was the son of Draper and former Warden, Richard Rennoldes the elder. See Johnson, *History*, ii. 469–70.

[284] Richard Thompson was a Draper. See Boyd, *Roll*.

[285] Stephen Malyn was a Draper. See Boyd, *Roll*.

Item paid to Henry Blower, Wax Chandler,
for three standing dishes viz. a boar's head
the arms and supports of the Company and
the other the helmet and crest   36*s.*
Item paid to Henry Starr our Labourer
for two days at 8*d.* per day and to Jarmen
another labourer for two days at 10*d.* per
day, both attending for the carriage of plate
and hangings and other things necessary
about the house   3*s.*
Item paid for the mending of a lid of one
of John Lowen's[286] pots the same being
fallen of   2*s.*
Item paid to them that made the speeches
at the bringing in of the boar's head and to
the child that took pains therein in all   8*s.*   8*d.*
Item paid to Robert Richards for summage
by him disbursed for the bringing in of two
hogshead of wine and laying the same into
the cellar   12*d.*

| | Sum part | 59*s.* | 2*d.* |
| Sum total | £92 | 11*s.* | 4*d.* |

Deductions Allowances of the house   £20
Quarterage money received at the potation
of the Company   41*s.*   4*d.*
Quarterage money received of the Clerk
gathered by him   24*s.*

Sum of the deductions   £23   5*s.*   4*d.*

So the whole to be divided into four parts
amounts to   £69   6*s.*

And so every Master Wardens' parts
cometh to   £17   6*s.*   6*d.*

f.99r. **Bucks received by generality**
Sent by the Lord Treasurer – one buck
Sent by Master Alderman Barnam – one buck
Sent by Master Doctor Gybbon – one buck

Sum is – three bucks

[286] John Lowen served as Warden of the Drapers' Company in 1575–6, 1583–4, and 1587–8. See Johnson, *History*, ii. 471–2.

Bucks by particularity
From Mr Branche
From Mr Calthorppe – two bucks
From Mr Diconson – one buck
From Mr Garwaye – two bucks

Sum is [-]

Sum in all [-]

Whereof two were baked abroad for red deer and came not to the hall but in pasties and were – seven pasties
Of the rest were baked in the Hall and at the cooks – fifty-one pasties

<u>Sum of all – fifty-eight pasties</u>

Which were spent and given away as follows:
Spent on Sunday at dinner – two pasties
Spent on Monday at dinner – twenty pasties
Spent on Monday in red deer – six pasties
Spent on Tuesday dinner – seven pasties
Given away – twelve pasties
Delivered by the Steward to the Master
Wardens themselves – eleven pasties

Sum – fifty-eight pasties

f.99v. Four messes	**Potation for the Masters on Saturday at night**

Spiced cakes and buns
Bisketts and caraways
Codling and plums
Comfits two dishes
Pears and gennetings

Twelve messes **Potation for the Masters and whole Livery on Sunday at night**
Spiced cakes and buns
Bisketts and caraways
Codlings and plums
Comfits two dishes
Pears and jennetyngs
Comfits two dishes
And filberts

Two messes **For the Wardens' wives and Master Bachelors**
As above

For servants
Manchets
Pears
Plums
Codling

Two messes
single

Sunday for dinner for the four Masters the Wardens their wives, officers of the house etc.
Brawn and mustard
Boiled capon
Roasted beef
Roasted veal
Baked venison
Roasted capon

For servants
Mutton and pottage and roasted beef

f.100r.

Monday at dinner prepared twenty-two messes of meat as follows:

First course
Four messes

For the high table in the hall
A wax dish of a boar's head
Brawn and mustard
A wax dish of the Drapers' arms
Boiled capon
Roasted capon
Roasted swan
Baked venison
Pike in herblade
Roasted capon
Custard

First course
Five messes
double

For the second table in the hall
As above, quarter wax dishes

First course
Five messes
double

For the third table in the hall
As above, quarter wax dishes and one goose instead of a swan

First course
Three messes
double

In the parlour
As above, quarter goose in the place of swan

One mess

For the Master Wardens in the parlour
As above, quarter

One mess **For the cooks**
As above single

Two messes **Received into the larder**
Viz. one mess double and one mess single

f.100v. **Second course At the high table in the hall**
Four messes A standing dish with the Company's crest
Partridges
Red deer whole pasties
Sturgeon
Marchpane

Second course At the second table in the hall
Five messes As above

Second course At the third table in the hall
Five messes As above

Second course At the table in the parlour
Four messes As above, quarter pigeons

Hippocras and wafers through the house

Monday at night supper
Two shoulders of mutton whole and roots
and cucumbers with cold meat

Tuesday at dinner

First course At the high table in the hall
Four messes A standing dish of a boar's head
double Brawn and mustard and puddings
A standing dish of the Drapers' arms
Boiled capons
Roasted cygnet
Baked venison
Pikes
Roast capon
Custards

f.101r. **First course At the second table**
Three messes As above saving goose instead of swan

Second course At the high table four messes
Four messes A standing dish of the helm and crest of
the Company
Pigeons
Red deer

130

Sturgeon
Marchpane

Second course   **At the second table**
Three messes   As above – except standing dish

Hippocras and wafers

ANNIS 1570 AND 1571

In the time of John Quarles, Master of the
Craft, and

William Dumer
Johnis Sutton[287]
Johnis Tatton[288]   } Wardens
Johnis Noble[289]

**Quarter
Dinner**

Expenses of the first Quarter Dinner kept
the twenty-first day of November 1570, and
the thirteenth year of the reign of Elizabeth,
for nine messes of meat as follows:

f.103r. **Quarter
Dinner**

**Expenses of the second Quarter Dinner
kept the nineteenth day of March 1570
being in lent, for eight messes of meat as
follows:**

First paid for three rondes of sturgeon	7s.	
Item for four old lings at 3s. the piece	12s.	
Item for four green fishes at 20d. the piece	6s.	8d.
Item for five great roasting eels	11s.	
Item for eight pikes at 2s. 6d. the piece	20s.	
Item for eight carps at 28d. the piece	12s.	
Item for eight tenches[290] at 15d. the piece	10s.	
Item to Cartwright and Hill as porters		12d.

Paid to the Cook for spinach – 11d, for
sorrel – 2d, for alexander buds – 10d, for
a quart of salad oil – 16d, for sweet herbs
for puddings – 4d, for di cwt. roasting
lamperns – 4s, for 2cwt. of smelts – 3s. 4d,
for half a peck of flour – 4d.   10s.   10d.

---

[287] John Sutton served as Warden of the Drapers' Company in 1562–3 and 1570–1. See Johnson, *History*, ii. 469–70.

[288] John Tatton served as Warden of the Drapers' Company in 1570–1. See Johnson, *History*, ii. 470.

[289] John Noble served as Warden of the Drapers' Company in 1570–1. See Johnson, *History*, ii. 470.

[290] Tench: a deep-bodied freshwater fish related to the carp.

Paid more to him for nine lampern pies at
14*d.* the piece – 10*s.* 6*d,* for nine eel pies
at 16*d.* the piece – 12*s,* for eight custards
at 2*s.* 4*d.* the piece – 18*s.* 8*d,* for eight
marchpanes at 3*s.* 6*d.* the piece – 28*s.* Item
to him for dressing of the dinner – 6*s.*   £3   15*s.*   2*d.*
Paid to John Catcher, Pewterer, for the hire
of six garnish of vessel at 10*d.* the garnish   5*s.*
Paid for grocery viz. for 2oz. pepper – 5*d,*
for large mace 1oz. di – 18*d,* for cinnamon
1oz. – 4*d,* for sugar fine 6lb. – 6*s,* ginger
1oz. – 4*d,* dates 1lb. – 8*d,* currants 2lb.
di – 10*d,* prunes 1lb. di – 3*d,* dates di lb. –
5*d,* 1lb. – 4*d,* cinnamon 1oz. – 5*d,* ginger
1oz. – 5*d,* nutmeg 1oz. – 6*d,* for a quarter
of bisket – 4*d.*   14*s.*   3*d.*
Paid to the Butler for a kilderkin of ale –
3*s,* and for a kilderkin of beer – 3*s.* Item
for his pains and his under servants – 4*s,*
and for carriage of the plate – 8*d.*   10*s.*   8*d.*
Paid for oranges – 3*d,* for two dozen
of trenchers – 10*d,* for salad herbs and
parsley – 12*d,* for sweet butter – 2*s.* 4*d,*
for barrelled butter – 2*s.* 3*d,* and sweet
butter by the lb. – 3*s.* 11*d,* for eggs – 8*d,*
for yeast – 6*d,* for a pint of barberries – 6*d,*
and more for parsley, salad herbs and
flowers – 9*d,* for rushes – 4*d.*   11*s.*   1*d.*

                                                   Sum   £10   6*s.*   8*d.*

f.103v.   Paid to the Goodwife Holmes for herself
and Goodwife Eles, washing the dishes
and making clean the house   18*d.*
Paid to Anthony Ratclyf[291] for eight gallons
of claret wine and three quarters at 16*d.* the
gallon – 11*s.* 8*d,* for a gallon of white wine
– 16*d,* a quart of malmsey – 5*d,* four gallons
of sack at 20*d.* the gallon – 6*s.* 8*d.* Item for
wine from the white house – 5*s.*   25*s.*

[291] Anthony Ratclyf (or Ratclyffe) was a Merchant Taylor. He was an Alderman from 1566
and served as Sheriff in 1585–6. See Beaven, *Aldermen,* ii. 42.

133

Paid to Awgar[292] for half a peck of fine
salt – 5*d*, for a pottle of vinegar – 3*d*, for
a pottle of vergys – 3*d*, for mustard – 6*d*,
for a pot for it – 2*d*, for onions – 1*d*, for a
broom – 1*d*, for half a peck of fine white
salt for the table – 3*d. ob*, for a pint of
white vinegar – 2*d*, for taps for ale and
beer – *ob*. Item for a ladle – 1*d*, for a
boiling pot – 2*d*.   2*s*.   4*d*.
Paid for nine dozen of bread   9*s*.
Item paid to Robert Richards for twenty
fagots and four sacks of coal   3*s*.   6*d*.

                                        Sum   41*s*.   4*d*.

                          Sum total £12   8*s*.

Quarter **Dinner**	**Expenses of the third Quarter Dinner** **kept the twelfth day of June 1571,** **for eight messes of meat prepared as** **follows:**

First paid to Robert Mason, Poulterer, for
ten capon roosters at 22*d*. the piece – 18*s*.
4*d*, for sixteen green geese – 16*s*, for two
dozen di of chickens to boil at 5*s*. the
dozen – 12*s*. 6*d*, for two dozen of rabbits
runners at 4*s*. the dozen – 8*s*, for a dozen
of tame pigeons – 4*s*.   59*s*.   2*d*.
Paid to Triegle the Cook for eight chicken
pies at 3*s*. the piece – 24*s*, for eight
custards at 2*s*. 4*d*. the piece – 18*s*. 8*d*, for
eight marchpanes at 3*s*. 4*d*. the piece –
26*s*. 8*d*, for a salmon and a half – 24*s*, for
four rondes of sturgeon – 10*s*, for a sirloin
of beef – 6*s*. 6*d*, for six long marrowbones
– 3*s*, for butter and eggs – 4*d*, for his pains
dressing the dinner – 6*s*.   £5   19*s*.

                                        Sum   £8   18*s*.   2*d*.

---

[292] Nicholas Awgar, a Draper who practised as a chandler. He served as Warden of the Drapers' Company in 1573–4, 1581–2, and 1585–6. See Johnson, *History*, ii. 470–1.

Paid to Henry Cowdale for bread	8*s.*	
Paid to Nicholas Awgar for half a peck of white salt – 2*d,* for a pottle of vinegar – 4*d,* for packthread – 1*d,* for cart salt – 2*d,* for broom – 1*d,* for a pottle of vergys – 3*d,* for a pot – 1*d,* for vinegar – 2*d,* for white vinegar of the best – 4*d.*		20*d.*
Paid to Buckle of the Bishoppes Hed for claret wine and white set there	18*s.*	8*d.*
Paid to the grocer for 3lb. three quarters of valence sugar – 4*s,* for 3lb. of other sugar – 4*s,* for 3lb. of other sugar – 2*s.* 6*d,* large mace 1oz. – 12*d,* cinnamon 1oz. – 5*d,* biskett di lb. – 8*d,* currants 2lb. – 8*d,* prunes 2lb. – 5*d,* dates 1lb. – 8*d,* pepper 2oz. – 5*d.*	10*s.*	9*d.*
Paid for six sacks of coals	3*s.*	
Paid for butter		18*d.*
Paid for cloves for the perfume		1*d.*
Paid for a bundle of rushes		4*d.*
Paid for vinegar more		1*d.*
Paid for a quart of sweetwater	2*s.*	
Paid to the Butler for two stands of ale – 6*s,* for a kilderkin of beer – 3*s,* for his pains – 4*s.* and for carriage of the plate – 8*d.*	13*s.*	13*d.*
Paid for three gallons di of sack	7*s.*	
Paid to Goodwife Holmes for herself and the Goodwife Elys, washing the dishes and making clean the house		18*d.*
Paid to George Hill and Cartwright serving as porters, although not called nor other years accustomed		12*d.*
Paid to John Catcher the Pewterer for six garnish of vessels at 10*d.* the garnish	10*s.*	

Sum	£3	14*s.*	4*d.*
Sum total	£12	12*s.*	5*d.*

FEAST DINNER }ANNO 1571

The tenth year in the reign of Queen
Elizabeth the first of England, France and
Ireland etc. Sixth August Monday

Mr John Quarles	our Master

Mr William Dumer	
Mr John Sutton	} our four
Mr John Tatton	Master Wardens
Mr John Noble	

**Provision of the same Great Dinner
and for the potations on Saturday
and Sunday as also for the dinner on
Tuesday the day next following after the
Great Dinner:**

Poulterer Paid to Robert Mason our Poulterer for
these parcels:

Sunday at   First paid for boiling capons and roosters
dinner   four at 2s. the piece one with another   8s.
             Item for twelve pigeons at 20d. the dozen   20d.
             Item for di cwt. of eggs   16d.

Monday   Item for forty-two capons boilers and
             forty-two roosters at 2s. the piece one with
             another   £8   8s.
             Item for ten cygnets bought by him abroad
             and for scalding of them at 8s. 4d. the
             piece one with another   £4   3s.   4d.
             Item for twelve geese at 20d. the piece   20s.
             Item for forty partridges at 10d. the piece   33s.   4d.
             Item for six dozen of pigeons   10s.
             Item for 1cwt. of eggs   2s.   8d.
             Item for three roasting capons for supper   6s.

Tuesday   Item for twenty-one boiling capons and
             twenty-one roosters at 2s. the piece one
             with another   £4   4s.
             Item for three cygnets at 8s. 4d. the piece   25s.
             Item for eight geese at 20d. the piece   13s.   4d.

	Item for five dozen pigeons at 20*d.* the dozen	24*s.*	
	Sum paid £24	9*s.*	

f.105r. **Butcher**	Paid to Sawyer, Butcher, for the parcels following:			

Sunday at dinner	First for a sirloin and a rib of beef weighing 6st. and 4lb. at 12*d.* the st.		6*s.*	6*d.*
	Item for a quarter of mutton		2*s.*	
	Item for a breast of veal			12*d.*
	Item for 30lb. of suet at 3*d.* the lb.		7*s.*	6*d.*
	Item for two long marrowbones			12*d.*
	Item for a peck of pricks			6*d.*

Monday	Item for twenty long marrowbones	10*s.*	
	Item for 32lb. of suet at 3*d.*	8*s.*	
	Item for two whole muttons	16*s.*	
	Item for two sirloins of beef weighing 11st. 7lb. of beef at 12*d.* the st.	11*s.*	10*d.*

Tuesday	Item for half a sheep	4*s.*	
	Item for a sirloin of beef weighing 6st. at 12*d.* the st.	6*s.*	
	Item for 28lb. of suet at 3*d.* the lb.	19*s.*	6*d.*
	Item for long guts and blood for puddings	2*s.*	
	Item for eight long marrowbones	4*s.*	

For the poor	Item for 26st. of beef for the poor on Tuesday at 12*d.* the st.	26*s.*	

A boar	Item paid him for a boar price – 50*s,* for seething of the same boar – 10*s,* and for saucing drink thereto – 2*s.*	£3	2*s.*	

	Sum paid	£9	7*s.*	10*d.*

Baker	Paid to the Baker for these things following:		

Saturday at potation	First for one dozen of rolls		12*d.*

Sunday at dinner	Six dozen of rolls for dinner	6*s.*	

Monday	Eleven dozen of rolls	11*s.*	
	Twelve dozen of half penny white bread	12*s.*	
	Two dozen of wheaten bread	2*s.*	

137

	Seven dozen of stale white to great etc.	12*s.*	
Tuesday	Four dozen white in the morning	4*s.*	
	Eleven dozen in the afternoon white and		
	wheaten for the poor	11*s.*	

Meal and flour
Item for three bushels di of rye meal — 6*s.* 6*d.*
Item for sixteen bushels of wheat flour at
2*s.* 8*d.* the bushel — 42*s.* 8*d.*

Wednesday
Item for di dozen of white bread for
breakfast on Wednesday — 6*d.*

Sum paid £5 3*s.* 8*d.*

f.105v. **Grocer** Paid to Henry Falks, Grocer, those parcels following:

First for 14lb. 1oz. of pepper at 3*s.* the lb. — 42*s.* 3*d.*
Sugar middle 54lb. at 10*d. ob.* the lb. — 47*s.* 3*d.*
Saffron 2oz. at 14*d.* the oz. — 2*s.* 4*d.*
Cloves 8oz. at 5*d.* the oz. — 3*s.* 4*d.*
Currants 12lb. at 4*d.* the lb. — 4*s.*
Prunes 10lb. at 2*d. ob.* the lb. — 2*s.* 1*d.*
Dates 10lb. at 11*d.* the lb. — 5*s.*
Sugar fine 17lb. di at 13lb. — 18*s.* 11*d.*
Cinnamon large 2lb. three quarters at 5*s.* the lb. — 13*s.* 9*d.*
Cinnamon in powder 7oz. at 4*d.* the oz. — 2*s.* 4*d.*
Nutmeg 12oz. at 5*d.* the oz. — 5*s.*
Cloves and mace 2oz. at 8*d.* the oz. — 16*d.*
Ginger white 2lb. at 3*s.* 8*d.* the lb. — 9*s.* 4*d.*
Mace large picked 4oz. at 13*d.* oz. — 4*s.* 4*d.*
Sanders powder 1oz. di — 4*d.*
Coriander 4oz. at — 6*d.*

Sum paid £8 2*s.*

Comfits Paid for comfits of diverse sorts by the pound bought by the Master Wardens' wives and bisketts and caraways — 14*s.* 9*d.*
Item for a lb. di of comfits bought by the Steward — 2*s.* 3*d.*

Sum paid 17*s.*

Spicebread Paid by the Wardens' wives for spice, butter, bread and ale for the same in all — 14*s.* 8*d.*

138

Marchpanes	Paid to Triegle the Cook for six marchpanes of the largest sort at 3*s.* 8*d.* the piece and for twenty-four marchpanes of another sort at 3*s.* 6*d.* the piece	£5	6*s.*	
Custards	Item paid to him for thirty-one custards at 2*s.* 5*d.* the piece	£3	14*s.*	6*d.*
Lard	Item paid to him for 30lb. of lard at 8*d.* the lb.		20*s.*	
	Sum paid	£10	2*s.*	
f.106r. **Pikemonger**	Paid to Ravens, Pikemonger, for twenty pikes on Monday at dinner and seven on Tuesday of the scantlings accustomed		56*s.*	
Sturgeon	Paid to Blage dwelling at the Kings Headd and the Castle in Fyshe Stret for two firkins of fresh sturgeon at 26*s.* 8*d.* the firkin		53*s.*	
Wafers	Paid to Mrs Wharton for thirteen boxes of wafers at 2*s.* the box		26*s.*	
Wine	Paid to Buckel of the Bishoppes Hedd for eight gallons one pottle of muscadel at 2*s.* 4*d.* the gallon – 19*s.* 10*d,* one gallon and a pottle malmsey at 20*d.* the gallon – 2*s.* 6*d,* three gallons of white wine at 16*d.* the gallon – 4*s.*		26*s.*	4*d.*
	Item paid by Mr Noble and repaid him again for twenty-one gallons three pints of sack at 2*s.* the gallon		42*s.*	8*d.*
	Item paid to Mr Colclough for two hogsheads of claret wine	£6	5*s.*	
	Sum	£9	14*s.*	
Ale Brewer	Paid to Mathew Marten for three barrels of ale at 6*s.* the barrel – 18*s,* and for one barrel of small ale – 4*s.*		22*s.*	
Beer Brewer	Paid to Campion, Beer Brewer, for two hogsheads of court beer at 5*s.* the barrel and for two barrels of beer of 4*s.* the barrel		23*s.*	

Linen cloth	Paid to Nicholas Layfeld[293] for fifty-two ells three quarters of lockeram at 13*d.* the ell for aprons		57*s.*	2*d.*
	Item for two ells of Holland for the Sewer and Carver at 2*s.* ell		4*s.*	
	Item for six ells soultage at 7*d.*		3*s.*	

Sum paid £3 4*s.* 8*d.*

f.106v. **Butter** Paid for 80lb. of butter bought in the market at 3*d.* the lb. 20*s.*

Pewterer Paid to the Pewterer for the hire of twenty garnish of vessels at 10*d.* the garnish — 16*s.* 8*d.*
Item for the hire of twelve dozen of banqueting dishes at 6*d.* the dozen — 3*s.* 6*d.*
Item for the loss of one platter, one plate and one banqueting dish, all weighing 8lb. at 6*d.* the lb. — 4*s.*

Sum paid 24*s.*

Chandler Paid to Nicholas Awgar, Chandler, as follows:

First for eighteen green pots lost and broken at 9*d.* the dozen and for occupying of six pots redelivered – 2*d.* — 15*d.* ob.
Item for eleven pottle pots at 12*d.* the dozen and for the occupying of the seven at 4*d.* the dozen — 13*d.*
Item for six earthen candlesticks — 6*d.*
Item for the occupying of four steynes — 2*d.*
Item for two chafers and occupying of four — 8*d.*
Item for occupying of eight pans — 2*d.*
Item for two links — 8*d.*
Item for white salt one bushel — 18*d.*
Item for di bushel of oatmeal — 14*d.*
Item for 1lb. of packthread — 7*d.*
Item for di bushel of bay salt — 6*d.*
Item for 6lb. of candles — 16*d.*
Item for di peck of fine salt — 8*d.*
Item for a peck of picked oatmeal — 12*d.*
Item for a gallon of red vinegar and a pot — 8*d.*
Item for onions — 7*d.*
Item for mustard and a pot — 15*d.*

[293] Nicholas Layfeld (or Layfield) was a Draper. See Boyd, *Roll.*

Item for two birchen brooms – 2*d*. and for green brooms – 2*d*. in all		4*d*.	
Item for four boiling pots		10*d*.	
Item for two gallons of white vinegar	2*s*.	4*d*.	
Item for a peck more of white salt		5*d*.	
Item for di a peck more of oatmeal		3*d*.	*ob*.
Item for three chafers		9*d*.	

Sum paid   <u>20*s*.</u>

Turner's ware

Paid for thirty dozen of trenchers at 6*d*. the dozen – 15*s*, for four Dansick trays, two dozen ashen cups, one dozen of taps, a pail and one coal shovel together – 11*s*. 4*d*. and two baskets – 8*d*.   27*s*.

f.107r. **Musicians**

Paid to the Waits of the City for their pains attending here in the hall the two days viz. Monday and Tuesday playing upon diverse instruments   20*s*.

Strainers

Paid to the Steward for two strainers by him bought   12*d*.

Flowers and herbs

Paid to Mrs Dumer[294] for flowers   2*s*.
Item paid to the Steward for herbs by him bought for the puddings – 12*d*, and for cucumbers and oil – 4*d*.   16*d*.

Sum   <u>3*s*.</u>   <u>4*d*.</u>

Fruit

Paid to the Steward for pears and plums by him bought   2*s*.   9*d*.
Item for codlings   18*d*.

Sum   <u>4*s*.</u>   <u>3*d*.</u>

Milk

Paid to the Steward for a gallon di of milk by him bought for the puddings   6*d*.

Officers' wages

Paid to Triegle the Cook for his pains with others under him the two days dressing the dinners etc.   40*s*.
Paid to Edmond Wright the Butler for his pains and five other serving with him in all   26*s*.   8*d*.

---

[294] Kinborough (or Katherine) Dummer (née Brydges) was the wife of William Dummer, Warden of the Drapers' Company. See VCH, *Hants*, iii. 358–9.

Paid to the Steward for his pains during those two days as also in providing of things necessary before	40*s.*		
Paid to Fulke the Common Crier for his pains serving as Sewer		6*s.*	8*d.*
Paid to Thomas Cartwright – 3*s*, Robert Selby – 3*s*, John Taylor – 3*s*, Robert Brushwood – 3*s*, George Shaw – 3*s*, George Hill – 3*s*, all porters	18*s.*		

Sum   £6   11*s.*   4*d.*

f.107v. **Preacher**	Paid to Mr Noble to give to Mr Crowley for his pains in preaching the two days viz. Sunday at afternoon and Monday in the forenoon at St. Michael's	13*s.*	4*d.*
Women in the kitchen	Paid to Goodwife Holmes – 2*s.* 6*d*, to Dyanis Eles – 2*s.* 6*d*, to Phillipp's wife – 2*s*, serving in the kitchen washing of dishes and cleansing and washing of the house	7*s.*	
Raker	Paid to the Raker of the Ward for carriage the garbage and other offal away in reward		8*d.*
Clerks of St. Michael's	Paid to the Clerks of St. Michael's in reward	5*s.*	
Extra-ordinary charges	Paid to Stephen Malin and another in consideration of their pains drawing of drink and carriage of plate to and fro	5*s.*	
	Item to Thompson for his pains drawing of wine in the cellar	3*s.*	
	Item to him for two small taps		2*d.*
	Item to Henry Star in reward	2*s.*	6*d.*
	Item to the labourers in the kitchen serving the cooks in reward no precedent there of before had	2*s.*	
	Item to Robert Beaumond the Steward for bay salt – 1*d*, for three gallons of red wine – 4*s.* 6*d*, for bringing the sturgeon to the hall – 4*d.* and for a padlock – 4*d.*	5*s.*	3*d.*

142

Item paid to Robert Richardes for summage by him disbursed for boat hire to Chelsey and for their drinking at Westminster coming home – 5*s*, and for carriage and laying down of two hogsheads of wine into the cellar being received of Mr Colclough – 11*d*, and given in reward as the Sexton of St. Dunston's in the East for opening the church door to see Sir Richard Champion's tomb[295] – 4*d*.	6*s*.	3*d*.

f.108r.

Item paid by Mr Tatton for charges going for the pikes		6*d*.
Item paid to Gode the Cooper for two canes for to set the wine abroche[296] and for his pains setting the same abroche		8*d*.

Sum of the extraordinary	24*s*.	2*d*.

Rewards for bucks

Paid for Robert Beaumond the Steward in reward to Mr Quarles' servant for bringing on buck	2*s*.
Item more by him in reward to Master Warden's man for bringing of a brace of bucks	10*s*.
Item paid by Mr Tatton to Mr Doctor Gibbon's man in reward for bringing of a buck sent by his Master	5*s*.
Item to Mr Candeler's servant for a buck sent by his Master	5*s*.
Item in charges in serving the warrant received from the Lord Treasurer	9*s*.

Sum in reward	31*s*.

Allowance for venison among themselves

Paid and allowed to Mr Dumer for a stag and two bucks brought by him more than the other	49*s*.
Item paid and allowed to Mr Noble for our bucks brought by him above the ordinary	10*s*.

Sum	59*s*.

---

[295] Sir Richard Champion died in 1568. Orlin holds that the incumbent Master, Francis Barnham, led prominent members of the Company to view the tomb. Barnham had been apprenticed to Champion. See Orlin, *Locating Privacy*, 224.

[296] Abroach: to pierce the container of wine, to vent it or let it run out of the container.

Wood and coal	Paid to Mr Richardes the Renter as money by him disbursed viz. for twenty-four sacks of coals at 9*d.* the sack		18*s.*	
	Item for di cwt. billets – 6*s,* and for 1cwt. di of fagots for the ovens etc. – 7*s.* 6*d.*		13*s.*	6*d.*
	<div align="right">Sum</div>		<u>31*s.*</u>	<u>6*d.*</u>
	<div align="right">Sum total</div>	<u>£101</u>	<u>17*s.*</u>	<u>11*d.*</u>

f.108v. **Deductions**

The allowance of the house of ordinary towards the same dinner	£20		
Item quarterage money received by the Wardens themselves at the potation		45*s.*	4*d.*
Item the quarterage of the rest being then absent sold to Warner the Clerk and he to receive the same for the which he paid in ready money		12*s.*	
<div align="right">Sum of the deductions</div>	<u>£22</u>	<u>17*s.*</u>	<u>4*d.*</u>
So the whole to be divided into four parts amounts to	£99		7*d.*
And so every of the Master Wardens' parts amounts to	£19	15*s.*	1*d. ob. qt*

ANNIS 1571 AND 1572

In the time of Ffrancissi Barnam
Alderman, Master of the Craft, and

Nicholai Whelar
Ricardi Rennoldes
William Vaghan } Wardens
Johis Wight[297]

**Quarter
Dinner**

**Expenses of the first Quarter Dinner
kept the sixth day of December 1571
being Thursday, for eight messes of
meat as follows:**

First for six sacks of great coal at 9*d.* the sack amounts to	4*s.*	6*d.*
Item for a kilderkin of beer – 2*s.* 8*d.* and for a kilderkin of ale – 3*s.* in all	5*s.*	8*d.*
Item for eight dozen trenchers at 6*d.*	4*s.*	
Item for two rondes of brawn – 6*s.* 8*d.* and for saucing drink to the same – 2*d.*	6*s.*	10*d.*
Item for a birchen broom for the kitchen		1*d.*
Item for a sirloin of beef	2*s.*	4*d.*
Item for five long marrowbones	2*s.*	4*d.*
Item for 6lb. of butter		21*d.*
Item for a pint of rosewater		12*d.*
Item for a pint of barberries 2*d.* and for white salt – 4*d.*		6*d.*
Item for half a lb. of pepper to bake venison		18*d.*
Item for 6lb. of suet for the same		18*d.*
Item for bringing the venison		8*d.*
Item for candles for the kitchen		1*d.*
Item for a sack of small coal		5*d.*
Item for mustard 1*d.* *ob.* and for a quart of vinegar 2*d.*	3*d.*	*ob.*
Item for vergys – 1*d,* for 3lb. of salt butter – 9*d,* for a pipkin – 2*d.* and two other pots – 2*d.*	14*d.*	*ob.*

---

[297] John Wight served as Warden in the Drapers' Company in 1571–2, 1579–80, and 1584–5. See Johnson, *History*, ii. 471–2.

Item to Goodwife Holmes for her pains in the kitchen – 6*d*. and to another poor woman with child being also in the kitchen – 8*d*.			14*d*.
Item to Cartwright for his pains			6*d*.
Item paid to the Butler for his fee		4*s*.	
Item to Mr Ratclyf for six gallons claret wine		8*s*.	
Item to him for one pottle white wine			8*d*.
Item for a gallon of malmsey			20*d*.
Item for a pottle of muscadel			14*d*.
Item for three gallons of sack		4*s*.	9*d*.
Item for the hire of five garnish of vessels		4*s*.	
Item for parsley for the kitchen			1*d*.
Item for seven dozen of bread		7*s*.	

f.109v.

Item paid to Mason the Poulterer for twenty capons, one turkey, seven geese, two dozen green plovers, six woodcocks, eight dozen of larks with six penny worth of eggs — £3 10*s*.

Item paid to Treagle the Cook for eleven minced pies at 16*d*. the pie – 14*s*. 8*d*, for baking of five pasties of venison at 10*d*. the piece – 4*s*. 3*d*, for eight custards at 2*s*. 4*d*. the piece – 18*s*. 8*d*, for eight quince pies at 3*s*. the piece – 24*s*. for his pains in dressing the dinner – 6*s*. — £3 7*s*. 6*d*.

Item paid to the Grocer for an oz. of large mace – 12*d*. for 1oz. of cinnamon – 5*d*, for 2oz. of pepper – 5*d*, for 1oz. ginger – 4*d*, for 1lb. of dates – 8*d*, for half a pound bisketts – 7*d*, for 2lb. of currants – 9*d*, for 2lb. damask prunes – 6*d*, for 3lb. fine sugar – 3*s*. 4*d*, for 2lb. middle sugar – 23*d*. — 9*s*. 10*d*.

Sum total of the whole charge of this
quarter dinner amounts to   £10   15*s*.

Whereof

Allowed towards the same by the house	£8		
Master Warden Vaghan		27*s*.	6*d*.
Mr Wright		27*s*.	6*d*.

146

FEAST DINNER } ANNO 1572

In the fourteenth year in the reign of
Queen Elizabeth

Mr Alderman Barnam our Master

Mr Nichlas Whelar
Mr Richard Rennoldes   } our four
Mr William Vaghan   Masters the
Mr John Wight   Wardens

**Provision of the same dinner and for
the potation on Sunday at night as also
for the dinner on Tuesday the next day
following the Great Dinner.**

Poulterer	Paid to Robert Mason for these parcels following:			
Sunday at dinner	First paid for two geese at 20*d.* the piece		3*s.*	4*d.*
	Item paid for four capons, two roosters and boilers at 2*s.* the piece one with another		8*s.*	
Monday at dinner	Item paid for forty-two boiling capons – 32lb, roasting capons at 2*s.* the piece	£7	13*s.*	
	Item paid for ten pullets at 14*d.* the piece		11*s.*	8*d.*
	Item paid for thirteen geese at 20*d.* the piece		21*s.*	13*d.*
	Item paid for eight cygnets at 8*s.* the piece alive, and for scalding of them at 4*d.* the piece	£3	6*s.*	8*d.*
	Item paid for four dozen of partridges price		42*s.*	
Dinner on Thursday	Item paid for six dozen of pigeons at 20*d.*		10*s.*	
	Item paid for 6cwt. of eggs on Sunday and Monday		14*s.*	3*d.*
	Item paid for twenty boiling capons and fourteen roasting capons at 2*s.* the piece one with another	£3	8*s*	
	Item for six pullets at 13*d.* the piece		7*s.*	
	Item for eleven geese at 20*d.* the piece		18*s.*	4*d.*
	Item for five dozen of pigeons at 20*d.*		8*s.*	4*d.*
	Item for 1cwt. of eggs price		2*s*	5*d.*
	Sum	£21	9*s.*	8*d.*

147

	Item paid for sixteen pewits[298] at 15*s.* the dozen	20*s.*	

f.111v **Butcher**	Paid for three buttocks of beef weighing 10st. at 13*d.* the st, bought to bake for red deer	11*s.*	8*d.*
Sunday at dinner	Item for a sirloin of beef weighing 5st. at the same price, roasted on Sunday	5*s.*	10*d.*
	Item for a hind quarter of mutton, a neck and a leg	4*s.*	8*d.*
	Item for two long marrowbones		14*d.*
Monday at dinner	Item for sirloins of beef weighing 10st. at 14*d.* the st.	11*s.*	8*d.*
	Item two whole muttons for the waiters' breakfast	20*s.*	
	Item paid for twenty long marrowbones at 7*d.*	11*s.*.	8*d.*
	Item paid for 70lb. of suet at 3*d. ob.* the lb.	20*s.*	5*d.*
Tuesday at dinner	Item paid for a sirloin of beef weighing 4st. at 14*d.* the stone	4*s.*	8*d.*
	Item paid for ten long marrowbones at 7*d.*	5*s.*	10*d.*
	Item for 32lb. of suet at 3*d. ob.* the lb.	9*s.*	4*d.*
	Item paid for blood and guts for pudding		8*d.*
	Item for a peck of pricks for the kitchen		
	Item paid for a boar for brawn	£3	
	Sum	£8	7*s.* 7*d.*

Baker	Paid to Heath the Baker as follows:		
Saturday's potation	For a dozen of rolls at three for a penny		12*d.*
Sunday at dinner and at potation	For two dozen of the same rolls	2*s.*	
	For a dozen penny white for dinner		12*d.*
	For a dozen white stale		12*d.*
	For a dozen penny wheaten for dinner		12*d.*
	For a dozen half penny white bread		12*d.*

---

[298] Pewit: a green plover (or lapwing).

Monday dinner	For eight dozen penny stale white for the cooks	8s.		
	For ten dozen of rolls three for a penny	10s.		
	For ten dozen of half penny white bread new	10s.		
	For two dozen of penny wheaten bread	2s.		
Tuesday	For two dozen penny white bread stale	2s.		
	For three dozen penny white bread new	3s.		
	For one dozen penny wheaten	12d.		
	For six dozen rolls, three a penny	6s.		
	Sum	49s		

Spice bread	Paid to Wall's wife for eleven dozen of cakes and buns at 2s. the dozen, one dozen di of cakes and one dozen di of buns for the potation on Saturday at the secret nomination of the Master and Wardens, the rest being four dozen cakes, four dozen buns at the great potation on Sunday at night	22s.		
f.112r **Pikemonger**	Paid to Jeffrey Willins for eighteen pikes for Monday at dinner at 22d. the piece, and for ten pikes on Tuesday at dinner rebating 16d. the whole	50s.		
Fruits	Paid to the Steward for fruit by him bought viz. 4cwt. genetings at 13d. the cwt.	3s.		
	Pears 3cwt. at 12d. the cwt.	3s.		
	Plums 7cwt. at 6d. the cwt.		6d.	
	Katherin pears[299] 1cwt. at 14d. the cwt.		14d.	
	Codlings 1cwt. di at 16d. the cwt.	2s.		
	Sum	12s.	8d.	

Comfits	Paid for almond comfits one lb. di at 15d. the lb.		22d.	ob.
	Orange comfits 2lb. at 2s. the lb.	4s.		
	Ginger comfits 1lb. quarter at 2s. the lb.	2s.	6d.	
	Dredge comfits 1lb. at 2s. the lb.	2s.		
	Cinnamon comfits at 2s. 1lb. di	3s.		
	Coriander comfits 1lb. di at 15d. the lb.		22d.	ob.
	Bysketes 2lb. di at 14d. the lb.	2s.	11d.	
	Sum	19s.	4d.	

Grocer	Paid to the Grocer for spice as follows:		
For hippocras	Cinnamon 2lb. three quarters at 4s. 8d. the lb.	12s.	10d.

---

[299] Katherin (or Catherine) pear: an early variety of small pear.

Ginger 1lb. di	7s.	
Nutmeg 6oz.	7s.	
Coriander seeds 6oz.		3d.
Pepper 14lb. at 2s. 10d. the lb.	39s.	8d.
Cloves and mace 6oz.	4s.	
Mace large 8oz.	8s.	
Ginger 14oz.	4s.	1d.
Cinnamon 10oz.	2s.	11d.
Nutmeg three quarter lb.	3s.	9d.
Sanders 1oz.		2d
Saffron 2oz.	2s.	8d.
Dates 10lb.	6s.	8d.
Cloves 2oz.	5s.	10d.
Sugar fine 20lb. at 13d. the lb.	21s.	8d.
Sugar middle 64lb. at 10d. quarter the lb.	53s.	10d.
Cap paper three quires		15d.

| | Sum | £8 | 19s. | 10d. |

f.112v. **Cream**   Paid for ten gallons of cream on Monday for dinner at 14d. the gallon and for four gallons cream on Tuesday in all fourteen gallons at 14d. the gallon for the custards – 16s. 4d, and for a gallon of milk for the pudding on Tuesday – 4d.

         16s.   8d.

Lard   Paid for 27lb. of lard for the red deer and wildfowl at 8d. the lb.

         18s.

Beer Brewer   Paid to John Byrd for three barrels of beer of 10d. the barrel and for two barrels of beer of 4s. the barrel

         23s.

Ale Brewer   Paid to Mathew Marten for three barrels of ale at 6s. the barrel   18s.
Item for a barrel of small ale at 4s. the barrel   4s.
Item for two pails of yeast for the cooks   12d.

| | Sum | 23s. |

Wood and coal   Paid for a quartern of billets   3s.
Item for 2cwt. of fagots at 5s. the cwt.   10s.
Item paid for twenty-four sacks of coals   15s.   3d.

| | Sum | 28s. | 3d. |

Pewterer	Paid to Catcher the Pewterer for the hire of eighteen garnishes of vessels and di at 10*d.* the garnish	15*s.*	5*d.*
	Item for six dozen of banqueting dishes	2*s.*	4*d.*
	Item for a banqueting dish lost		8*d.*
	Sum	17*s.*	4*d.*

Sturgeon	Paid to Mrs Clove for two firkins of fresh sturgeon at 21*s.* the firkin	42*s.*	

Wafers	Paid to Mrs Wharton for ten boxes of wafers on Monday at dinner and five boxes on Tuesday at dinner at 2*s.* the box	30*s.*	

f.113r. **Chandler**	Paid to Mr Awgar for these things viz.:			
	First for two gallons of red vinegar and for a bushel two pecks of white salt, in all		23*d.*	
	Item for half a bushel of bay salt		6*d.*	
	Item for a lb. of packthread		7*d.*	
	Item for 6lb. of cotton candle		18*d.*	
	Item for three pecks of oatmeal		21*d.*	
	Item for two links		8*d.*	
	Item for a peck of fine white salt		8*d.*	
	Item for mustard for Sunday, Monday and Tuesday		20*d.*	
	Item for onions		6*d.*	
	Item for two gallons and a pottle of vergious		15*d.*	
	Item for two gallons a quarter of white vinegar	3*s.*		
	Item for four perfuming pans		12*d.*	
	Item for the occupying of four steynes		2*d.*	
	Item for the occupying of six chafers		3*d.*	
	Item for two chafers lost and broken[300]		6*d.*	
	Item for the occupying of three gallon pots		1*d.*	*ob.*
	Item for five gallon pots broken		10*d.*	
	Item for the occupying of five pottle pots		2*d.*	
	Item for eight pottle pots lacking		8*d.*	
	Item for the occupying of five green pots		2*d.*	
	Item for twenty green pots broken and lacking		15*d.*	*ob.*
	Item for the occupying of six pans		2*d.*	
	Item for two pans lacking and gone		4*d.*	
	Item for eight candlesticks of earth		8*d.*	
	Item for four boiling pots		10*d.*	
	Item for two ladles		2*d.*	
	Sum	£5	2*s.* 8*d.*	*ob.*

[300] A fair number of chafers, pottle pots, green pots and pans, hired from the Chandler, were broken or lost in the making of the dinner, indicating the intensity of activity in the kitchen.

Marchpanes	Paid to Treegle the Cook for four marchpanes at 4*s.* the piece Item for twenty-six parchpanes at 3*s.* 4*d.*			
	Sum	£5	2*s.*	8*d.*
Flour and Meal	Paid to the Cook for eighteen bushels of flour for the bakemeats at 3*s.*		54*s.*	
	Item paid for two bushels of wheatmeal for the baking of red deer		7*s.*	4*d.*
	Item for four bushels one peck of flour		15*s.*	7*d.*
	Sum	£3	16*s.*	11*d.*
Trenchers and trays	Paid for twenty-four dozen of trenchers at 6*d.* the dozen – 12*s,* and more to Mr Vaghan and Mr Wight for eleven dozen of trenchers by them furnished – 4*s.* 8*d.*		15*s.*	8*d.*
	Item for four trays at 18*d.* the piece – 6*s.* Item for two dozen of ashen cups at 12*d.* the dozen – 2*s,* for a cup for the hippocras and for taps for ale and beer – 6*d,* for a coal shovel – 4*d,* for a basket to preserve spices – 2*s.*		10*s.*	10*d.*
	Sum		26*s.*	6*d.*
f.113v **Wine**	Paid to Mr Rennoldes for a hogshead and six tiers of Gascon wine	£5		
	Item paid for two gallons of white wine for the sturgeon – 2*s.* 8*d,* for twenty gallons of claret and red wine for the hippocras – 26*s.* 8*d.* Item for four gallons of white and claret wine for the broths – 5*s.* 4*d.*		34*s.*	8*d.*
	Item paid for eighteen gallons of sack at 22*d.* the gallon		33*s.*	
	Item paid for eight gallons di of muscadel at 2*s.* 10*d.* the gallon		24*s.*	
	Sum	£9	11*s.*	8*d.*
Butter	Paid for a hundred weight of butter in the market at 3*d.* the lb.		25*s.*	

Linen cloth	Paid to Nicholas Layefield[301] for forty-six ells lacking a quarter of lockeram at 13*d.* the ell, for two ells of Holland at 2*s.* the ell, for the Sewer and Carver and for eight ells of Harfords at 7*d. ob.* for the kitchen	58*s.*	6*d.*
Strainers	Paid for strainers for the cooks in the kitchen		12*d.*
Tapestry	Paid to Mr Gunter[302] in Cornhill for the hire of certain stories of tapestry to hang the great parlour with all	20*s.*	
Butler	Paid to Edmond Wright the Butler for himself and others with him serving Sunday, Monday and Tuesday for their pains taking charge of plates and napery	26*s.*	8*d.*
Cook	Paid to Triegle the Cook for his pains and others with him the same day	40*s.*	
Steward	Paid to Robert Beaumond the Steward for pains the same time	40*s.*	
.114r. Sewer	Paid to Christofer Fulke the Sewer for his pains serving those two days	6*s.*	8*d.*
Musicians	Paid to the Waits of the City for their attendance for Monday and Tuesday	20*s.*	
Preachers	Paid to Mr Porder[303] preaching before the Company on Sunday at afternoon at St. Michael's – 6*s.* 8*d,* and to Mr Crowley preaching on Monday before them at St. Michael's before noon – 10*s.*	16*s.*	8*d.*
Porters	Paid to those hereafter following serving as porters at the gate and other places to whit John Tatam – 2*s,* Robert Selby – 3*s,* George Shaw – 3*s,* Robert Brushwood – 3*s,* Robert Hyve – 3*s.* and George Hall – 3*s.*	18*s.*	

---

301 Nicholas Layefield was a Draper. See Boyd, *Roll.*

302 Mr Gunter also hired out his hanging to the Company in 1561–2 (DCA, WA 1561–2, f.7r.). He may have been Francis Gunter, a Skinner from the parish of St. Michael's Cornhill (TNA, PROB 11/72/623).

303 Richard Porder was a London preacher and writer with puritan sympathies, associated with St. Peter's, Cornhill, and St. Paul's. See Orlin, *Locating Privacy*, 272–4; D. J. Crankshaw, 'Community, City and Nation, 1540–1714' in D. Keene, A. Burns and A. Saint (ed.) *St. Paul's: The Cathedral Church of London, 604–2004* (London and New Haven: Yale University Press, 2004), 52.

Women in the kitchen	Paid to Goodwife Holmes to Dennys Eeles and to Goodwife Thompson, all three washing dishes etc. in the kitchen, to every of them – 2s. 6d.	7s.	6d.
Clerks of St. Michael's	Paid to the Clerks of St. Michael's in Cornhill by the way of reward	3s.	6d.
Raker of the Ward	Paid to the Raker for carriage away of the garbage and other offal, that is cast out of the kitchen by the way of reward		10d.
Poor prisoners etc.	Paid and delivered to the poor about the hall and sent to the prisoners in money	40s.	6d

f.114v. **Rewards for bucks sent in generality**

Paid and given in reward to him that brought a brace of bucks from the Lord Marquess of Wynchester	13s.	4d.
Item to the bringer of a buck from Mr Mershe[304]	5s.	
Item to the bringer of a buck from Prestwiche[305]	3s.	4d.
Item to the bringer of a buck from Mr Alderman Barnam	6s.	8d.
Item to the bringer of a buck from Doctor Gybbon	5s.	
Item to the bringer of a buck from Mr Warder	5s.	
Item to the bringer of two bucks from Mr Elkinton[306]	5s.	
Item to the bringer of a buck from Mr Swan[307]		
Item to the bringer of a buck from Mr Champion[308]		
Sum	43s.	4d.

Brooms	Paid for green brooms and birchen brooms in all	4d.

[304] Possibly Nicholas Marshe, a Draper. See Boyd, *Roll*.

[305] Prestwiche is described 'of our Company' on the next page, though his membership is not confirmed by Boyd.

[306] John Elkington (or Elkinton) was a Draper who bound an apprentice 'out of this house' in 1573. See Boyd, *Roll*.

[307] Possibly John Swan, a Draper who served as Fourth Warden in 1537–8. See Johnson, *History*, ii. 469. Or Francis Swan, a Draper who served as Third Warden in 1576–7. See Johnson, *History*, ii. 471.

[308] Likely Richard Champion junior, son of Sir Richard Champion, who was a Draper. See Boyd, *Roll*.

Paid for carriage of the sturgeon from the place they bought it to the hall		3*d.*
Item for carriage to the hall of the fruit		2*d.*
Item for carriage the hire of trenchers		2*d.*
Item for carriage of rushes to the hall		8*d.*
Item for fish, bread and drink for the Steward's dinner on Saturday with the officers and labourers	2*s.*	
Item for carriage of sack to the hall		3*d.*
Item for baking of twenty-four pasties venison at the Cook's house at 2*d.* the piece	4*s.*	
Item paid to Stephen Malyn for his pains – 3*s,* and to two other beadles – 2*s.*	5*s.*	
Item to Henry Starr our Labourer in reward in consideration of his poverty	2*s.*	6*d.*
Item paid to the Sheriff's officers for their pains there serving and carving	10*s.*	
Item to Anthony Clerk in reward		12*d.*
Item paid for the charges of carriage and portage of the wine laid in the cellar	3*s.*	7*d.*
Item paid for radish roots etc.		3*d.*

Sum		29*s.*	10*d.*
Sum Total	£98	4*s.*	3*d.*

f. 115r.

Deductions Allowed to the Mr Wardens by the house towards the same great dinner £20
Item of our quarterage money gathered of the whole Livery amounts to
Item for a brace of bucks allowed to them by the house wherein Richard Candler dwelt and now Isaac Taylor 40*s.*

Bucks by generality From the Lord Marquess of Wynchester
From Mr Marshe
From Prestwiche of our Company
From the Lady Champion
From Mr Alderman Barnam
From Mr Doctor Gybbon
From Mr Wardure
From Mr Elkinton of our Company

Sum – eleven bucks

Bucks for Mr Whelar	From Reading
	From Wyndsore
	From Mr Turner
	Sum – three bucks

f.115v. **Bucks for Mr Rennoldes** — From John Hall – one

Bucks from Mr Vaghan — From [-] – one

Bucks for Mr Wight
On Friday – one
One Saturday – one

Whereof were made 113 pasties, two of the said pasties were baked for red deer

Red deer made of beef – six pasties
Of di a stag made – four pasties
Of a haunch of fallow deer – two pasties
From Mr Vaghan out of the country[309] – two pasties

Fourteen pasties

Spent on Monday and Tuesday – seven
The remainder to Mr Wardens – seven

Fourteen pasties

Four messes — **Potation for the Masters on Saturday at the secret nomination**
Special cakes and buns of each – three
Plums and genetings
Pears and genetings
Bysketes and caraways
Comfits two dishes each mess

Twelve messes — **Potation for the Masters and Livery on Sunday at night after the sermon**
As above

---

[309] 'Out of the country' suggests the absence of Mr Vaghan at the time of the Election Dinner.

f.116r.   **The Order of Service**

Two messes   **Dinner on Sunday for the Masters the**
single   **Wardens, the officers, and servant**
                Brawn and mustard
                Boiled legs of mutton
                Boiled capons
                Roast goose
                Roast beef
                Baked venison
                Roast capon

                For the cooks and servants
                Boiled mutton
                Roasted beef
                Baked venison

                Breakfast on Monday for the Bachelors
                and waiters
                Mutton and pottage

First course   **Dinner on Monday at the high table**
Four messes   Brawn and mustard
                Boiled capons
                Roasted swan
                Baked venison
                Pike
                Roasted capon
                Custard

First course   **At the second table**
Four messes   Brawn and mustard
                Boiled capon
                Roasted swan or goose
                Baked venison and pike
                Roasted capon
                Custard

                At the third table
                In all as before

Second course   **At the high table**
Four messes   Pewits
                Partridges
                Red deer
                Sturgeon
f.116v.   Marchpane

Second course   **At the second table**
Five messes   Partridges or pigeons

157

Red deer
Sturgeon
Marchpane

Second course **At the third table**
Five messes   Partridges and pigeons
Red deer
Sturgeon
Marchpane

First and
second
courses   **At the table in the great parlour**
One mess   As above as to the side tables in the hall

Three messes   **For the Bachelor waiters**
Brawn and mustard
Boiled capon
Baked venison

Lady Chester
One single mess home to her house

Mrs Kyddermister[310]
A boiled capon
Roasted capon
A pastry of venison

Mr Swan
A pasty of venison

---

[310] Possibly the widow of John Kydermyster, a Draper who died prematurely in 1545 (TNA, PROB 11/30/559). See Boyd, *Roll.*

ANNIS 1572 AND 1573

In the time of Johnis Branche Alderman,
Master of the Craft, and

Martini Calthorp
Georgii Brathwait
Anthonii Prior[311]   } Wardens
William Megges[312]

Quarter   **Expenses of the first Quarter Dinner kept**
Dinner   **the twenty-fifth day of November 1572**
             being Tuesday, for mess of meat follows:

             [-]

f.120r. **Feast Dinner**   In the fifteenth year in the reign of Queen
} Anno 1573   Elizabeth

Mr Alderman Branche our Master

Mr Martyn Calthorpp
Mr George Brathwait   } our four Masters the
Mr Anthony Pryor   Wardens
Mr William Megges

Provision of the same dinner and for the
potation on Sunday at night etc.

Grocer   Paid first to the Grocer for 41lb. sugar at
Wafers   8d. the lb. – 27s. 4d, 8lb. of sugar at 9d. the
             lb. – 6s, for 16lb. di of fine sugar at 12d. the
             lb. – 16s. 6d, for 10lb. of pepper at 2s. 10d.
             per lb. – 28s. 4d, for one pound of nutmeg –
             5s. 4d, 3oz. of large mace – 3s, 1lb. 6oz. of
             ginger – 4s. 7d, 2lb. 6oz. cinnamon – 11s.
             1d, for sanders – 1d, 1oz. of saffron – 17d,
             6lb. of currants – 3s. 9d, 5oz. of cloves – 2s.
             1d, 6lb. of prunes – 18d, 2qts. of barberries
             – 16d, ten boxes of wafers – 20s, 2oz. of
             coriander seeds – 2d, 2lb. of dates – 5s.   £6   17s.   6d.

---

[311] Anthony Prior (or Pryor) served as Warden of the Drapers' Company in 1572–3. See
     Johnson, *History*, ii. 471.

[312] William Megges (or Meggs) served as Warden of the Drapers' Company in 1572–3,
     1578–9, and 1582–3. He was Master in 1590–1. See Johnson, *History*, ii. 471–2.

Comfits	Item paid for 2lb. of cinnamon comfits – 3s. 8d, 1lb. of ginger comfits – 22d, 1lb. of dredge comfits – 22d, 1lb. of musk comfits – 18d, 1lb. of caraways – 14d, 2lb. of byskettes – 2s. 4d, 1lb. di of almond comfits – 21d, 1lb. di of coriander comfits – 21d, half a lb. of orange comfits – 11d.	16s.	9d.
Fruit	Item for 4cwt. of pears – 4s, 2cwt. of genetings – 20s. Item more 1cwt. of genetings – 12d, 1cwt. of codlings – 12d, 14lb. of cherries at 3d. the lb. – 3s. 6d, di cwt. codling – 12d.	12s.	2d.
Spicebread	Item to Mrs Wall for ten dozen cakes and buns	20s.	
Wood and coal	Item for a quarter of billets – 3s, cwt. di of fagots – 7s. 8d. for twenty sacks of coals at 8d. the sack and 4d. over – 13s. 8d.	24s.	4d.
	Sum of page £10	10s.	9d.
f.120v. **Beer**	Item paid for two barrels of beer at 5d. the barrel and one barrel of 4s.	14s.	
Ale	Item for two barrels of ale of 6s. the barrel and one barrel of 4s.	16s.	
Trenchers, trays and ashen cups	Item for four small trays – 2s, for two dozen of ashen cups – 2s, for twenty-four dozen of trenchers at 6d. ob. the dozen – 13s.	17s.	
Butter	Item paid for four dozen and 2lb. of butter at 3s. 4d. the dozen	13s.	
Reward for bringing venison	Item given in reward to those that did bring venison to whit, to Doctor Gybbon's servant – 3s. 4d, to Elkington's man – 5s, to Mr Lucas' man – 12d, to Mr Carowe's servant – 12d.	10s.	4d.
Butcher	Item paid for three sirloins of beef, a mutton three quarters and a leg, weighing in all 30st. and di at 17d. the st.	35s.	6d.
	Item for 50lb. of suet at 3d. the lb. – 12s. 6d, for fourteen long marrowbones at 4d. the piece, 4d. less – 9s.	21s.	6d.

160

Poulterer	Item paid to Robert Mason, Poulterer, for five dozen and four capons at 2*s*. 1*d*. the piece – £6. 13*s*. 4*d*, for nine geese at 20*d*. the piece – 15*s*, two cygnets at 7*s*. the piece – 14*s*, four dozen of pigeons at 20*d*. the dozen – 6*s*. 8*d*, for 3cwt. of eggs at 3*s*. the cwt. – 9*s*.			error in the
		£8	18*s*.	capons
	Item paid to Otwell Strenell for eight cygnets at 6*s*. 8*d*. the piece – 53*s*, for four dozen of quails at 12*s*. the dozen – 43*s*.	£5		12*d*.
Red deer	Paid for 7st. of beef and di for to be baked for red deer – 8*s*, for 16lb. of lard for the same at 8*d*. the lb. – 10*s*. 8*d*, for two bushels of meal for the paste – 6*s*, for a lb. and a *qt*. of pepper – 3*s*. 6*d*, for 2oz. of nutmeg – 8*d*, for 2oz. of cinnamon – 7*d*, 2oz. of cloves – 7*d*, an oz. of ginger – 4*d*, 12lb. of suet at 3*d*. the lb. – 3*s*.		33*s*.	4*d*.

	<u>Sum of page</u>	<u>£22</u>	<u>6*d*.</u>

f.121r.	**Flour**	Item paid for sixteen bushels of flour at 3*s*. 8*d*. the bushel	58*s*.	8*d*.
	Marchpanes	Item paid to Treegle the Cook for sixteen marchpanes at 3*s*. 4*d*. the piece	53*s*.	4*d*.
	Cook's wages	Item paid to the Cook for his pains dressing the dinner – 30*s*, for baking of ten pasties of venison in his ovens – 20*d*.	31*s*.	8*d*.
	Chandler	Item paid for occupying of four steynes – 4*d*, for chafer pots – 3*d*, for eleven pottle pots – 11*d*, twenty green pots – 14*d*, for occupying six great pans – 3*d*, for four boiling pots – 16*d*. for di a bushel of bay salt – 10*d*, for 6lb. of candles – 18*d*, for four taps – 2*d*, for di 1lb. of packthread – 4*d*, a pottle of sand – 2*d*, a peck of oatmeal – 7*d*, for a bushel of white salt and a pan – 2*s*. 6*d*, for 7qts. and a pint of vinegar – 18*d*, for two gallons of vergious with two pots – 16*d*, two links – 8*d*, two gallons and a pint of vinegar white and two pots – 2*s*. 9*d*, a *qt*. of mustard and two pots to put it in – 6*d*, for onions – 8*d*, more for oatmeal and a pot – 3*d*, for a gallon pot – 6*d*, for di a peck of pricks – 3*d*.	18*s*.	9*d*.

Pewterer	Item paid for the hire of twenty-two garnish of vessels at 10*d.* the garnish, 4*d.* less		18*s.*	
Sturgeon	Item paid for a firkin of fresh sturgeon with 2*d.* for the carriage thereof to the hall		24*s.*	2*d.*
Pikemonger	Item paid for sixteen pikes at 22*d.* the piece		29*s.*	4*d.*
Wine	Item paid for one hogshead of wine – £4, for fourteen gallons of sack – 28*s,* for two gallons of white wine – 3*s.* 4*d,* for six gallons and a pottle of red wine at 20*d.* the gallon – 10*s.* 10*d,* and for a cane to draw the Gascon wine withall – 2*d.*	£6	10*s.*	4*d.*
Aprons	Item for four aprons for the women in the kitchen washing dishes		2*s.*	6*d.*
Cap paper	Item for a quire of cap paper for the cooks			4*d.*
	Sum of page	£18	7*s.*	1*d.*
f.121v. **Gooseberries**	Item paid for gooseberries for the cooks			4*d.*
Bread	Item paid for thirty-three dozen of bread		33*s.*	
Porters	Item paid to five of the Company serving as porters at the gate at 2*s.* the piece		10*s.*	
Women in the kitchen	Item paid to women giving their attendance washing the dishes in the kitchen and washing the house etc. to whit to Mother Holmes for four days at 6*d.* per day – 2*s,* to Goodwife Eelys for four days – 2*s,* to Goodwife Morys for two days – 12*d,* to Goodwife Markes for one day – 6*d.*		5*s.*	6*d.*
Brooms	Item paid for brooms			4*d.*
Scavenger	Item paid to the scavenger			8*d.*
Clerks of St. Michael's	Item paid to the Clerks of St. Michael's		3*s.*	4*d.*
Musicians	Item paid to the musicians – 10*s.* and more in reward to Segar – 3*s.* 4*d.*		13*s.*	4*d.*
Writing paper	Item for writing paper			1*d.*

Butlers	Item paid to the Butler for his wages	26s.	8d.
Cream	Item paid for six gallons of cream	8s.	
Preacher	Item paid to Mr Gateacre[313] for his sermon made before the Company at St. Michael's on Sunday at afternoon	6s.	
	Item paid to be released of the bargain made for a boar	5s.	

	Sum	£10	12s.	3d.
	Sum total of the whole together	£56	10s.	7d.

Sum gathered at the potation and other allowance towards the said dinner in all	£12	7s.	2d.

Mr Calthorp	£11	10d. ob. qt.
Mr Brathwayt	£11	10d. ob. qt.
Mr Pryor	£11	10d. ob. qt.
Mr Megges	£11	10d. ob. qt.

---

[313] Thomas Gateacre (or Gatacre, or Gataker) was a clergyman in the Church of England. He served as MP in 1554. After time in Louvain, Oxford, and Cambridge, he was a priest at St. Edmund, Lombard Street, Christchurch, Newgate Street and was the domestic chaplain of the Earl of Leicester. See *HP Commons, 1509–1558*, ii. 195–6; *Oxford DNB*.

FEAST DINNER } ANNO 1574

In the sixteenth year of the reign of Queen
Elizabeth, Sir Richard Pipe Knight, then
being Master of this Company

Mr William Dumer
Mr William Thorowgood
Mr Nicholas Awgar
Mr Thomas Whelar

} our four Master
Wardens

**Provision of the same dinner and for the
potation on Sunday at night before:**

Fruit	Paid to Goodwife Sturdy for 3cwt. of pears – 5s, 3cwt. genetings – 3s, 1cwt. di of codling – 3s. Item to Mrs Thorowgood[314] for pears bought by her – 6d. And to Margery Shore for 9lb. of cherries at 4d. the lb. – 3s.	14s.	6d.
Comfits	Item paid to Raff King,[315] Comfit-Maker, for comfits of diverse sorts bought for the potation on Sunday at night viz. 2lb. of cinnamon comfits, ginger 1lb, dredge 1lb, musk comfits 1lb, orange di lb. in all 5lb. di at 22d. the lb. – 10s. 1d, for caraways 1lb. for byskettes 1lb, almond comfits 1lb. di, corianders 1lb. di in all 5lb. at 14d. the lb. – 5s. 10d, And for a lb. of fine sugar and di for the same potation – 18d.	17s.	4d.
Spicebread	Item paid to Mrs Wall for nine dozen spicebread, half cakes and half buns at 2s. 6d. the dozen	22s.	6d.
Wood and coal	Item for ten sacks with coal bought at 8d. the sack – 6s. 13d. and for three quarters of fagots with the carriage – 5s.	11s.	8d.

---

314 Mrs Thorowgood was married to William Thorowgood, who served as Warden of the
Drapers' Company. Orlin suggests she was involved in the silk trade. See Orlin, *Locating
Privacy*, 288.
315 Possibly Ralph King, also a Draper. See Boyd, *Roll*.

Butcher	Paid to Frannces Greene, Butcher, for 26st. and 6lb. of beef at 14*d*. the st. – 31*s*, for 6lb. of suet – 2*s*, for twenty-two marrowbones at 3*d*. the piece – 5*s*. 6*d*, and for one mutton – 10*s*.		48*s*.	8*d*.
Poulterer	Paid to Mason, Poulterer, for four swans at 8*s*. the piece – 32*s*, for eleven geese – 20*s*, for five dozen of chickens – 26*s*, for two dozen and three partridges – 21*s*, for one pullet – 18*d*, for five dozen of pigeons – 8*s*. 4*d*, and for 3cwt. eggs – 9*s*, and for three dozen and [-] capons bought by Mr Whelar – £8. 19*s*.	£9	15*s*.	10*d*.
Beer and ale	Paid for a barrel and a half of beer – 12*s*, and for a barrel of the best ale – 8*s*, and for a kilderkin of small ale for the kitchen – 3*s*.		23*s*.	

	Sum of page	£16	14*s*.	6*d*.

f.122v. **Grocer**	Paid to the Grocer for spice for bakemeats and otherwise viz. large maces at 12*d*. the oz. for 3oz. – 3*s*, pepper di a lb. – 27*d*, saffron di oz. – 10*d*, cloves 2oz. – 12*d*, nutmeg 7oz. – 2*s*. 6*d*, 2oz. cinnamon – 8*d*, ginger 2oz. – 6*d*, 6lb. of prunes – 21*d*, currants 6lb. – 2*s*. 6*d*, dates 3lb. – 6*s*, sugar middle – 13lb. at 10*d*. the lb. – 10*s*. 10*d*, sugar fine 4lb. at 13*d*. the lb. – 4*s*. 4*d*, bysketts 1lb. – 15*d*, more for fine sugar 9lb. di at 11*d*. *ob.* the lb. – 9*s*. 1*d*	£2	5*s*.	8*d*.
Marchpanes	Paid for four marchpanes of the largest sorts at 3*s*. 4*d*. the piece – 12*s*, and for ten of another sorts at 2*s*. 6*d*. the piece – 25*s*.		37*s*.	
Hippocras	Paid for ten gallons, one pottle and a pint of hippocras at 5*s*. the gallon		53*s*.	
Wafers	Paid to Henry Newton's wife for three boxes of wafers – 6*s*, and to James Wharton's wife for five boxes – 10*s*, and more to her for taking again two boxes being bespoken and not spent – 6*d*.		16*s*.	6*d*.

Wine of all sorts	Paid to Mr Ratclyf for wine set there for the hall, Sunday, Monday and Tuesday viz. on Sunday at afternoon for the potation three gallons one pottle of claret wine at 2*s.* the gallon – 7*s*, two gallons di of sack at 2*s.* 4*d.* the gallon – 5*s.* 10*d*, on Monday the second of August – eighteen gallons one pint of claret wine and one gallon of white at 2*s.* the gallon – 38*s.* 4*d*, eight gallons three quarters of sack at 2*s.* 4*d.* the gallon – 20*s.* 5*d*, and more on Tuesday one pottle of claret wine – 12*d.*	£3	12*s.*
Baker	Paid to Heath the Baker for twelve dozen of bread – 12*s,* and to Storer, Baker, for thirteen dozen of Bread and di – 13*s.* 6*d.*	25*s.*	6*d.*
Sturgeon	Paid for a firkin of fresh sturgeon	26*s.*	8*d.*
Fresh salmon	Paid for three salmons di whereof two cost – 16*s.* 8*d*, and the one and di cost – 16*s,* and for carrying the same to the hall – 4*d.*	33*s.*	
Pikemonger	Paid to the Pikemonger, William Harres, for fourteen pikes	25*s.*	
	Sum	£16 14*s.*	4*d.*
f.123r. **Butter**	Paid for 36lb. of butter bought by Mr Whelar whereof 30lb. at 3*d. ob.* and 6lb. at 4*d.* the lb.	10*s.*	9*d.*
Flour	Paid for two bushels di of fine flour whereof two bushels cost 4*s.* 8*d.* the bushel and the di bushel after 5*s.*	11*s.*	10*d.*
Cream	Paid for six gallons of cream for custards at 14*d.* the gallon	7*s.*	
Sweet water	Paid for a pottle of washing water and a pint of rosewater for the Cook	3*s.*	4*d.*
Washing coverpanes[316]	Paid for washing the coverpanes	3*s.*	
Trenchers	Paid for sixteen dozen of wooden trenchers	8*s.*	

[316] Coverpane: a cloth that covers, likely used as tablecloth, possibly decorated.

Preacher	Paid to Mr Crowley for his pains in making two sermons before the Company on Sunday at afternoon and Monday afternoon	13*s.*	4*d.*
Cook	Paid to Stephen Treeagle the Cook for his pains dressing the dinner	26*s.*	8*d.*
Butler	Paid to Edmond Wright, Butler, for his pains and his Company	20*s.*	
Porters	Paid to John Taylor – 2*s*, to George Hall – 2*s*, to Robert Hyve – 2*s*, to John Rolles[317] – 2*s*, all porters attending at the gate and stair head etc. Sunday and Monday	8*s.*	
Musicians	Paid to John Michel, Musician, and his Company serving on Monday at dinner	8*s.*	
Clerks of St. Michael's	Paid and given in reward to the Clerks of St. Michael's in Cornhill	3*s.*	4*d.*
Cap paper	Paid for a quire of cap paper for the Cook for the bake meats		4*d.*
Goose-berries	Paid for gooseberries three quarts		12*d.*
Pewterer	Paid to the Pewterer for the occupying of ten garnish of vessels and two garnish of banqueting dishes at 10*d.* the garnish	10*s.*	
Labourers	Paid to Stephen Malyn and Robert Cheynn for three days labour each of them in making clean the house and going on errands at 8*d.* per day a piece – 4*s*, and to Mathew Tyson for carrying the cushions to and from the church – 4*d.*	4*s.*	4*d.*

Sum of page   £6 18*s.* 11*d.*

---

[317] John Rolles was a Draper. See Boyd, *Roll.*

f.123v. **Chandler**	Paid to the Chandler for things set from him as follows to whit, for one gallon and one pottle of red vinegar – 15*d*, and for a pot to put it in – 2*d*, for oatmeal – 4*d*. Item for a peck of fine salt – 6*d*, for two boiling pots – 3*d*, for onions – 2*d*, for di all of packthread – 4*d*, for two chafer pots – 6*d*, for occupying of three chafer pots – 2*d*, for five pottles pots which are lacking – 5*d*, for occupying of seven pottle pots – 2*d*, for occupying of six candlesticks and for one lacking – 2*d*, for occupying of two great pans with the salmon – 4*d*, for occupying of three small pans – 1*d*, for twelve green pots lacking and for the occupying of six – 9*d*, for a gallon and di of vergious with a pot – 12*d*, for occupying of two steynes – 2*d*, for a link – 4*d*. Item for a lb. of candles – 3*d*, for a peck of coarser salt white – 6*d*, for three quarts of white vinegar and three pots which went with the vinegar – 2*s*.	9*s*.	10*d*.
Women in the kitchen	Paid to Mother Holmes for two days for herself and another helping in the kitchen – 18*d*. Item to Goodwife Parkinson for three days washing the house before the dinner and after and also washing dishes in the kitchen the day of the Great Dinner at 6*d*. per day – 18*d*.	3*s*.	
Raker	Paid to the Raker of the Ward in reward for carrying away the rubbish put out of the kitchen		8*d*.
Extra-ordinary	Paid extraordinary viz. to Mother Stoughton widow a poor woman for strewing herbs in Finckes Lane – 12*d*, for rushes bought by Mrs Thorowgood over and beside the nine dozen allowed by the house of ordinary – 6*d*. Item paid for bread and drink for Monday at supper and Tuesday at dinner – 4*s*. 2*d*.	5*s*.	8*d*.
	Item more paid extraordinary to Mr Sheriff Pullison's Butler in reward for his attendance here at dinner – 2*s*, and for bringing and sending Mr Sheriff's plate hither and home again – 16*d*.	3*s*.	4*d*.

1574

f.124r.

Some total of the whole charges £41 10s. 3d.

The allowance of the house is	£8		
Item for quarterage gathered		56s.	
Item received of the Clerk for quarterage of them that were absent agreed for		15s.	
Item of Isaack Taylor for a brace of bucks according to his lease		40s.	
Item for the alienation of the said Taylor's lease	£3	10s.	

Sum £17 12d.

Which being deducted there rests clear to be paid by them £24 9s. 3d.

To whit by

Mr Dumer	£6	2s.	3d. ob. qt.
Mr Thorowgood	£6	2s.	3d. ob. qt.
Mr Awgar	£6	2s.	3d. ob. qt.
Mr Whelar	£6	2s.	3d. ob. qt.

169

FEAST DINNER } ANNO 1575

The seventeeth year in the reign of Queen
Elizabeth, Mr Alderman Pullison then
being Master of this Company

Mr Rennoldes	
Mr Calverley	} our four Master
Mr Planckay[318]	Wardens
Mr Trott[319]	

**Provision of the same dinner and for the
potation on Sunday at night before:**

Fruit	Paid for fruit for the potation viz. 3cwt. of genetings – 2s. 2d, 1cwt. of plums – 14d, 3cwt. of pears – 3s. 11d, 2cwt. of codlings and di – 2s. 8d, for di a peck of filberts – 7d.	10s.	6d.
Spicebread	Paid to Mrs Wall for nine dozen and di of cakes and buns at 2s. the dozen	19s.	
Comfits	Paid to Raffe King for the banquet on Sunday at night viz. for 2lb. of cinnamon comfits, 1lb. of ginger comfits, 1lb. of orange comfits at 22d. the lb. – 7s. 4d, 1lb. of musk comfits – 20d, 1lb. of caraways – 15d, 1lb. di of coriander comfits – 22d. ob, byskettes 2lb. at 15d. a lb. – 2s. 6d, di lb. of fine sugar – 7d, for sanders – 1d. ob, for one lb. of almond comfits – 15d.	16s.	7d.
Wood and coal	Paid for two quarterns of fagots – 3s. 9d, for a quarter of billets – 2s. 11d, for twelve sacks of great coals at 8d. per sack – 8s, and for three sacks of thorn coals – 16d.	16s.	
Trenchers, trays and ashen cups	Paid for twenty-four dozen of trenchers at 6d. the dozen – 12s, for four trays – 4s, for a dozen of ashen cups – 16d.	17s.	4d.

---

[318] Henry Planckney served as Warden of the Drapers' Company in 1574–5. See Johnson, *History*, ii. 471.

[319] John Trott the younger served as Warden of the Drapers' Company in 1574–5, 1582–3, and 1586–7. See Johnson, *History*, ii. 471–2.

| **Spice for hippocras** | Paid for spice for the making of thirteen gallons of hippocras viz. three quarters of ginger – 2*s*. 2*d*, 1lb. di of cinnamon – 6*s*. 6*d*, 3oz. of cloves – 16*d*, 3oz. of nutmeg – 16*d*, 2oz. coriander seeds – 2*d*, 28lb. of sugar at 10*d*. the lb. – 24*s*. 4*d*. | | | |

| | <u>Sum of page</u> | <u>£5</u> | <u>14*s*.</u> | <u>3*d*.</u> |

| f.125r. **Wine** | Paid for wine of all sorts to whit for a tiers of Gascon wine bought of Mr Rennoldes – £3 6*s*. 8*d*, for cartage and portage of the same to the hall in to the cellar – 10*d*, for three gallons of red wine put to the making of hippocras – 6*s*, for eleven gallons three quarters of sack of Mr Colclough at 22*d*. the gallon – 21*s*. 13*d*, for bringing of the same home and broching – 6*d*, for two gallons of white wine for the cooks – 4*s*, for five gallons di of French wine – 11*s*. | £5 | 10*s*. | 8*d*. |

| **Poulterer** | Paid to Mason the Poulterer for four dozen di of capons to whit three dozen and six for Monday, twelve for Tuesday to dinner at 2*s*. the piece – £5 8*s*, for four cygnets at 8*s*. the piece – 32*s*, for 12 geese at 20*d*. the piece – 20*s*, for four dozen di of chicken at 6*s*. the dozen – 27*s*, for two dozen di of partridges at 10*s*. the dozen – 25*s*, for six dozen di of pigeons at 20*d*. the dozen – 10*s*. 10*d*, for 2cwt. di of eggs at 3*s*. the cwt. – 7*s*. 6*d*, and for the meat of two swans which our Master sent – 12*d*. | £11 | 5*s*. | |

| **Grocer** | Paid to the Grocer as follows for large mace a quarter of a pound – 3*s*. 8*d*, pepper di all – 16*d*, saffron di oz. – 12*d*, cloves 2oz. – 12*d*, nutmeg 6oz. – 2*s*, cinnamon 2oz. – 8*d*, ginger 2oz. – 5*d*, prunes 6lb. – 18*d*, currants 7lb. – 2*s*. 4*d*, sugar middle 5lb. at 14*d*. the lb. – 5*s*. 10*d*, more 6lb. fine – 7*s*. 6*d*, dates 3lb. di at 16*d*. the lb. – 4*s*. 8*d*, nutmeg more 4oz. di quarter – 2*s*. 3*d*, maces di oz – 6*d*, currants more 1lb. – 4*d*, sugar 2lb. – 2*s*. 4*d*, pepper 1lb. 2oz. – 3*s*, prunes more one pound – 3*d*, ginger 2oz. – 5*d*, cloves 1oz. – 6*d*, more for 5lb. of fine sugar – 6*s*. 3*d*. | | 47*s*. | 10*d*. |

Butcher	Paid to the Butcher for thirty-eight marrowbones – 9s. 9d, for 21st. and 3lb. of beef at 15d. the st. – 26s. 9d, for one mutton – 10s, for 16lb. of suet – 4s.	50s.	6d.

Sum of page   <u>£21</u>   <u>14s.</u>

f.125v. **Salmon and turbet**	Paid for turbet – 5s. 2d. and for a side of fresh salmon and the chin – 10s.	15s.	2d.
Pikemonger	Paid to William Harryson, Pikemonger, for fourteen pikes	25s.	
Sturgeon	Paid for a keg of sturgeon bought – 8s, the other firkin was given to Master Wardens by John Bodeley[320] and for carriage of the same sturgeon to the hall – 2d.	8s.	2d.
Neats tongue	Paid for twenty-six neats tongue to bake at 7d. the piece	15s.	2d.
Rye meal	Paid for a bushel di of rye meal to bake the same tongue with all	3s.	6d.
Marchpanes	Paid to Raffe King for eight large marchpanes at 3s. 4d. the piece – 26s. 8d, and for ten smaller marchpanes at 2s. 7d. the piece – 26s. 8d.	53s.	4d.
White vinegar	Paid for three pottles of white vinegar	2s.	
Butter	Paid for salt butter and fresh butter 54lb. at 3d. the lb. whereof 12lb. was for the baking of neats tongue	13s.	4d.
Beer and ale	Paid for two barrels of beer at 6s. the barrel and one kilderkin after 4s. the barrel – 14s, and to Mathew Martyn for two barrels of ale at 6s. the barrel – 12s.	26s.	

---

[320] As a merchant, John Bodeley (or Bodley) was a Draper, Merchant Adventurer, and founding member of the Eastland Company. As a religious radical, he was a leading Calvinist who was closely connected to the French and Walloon refugees' church in London during the 1570s. See *Oxford DNB*.

The Cook	Paid to Stephen Treeagle the Cook for three bushels one peck of flour for the bake meats – 11*s*, for five gallons of cream for custards – 6*s*. 5*d*, for a gallon of barberries – 2*s*. 8*d*, for 6lb. of lard – 4*s*, for baking of di a buck – 5*s*, for four custards – 10*s*, for his pains dressing the dinner – 30*s*, for two aprons – 23*d*.	£3	11*s*.	
Baker	Paid to Mrs Heath, Baker, for twenty-six dozen and a half of bread		26*s*.	6*d*.
Sweet water	Paid for washing water and rosewater		3*s*.	
	Sum of page	£13	2*s*.	2*d*.

f.126r. **Wafers**	Paid for nine boxes of wafers where of four boxes had of Wharton's wife and five of Newton's wife at 2*s*. the box		18*s*.	
Musicians	Paid to the musicians for one day		13*s*.	4*d*.
Butler	Paid to Edmond Wright, Butler, for his pains with four, serving the three days		26*s*.	8*d*.
Chandler	Paid to Thomas Awgar for Chandler's stuff in as by his bill		11*s*.	6*d*.
Pewterer	Paid to John Catcher, Pewterer, for the hire of vessels to whit eleven garnish of vessel at 10*d*. the garnish – 9*s*. 2*d*, seven dozen of banqueting dishes at 4*d*. the dozen – 2*s*. 4*d*, eight pottle pots – 6*d*.		12*s*.	
Flowers and herbs	Paid for flowers and herbs		2*s*.	6*d*.
Brooms, oranges etc.	Paid for brooms – 3*d*, for di cwt. of oranges – 8*d*, for small ale and beer set out of the doors – 6*d*.			18*d*.
Cap paper	Paid for a quire of cap paper			4*d*.
Linen cloth	Paid for two ells di of linen cloth for the Sewer and Carver – 2*s*. 10*d*. Item for four aprons for the butlers – 2*s*. 6*d*. for three aprons for the Clerk's wife and her two daughters – 3*s*, for four ells of Harfordes for the women in the kitchen at 7*d*. the ells – 2*s*. 4*d*.		10*s*.	8*d*.

Sewers and carver	Paid to the officers for their pains in sewing and carving		6s.	8d.
Women in the kitchen	Paid to Goodwife Holmes for her pains in the kitchen – 18d, and to Goodwife Parkinson and her maid – 3s. 6d, to whit for herself for five days dressing up the house before the feast and after and helping in the kitchen at 6d. per day and to her maid for three days at 4d. per day		6s.	
Labourer	Paid to Stephen Malyn for four days and Robert Cheynn for as many		5s.	
Porter	Paid to George Hills, Robert Hyve and John Rowles to whit Hills and Hyve for two days – 12d. a piece – 2s, to John Rowles and John Taylor for three days a piece – 3s.		5s.	
	Sum of page	£5	19s.	2d.

f.126v. **Clerks of St. Michael's**	Paid to the Clerks of St. Michael's in reward		3s.	4d.
Stowghton's widow	Paid to Stoughton's widow by the way of charity, for stowing Finckes Lane with herbs at the end next Cornehill			6d.
Labourers in the kitchen	Paid by the way of reward to the labourers in the kitchen			12d.
The Raker	Paid to the Raker of the Ward for carrying away the rubbish and offal of the fowl etc.			8d.
	Sum		5s.	6d.
	Sum total of the whole charges amounts to	£46	15s.	1d.

Whereof

Allowed by the house towards the same	£8		
Quarterage gathered at the potation		50s.	8d.
Agreed and received of the Clerk for all those that remain to pay their quarterage being absent at the potation		17s.	4d.

174

1575

Received of Richard Godard for the brace
of bucks which he giveth yearly for the
tenement he holds of the Company in
Colman Street   40*s.*

        Sum of the allowance   £13   8*s.*

Which being deducted the whole charges
of the same dinner will amount to   £33   7*s.*

To whit
Mr Rennoldes   £8   6*s.*   9*d.*
Mr Calverley   £8   6*s.*   9*d.*
Mr Planckny   £8   6*s.*   9*d.*
Mr Trott   £8   6*s.*   9*d.*

f.127r.

Memorandum that the proportion of two
Election Dinners cannot be gotten at
the Master Wardens' hands viz. the one
in anno 1576. Mr Nicholas Whelar, Mr
William Chester, Mr John Lowen and
Mr Lawrence Goff [321] then being the
four Master Wardens. The other in anno
1577, Mr George Brathwyt, Mr Mathew
Colclough, Mr Thomas Herdson and Mr
William Lowe[322] then Master Wardens

[321] Lawrence Goff served as Warden of the Drapers' Company in 1575–6, 1585–6, and 1589–90. He was Master in 1595–6. See Johnson, *History*, ii. 471–2.
[322] William Lowe served as Warden of the Drapers' Company in 1576–7. See Johnson, *History*, ii. 471.

FEAST DINNER } ANNO 1578

The twentieth year in the reign of Queen
Elizabeth, Mr Richard Pype[323] Alderman
then being Master of this Company of
Drapers

William Thorowgood	
Robert Diconson	} our four Masters
Symon Horsepoole[324]	Wardens
William Barnard[325]	

**Provision of the same dinner and for the
potation on Sunday at night before:**

Coals great and small	Paid for twelve sacks of great coal at 8*d.* the sack – 8*s,* and for five sack of small coal at 3*d.* the sacks – 15*d.*	9*s.*	3*d.*	
Fagots and billets	Paid for three quarters of cwt. of fagots after 5*s.* the cwt. – 3*s.* 9*d,* and for a quarter of a cwt. of billets after 12*s.* the cwt. – 3*s,* and in reward to a boy that brought them – 1*d. ob.*	6*s.*	10*d.*	*ob*
Fresh sturgeon	Paid for a firkin of sturgeon and for the bringing thereof to the hall	20*s.*	2*d.*	
Trenchers	Paid for twenty-four dozen of trenchers at 5*d.* the dozen – 10*s.* and for bringing them to the Drapers' Hall – 3*d.*	10*s.*	3*d.*	
Neats tongues	Paid for twenty-two neats tongue to bake at 8*d.* the piece	14*s.*	8*d.*	

[323] (Sir) Richard Pipe (or Pype) became Alderman in 1570. He translated from the Leather-sellers' Company to the Drapers' after serving as Sheriff in 1572–3. Pipe then served as Master of the Drapers' Company in 1573–4, 1577–8, and 1581–2. He was Lord Mayor in 1578–9. See Johnson, *History*, ii. 471, 481; Beaven, *Aldermen*, ii. 38.

[324] Simon (or Symon) Horsepoole served as Warden of the Drapers' Company in 1577–8, 1584–5, and 1588–9. He was Master in 1593–4. See Johnson, *History*, ii. 471–2.

[325] William Barnard served as Warden of the Drapers' Company in 1577–8. See Johnson, *History*, ii. 471.

Turner's ware	Paid for four great trays for the larders – 4*s,* for a dozen of ashen cups – 12*d,* for six taps for ale and beer – 2*d,* for quills and spigots and for setting the wine abroche – 6*d.*		5*s.*	8*d.*	
Butter	Paid for 8lb. of sweet butter to bake the neats tongue with all – 2*s.* 8*d,* and more for 50lb. of butter at 3*d. ob.* the lb. spent besides – 14*s.* 5*d.*		17*s.*	1*d.*	
Sack	Paid for twelve gallons three quarts of sack at 22*d.* the gallon – 23*s.* 4*d. ob,* for a rundlet – 14*d.* and for bringing the same to the hall – 2*d.*		14*s.*	8*d.*	*ob.*
	<u>Sum of page</u>	<u>£6</u>	<u>8*s.*</u>	<u>8*d.*</u>	
f.128r. **Sugar**	Paid for 20lb. di of sugar in powder for the kitchen at 11*d.* the lb.		18*s.*	9*d.*	*ob.*
Rewards for bucks	Paid to Mr Doctor Gibbon's son in reward bringing a buck from his father – 5*s,* and to Mr [-] servant in reward for bringing another – 3*s.* 4*d.*		8*s.*	4*d.*	
Swans	Paid to Mrs Heath for four swans bought of her at 8*s.* the piece		32*s.*		
Flowers and herbs	Paid for flowers and strewing herbs the three days		3*s.*	4*d.*	
Rosewater	Paid for a pint of rosewater – 10*d,* and for red rosewater – 4*d.*			14*d.*	
Clerks of St. Michael's	Paid to the Clerks of St. Michael's in reward		3*s.*	4*d.*	
Musicians	Paid to the Waits of the City for the two days		26*s.*	8*d.*	
Sewers and Carvers	Paid to Ellys, the Serjeant, for four serjeants and their yeomen for the first day and one sergeant and himself the second day in sewing and carving		10*s.*		
Bread	Paid to Hodges the Baker for twenty-seven dozen of bread spent the three days		27*s.*		

Wafers	Paid to Wharton's wife of our Company for nine boxes of wafers for the first and second day at 2*s.* the box		18*s.*	
Chandler	Paid to the Chandler Thomas Awgar for earthen pots of diverse sorts, salt, vinegar, verges chafer fetched as by his bill appears		17*s.*	
Hippocras	Paid to Robert Prannell for six gallons di pint of hippocras spent the two days at 5*s.* the gallon		30*s.*	4*d.*
Spicebread	Paid to Goodwife Wall for nine dozen of spice cakes and buns at 2*s.* 6*d.* the dozen		22*s.*	6*d.*

Sum of page £10 18*s.* 5*d.* *ob.*

f.128v. **Wine**	Paid to Gregory Shorter for a supply of Gascon wine besides one hogshead we had in the house to whit for four gallons at 20*d.* the gallon – 6*s.* 8*d,* and for a gallon and a quart of white wine for the kitchen set at the said Shorters – 2*s.* 1*d.*		8*s.*	9*d.*
Porters	Paid to George Hill, Thomas Sheford, John Taylor, George Shawe, Thomas Godson[326] and George Ffabyan[327] all porters for two days a piece whereof the first two had 2*s.* in reward and the other had 3*s.* 4*d.*		5*s.*	4*d.*
Grocers	Paid to Henry Ffankes, Grocer, for grocery wares bought of him as by his bill appears		37*s.*	
Marchpanes and comfits	Paid to Balthazer the Sugar Baker for sixteen marchpanes for both days and for comfits of all sorts for the banquet of Sunday at night	£3	8*s.*	8*d.*
Fruit	Paid for fruit as pears, plums, nuts, codling and such like for this banquet as by the bill appears		9*s.*	10*d.*
Poulterer	Paid to Robert Mason for poultry ware had him as by his bill appears	£9	5*s.*	3*d.*

---

[326] Thomas Godson was a Draper. See Boyd, *Roll*.
[327] George Fabian (or Ffabyan) was a Draper and a preacher based in Essex. See Boyd, *Roll*.

Butcher	Paid to Richard Bingham, Butcher, for beef and mutton as by his bill – 57s. 11d, and for guts to make puddings – 12d.	58s.	11d.
Pikemonger	Paid to the Pikemonger for six pikes at 21d. the piece – 10s. 6d.	10s.	4d.
Fresh salmon	Paid for three salmons viz. one at 22s. another at 20s. and the third at 13s. 4d.	55s.	4d.
The Cook	Paid to John Barton, Cook, supplying in the absence of Stephen Triegle for his pains and other things had of him as by his bill appears	£3	18d.
Preacher	Paid to Mr Crowley preaching two sermons	13s.	4d.

<u>Sum of the page</u> <u>£25</u> <u>14s.</u> <u>5d.</u>

f.129r. **Butler**	Paid to George Bland, Butler, for himself and three others with him the three days	26s.	8d.
Beer	Paid for two barrels of beer of 6s. the barrel and one kilderkin of 2s.	14s.	
Ale	Paid for two barrels of ale	12s.	
Linen cloth	Paid two ells of Holland for Carvers and Sewers at 20d. the ell – 3s. 4d, for twelve ells of three quarter cloths for sixteen aprons for cooks, butlers and other at 9d. the ell – 9s, and for four ells of [indarlenes][328] for the scullery at 5d. the ell – 20d.	14s.	
Pewterer	Paid to John Catcher, Pewterer, for vessels hired of him as by his bill	17s.	
Wheat flour	Paid to Mr Thorowgood for four bushels of flour to bake with all at 3s. the bushel	12s.	
Reward to the Clerk's daughters and sons	Paid to Bartholomew Warner's, our Clerk, two daughters for their pains in reward	3s.	4d.
	Item more in reward to his two sons for their pains in going in errands		8d.

[328] Illegible.

Fell and Jarmen	Paid to George Fell for his pains attending six days at the hall – 3*s*. 4*d*, and to John Jarmen for as many days giving his attendance there – 2*s*. 6*d*.	5*s*.	10*d*.	
Women in the kitchen	Paid to Goodwife Parkinson and another with her serving in the kitchen and dressing up the house before and after the dinners for three days apiece – 3*s*, to Alice Cooke for three days helping in like manner – 18*d*, and to Goodwife Holmes for two days helping in the kitchen – 12*d*.	5*s*.	6*d*.	
Carriage of things to the hall	Paid for bringing of things by diverse to the hall at sundry times		12*d*.	*ob.*
Reward to the Mr Bachelors	Paid to the four Master Bachelors of the Yeomanry in reward, with two pasties of venison given them to make merry with those that waited	6*s*.	8*d*.	
Raker of the Ward	Paid to the Raker of the Ward for carrying away the offal of the fowl		8*d*.	

Sum of page £5 19*s*. 4*d*. *ob.*

f.129v.

Sum total of all the whole charges of the
Great Dinner £48 11*d*.

Whereof

Allowed by the house towards the same	£8		
Quarterage gathered at the potation	£3	6*s*.	8*d*.
Quarterage remaining up and at the potation and agreed with the Clerk therefore		10*s*.	
Received for a brace of bucks from the great tenement in Colman Streat		40*s*.	

Sum of the allowances [-]

Which being deducted the whole charges
of the same dinner will amount to [-]

180

FEAST DINNER } ANNO 1580

In the twenty-second year in the reign of
Queen Elizabeth, Master Alderman Branch
then being Master of this Company

Brian Calverley
John Wright
John Jenny[329] and
John Hall

} our four
Masters the
Wardens

**Provision for the same dinner and banquet
on Sunday at afternoon and Tuesday the
day after the said dinner as follows:**

Comfits	Paid for comfits bought for the banquet on Sunday at afternoon of diverse sorts to whit aniseed comfits 2lb, almond comfits 2lb, coriander comfits 1lb. di, half a lb. caraways for 2lb. biskettes, all at 15*d.* the lb. – 8*s.* 9*d.* for 1lb.of musk comfits, 1lb. of cinnamon comfits, 1lb. of ginger comfits, and 1lb. of orange comfits at 22*d.* the lb. of every of them – 7*s.* 4*d.*	16*s.*	1*d.*
Fruit	Paid more for fruit for the same banquet to whit apples, pears, plums, geneting and a peck of filberts and codlings	7*s.*	2*d.*
Spicebread	Paid more to Goodwife Wall for four dozen of spice cakes and four dozen of buns	28*s.*	

[329] John Jenny served as Warden of the Drapers' Company in 1579–80 and 1586–7. See
Johnson, *History*, ii. 471–2.

Poulterer	Paid to Robert Mason for poultry ware had of him viz. six dozen capons at 22*d.* the piece – £3, sixteen geese at 20*d.* the piece – £6 12*s*, six swans at 10*s.* the piece – £3, sixteen geese at 20*d.* the piece – 26*s.* 8*d*, six pullets at 14*d.* the piece – 12*s*, twelve partridges and twelve quails – 20*s*, eight dozen di of pigeons at 20*d.* the dozen – 14*s.* 2*d*, four and three quarters of eggs at 2*s.* 10*d.* the cwt. – 13*s.* 6*d*, more for two capons and nine pigeons for Sunday bought by Mr Hall – 3*s.* 6*d*.	£13	16*s.*	10*d.*

	<u>Sum of page</u>	<u>£6</u>	<u>8*s.*</u>	<u>1*d.*</u>

f.130v. **Butcher**	Paid to Henry Bowers, Butcher, for flesh bought of him first for twenty neats tongues bought to bake – 13*s.* 4*d*, for 18st. and 5lb. of beef as per bill at 12*d.* the st. – 18*s.* 9*d*, for one whole mutton and a half – 12*s*, for 94lb. of suet at 4*d.* the lb. – 31*s.* 4*d*, for thirty-six marrowbones at 4*d.* the piece – 12*s*, for a fore quarter of veal – 3*s*, for pricks and blood to make puddings – 12*d*, sum abating 3*s.* 5*d.* in the whole and paid	£4	8*s.*
Baker	Paid for twenty-eight dozen of bread bought at the Bakers as follows viz. for Sunday at dinner in rolls and for the servants at potation – 12*d.* in wheaten bread – 12*d.* in penny white bread – 12*d*, on Monday in rolls – 6*s*, in manchets – 6*s*, in penny white bread stale – 4*s*, in wheaten bread – 2*s*, on Tuesday in rolls – 12*d.* in manchets – 3*s*, in wheaten bread – 2*s*, in penny white bread stale – 12*d*.		28*s.*
Ale and beer	Paid for one hogshead of beer of 6*s.* the barrel and one barrel of 4*s.* in all – 13*s*, and for two barrels of ale at 6*s.* the barrel – 12*s*.		25*s.*
Sturgeon	Paid for a firkin of sturgeon and wine to new pickle the same		28*s.*	8*d.*
Wood	Paid for three quarterns of fagots and a quartern of billets		7*s.*	6*d.*

182

Coal great and small and brooms	Paid for fifteen sacks of great coals at 9*d.* the sack – 11*s.* 3*d.* and more to Goodwife Holmes for small coals and for brooms – 2*s.* 8*d.*	13*s.*	11*d.*
Trenchers	Paid for twenty dozen of trenchers whereof ten dozen at 8*d.* the dozen and ten dozen at 7*d.* the dozen	12*s.*	6*d.*

Sum of page   £10   3s.   7d.

f.131r. **Grocer**	Paid to the Grocer for spice of diverse sorts as follows, first for 1lb. of cinnamon and 2oz. – 5*s.* 10*d,* for three quarters of all of ginger at 2*s.* the lb. – 18*d,* for three quarters of all of nutmeg at 6*s.* the lb. – 4*s.* 6*d,* for a quarter of a lb. of grains – 6*d,* for coriander seeds di lb. – 4*d,* for cloves at two times 2oz. – 16*d,* for 8lb. quarter of pepper at three times price 2*s.* 6*d.* the lb. – 20*s.* 7*d. ob,* for 1oz. saffron – 20*d.* for 4lb. of dates at 9*d.* the lb. – 3*s,* for 8lb. of currants at 4*d.* the lb. – 2*s.* 8*d,* for 12lb. of prunes – 2*s,* sanders – 3*d,* for two quires of paper – 7*d,* for sugar powder 1lb. – 12*d,* more for 1oz. of ginger – 1*d. ob,* large maces at two times 4oz. – 3*s.* 4*d,* middle mace 3oz. – 2*s,* more cloves 3oz. – 2*s.* 3*d,* more for 2oz. of cinnamon – 10*d.*	54*s.*	4*d.*
Sugar	Paid for 51lb. di of sugar bought by Mr Hall at three several times at 12*d.* the lb.	51*s.*	6*d.*
Butter	Paid for a firkin of butter bought by Mr Hall – 13*s.* 2*d,* more for sweet butter bought by him to whit 38lb. at three several times whereof 20lb. at 3*d. qt.* the lb. and 18lb. at 3*d,* sum as per bill – 10*s.* 8*d.*	23*s.*	10*d.*
Linen cloth	Paid for linen cloth bought of John Wethers[330] for towels for the Sewer and Carver to whit two ells quarter of Holland – 3*s.* 7*d,* and for aprons for the cooks, butlers and others to whit eighteen ells of Hambrough – 12*s.* 10*d,* and four ells of Harfords – 2*s.* 4*d.*	18*s.*	9*d.*

[330] Possibly John Withers, Draper. See Boyd, *Roll.*

Marchpanes	Paid to [-] for ten marchpanes bought of him at 2s. 8d. the piece – 26s. 8d. To Stephen Tryagle for two inch panes at 4s. the piece, and for eight inch panes at 3s. 4d. the piece less – 3s. 4d. in the whole – 34s. 8d.	£3		16d.
	Sum of page	£10	9s.	9d.

f.131v.	Lard	Paid for 13lb. of lard bought of our Cook Stephen Triegle for the larding of the neats tongues that were baked	8s.	8d.
	Cook	Paid to the said Stephen Triegle Cook for his pains and others with him dressing the said great dinner	40s.	
	Coverpanes washed	Paid for washing and new edging again of all the coverpanes	2s.	6d.
	Flour and meal	Paid for meal and flour as follows viz. for six bushels of flour at 2s. 8d. the oz. – 16d, for three bushels of flour at 3s. the bushel – 9s, for six bushels of meal and a half at 3s. the bushel – 19s. 6d. and for two bushels of meal at 3s. the bushel – 6s, more for three pecks of rye meal for the baking of the neats tongue – 22d.	52s.	4d.
	Pewterer	Paid to Catcher the Pewterer for the loan of sixteen garnish of vessel at 10d. the garnish – 13s. 4d. And more for the loan of six dozen of salad dishes – 2s. 2d.	15s.	6d.
	Pikemonger	Paid to the Pikemonger for pikes	41s.	
	Musicians	Paid to the musicians for both days	13s.	
	Fresh salmon	Paid for two fresh salmons – 33s. 4d. and for one fresh salmon – 20s.	53s.	4d.
	Cream	Paid for nine gallons di of cream for custards at 14d. the gallon	11s.	
	Wafers	Paid for eight boxes of wafers	16s.	
	Coal shovel	Paid for coal shovel		6d.
	Paper	Paid for a quire of paper for the kitchen		2d.

Wine	Paid for ten gallons and a pottle of sack – 21*s*. for five gallons of white wine – 8*s*. 4*d*, for two gallons of red wine bought by Higgens the Butler for the hippocras – 3*s*. 4*d*.		32*s*.	8*d*.
f.132r. **Rosewater**	Paid for a pottle of rosewater had of Mrs Full[331] – 2*s*. 4*d*. and for a quart of rose water – 12*d*.		3*s*.	4*d*.
Butler	Paid to Higgins the Butler for his pains and others the two days		26*s*.	8*d*.
Rewards for bucks	Paid and given in reward for bucks as follows viz. to Mr Mydleton's man that brought a buck – 10*s*, to Mr Doctor Gibbon's man that brought a buck – 5*s*, to Mr Alderman Pullison's man that brought a buck – 5*s*, to Mr Bates'[332] man a Draper that brought a buck – 10*s*, to Mr Reman's man of Chichester that brought a buck – 10*s*, to Mr Sheriff's[333] man that brought a buck – 3*s*. 4*d*, and given to Mr Wyke's man that brought a buck – 10*s*.	£2	15*s*.	10*d*.
Chandler	Paid for Chandler's ware bought of John Randall		26*s*.	
Clerks of St. Michael's	Paid and given to the Sexton and Clerks of St. Michael's in reward		3*s*.	4*d*.
Sewers and Carvers	Paid to Ellys, Serjeant, and other three officers with him waiting and carving in reward		6*s*.	4*d*.
Stoughton's widow	Paid to Stoughton's widow as a charity for strewing the street at Finckes Lane end towards Cornehill			12*d*.
The Clerk's daughters	Paid and given in reward to the Clerk's two daughters helping to dress up the house and Ladies' Chambers		3*s*.	4*d*.

[331] Possibly the wife of Hugh Full, Draper. See Boyd, *Roll*.
[332] Possibly Edward Bates, Draper. See Boyd, *Roll*.
[333] (Sir) Martin Calthorpe was Sheriff in 1579–80. See Beaven, *Aldermen*, ii. 40.

Porters	Paid to the two porters that kept the nether door – 2*s.* 7*d,* and to Rowlles and Whyte[334] other two porters for two days – 2*s.* 4*d.*	4*s.*	8*d.*
Jarmen, Taylor and Ffell	Paid to Jarmann our labourer John Taylor and George Ffell every of – 3*s,* clearing the house, hanging up of banners and other things for four days	9*s.*	
Women	Paid to women some helping to make clean the house before the dinner and cleansing the house and washing dishes in the kitchen. Some for four days, some for more and some for less.	7*s.*	

---

[334] Possibly William White, Alexander White or Robert White, Drapers. See Boyd, *Roll.*

QUARTER DINNER 1601

**Charges of a Quarter Dinner at
Drapers' Hall the seventh day of
December 1601**

Seven messes of meat, nine to the first table and five to the second table	In primis paid for twelve sacks of great coals		9s.	
	Paid Fflud[335] for four sacks of small coals		2s.	
	Paid seven bundles of rushes		2s.	
	Paid for half a cwt. of fagots		4s.	
	Paid for billets		2s.	
	Paid for spice		7s.	7s.
	Paid for thirteen of sugar		19s.	7s.
	Paid for twenty-four neats tongues	£1	3s.	8d.
	Paid for twelve dozen of trenchers		80s.	
	Paid for two whole sirloins and a double rib of beef weighing 12st. 6lb. at 20d. per st.	£1	1s.	4d.
	Paid for sixteen marrowbones		6s.	
	Paid for pepper 1lb. and di		5s.	3d.
	Paid for two bushels and di of flour		9s.	4d.
	Paid for 12lb. of suet		5s.	
	Paid for oranges and lemons		2s.	1d.
	Paid for wine for the cooks		2s.	10d.
	Paid for sanders and barberries		2s.	1d.
	Paid for six gurnets		12s.	
	Paid for three legs of mutton		4s.	
	Paid and given to the Cook		2s.	6d.
	Paid two sergeants and two yeomen		9s.	
	Paid for cloth to wipe pewter		4s.	2d.
	Paid for fifteen dozen of bread		15s.	
	Paid for a swan 10s, for a turkey 5s.		15s.	
	Paid for ten geese at 2s. 4d. per piece	£1	3s.	4d.
	Paid for twenty-four capons at 2s. 6d. per piece		18s.	
	Paid for two woodcocks at 10d. per piece		1s.	8d.
	Paid for seventeen partridges at 18d. per piece	£1	7s.	
	Paid for two smites 2s. 4d, for fourteen pigeons 10s. 6d.		12s.	10d.
	Paid for twelve dozen of larks 10d. per dozen		10s.	

---

335 Robert Fflud (or Floyd, Ffloid, Loyd), a Draper, was the porter at Drapers' Hall from 1571. He also served as a labourer. See Boyd, *Roll*. Also DCA, RA 1607–8, f.15r; RA 1621–22, f.12r.

187

Paid for eggs di cwt.		2s.	4d.
Paid for twenty-four minced pies at 22d. per piece	£2	4s.	
Paid for twelve custards at 3s. per piece	£1	16s.	
Paid for twelve quince pies at 4s. 8d. per piece	£2	16s.	
Paid for dressing the dinner	£1		
Paid for twelve marchpanes at 4s. and seven at 2s. 6d.	£1	17s.	6d.
Paid for twelve pikes, six at 3s. and six at 2s. 4d.	£1	12s.	
Paid for a barrel of beer 8s. and a barrel of ale 8s.		16s.	
Paid for 1lb. di oringado[336] 3s. and 2lb. lard 20d.		4s.	8d.
Paid the Butler for his pains		6s.	8d.
Paid for eight collars of brawn	£1	17s.	10d.
Paid for eighteen neats tongues		18s.	10d.
Paid for carriage of stools			8d.
Paid Ffloid for his pains			6d.
Paid four porters		4s.	
Paid Ffloid for brooms first and fagots		3s.	2d.
Paid to three women to make clean the hall and pantry		15s.	
Paid to Griffen for varges, vinegar and pots		13s.	8d.
Paid for 31lb. of butter to Griffen		14s.	2d.
Paid for ten gallons three quarts of claret wine at 2s.	£1	1s.	6d.
Paid for eleven gallons and one pint of sack at 3s. 2d,		19s.	4d.
Paid for six gallons and one quart of muscadel at 3s. 9d.	£1	3s.	6d.
Paid for three rundlets		3s.	4d.

f.133r. (appears beside "Paid for twenty-four minced pies")

[336] Oringado (or orangeado): candied orange peel.

188

QUARTER DINNER 1602

Charges of a Quarter Dinner at Drapers' Hall the eighth day of June 1602

Twelve messes of meat, nine to the first table and five to the second table	In primis paid for eight sacks of great coals		6s.	8d.

In primis paid for eight sacks of great coals		6s.	8d.
Paid for a barrel of beer		8s.	
Paid for grocery ware per bill	£1	7s.	10d.
Paid and given the officers		8s.	6d.
Paid for fourteen neats tongues	£1	5s.	5d.
Paid for fifteen marrowbones		6s.	8d.
Paid for three legs of mutton and pricks		5s.	3d.
Paid for two whole sirloins and a double rib of beef	£1	4s.	3d.
Paid for butter 7s. 11d, and for pipkins and pots		8s.	7d.
Paid the Cook for twelve chicken pies at 4s. 6d. the piece	£2	14s.	
Paid for twelve pippin pies at 3s.	£1	18s.	
Paid for twelve custards at 3s.	£1	16s.	
Paid for 1lb. of lard 10d. and flour 10d.		1s.	3d.
Paid for dressing the dinner	£1		
Paid for two pecks and a half of white salt			10d.
Paid for partridge 6d, for a gallon and a half of vinegar 9d, and for sweet herbs 2d.		1s.	5d.
Paid for portage of green rushes			4d.
Paid for fifteen dozen of bread		15s.	
Paid for four salmons	£2	6s.	
Paid for two congers[337]	£1		
Paid the Vintner for nine gallons and a half claret wine and four gallons of sack	£1	14s.	
Paid for seven marchpanes, five at 4s. and seven at 2s. 4d.	£1	17s.	6d.
Paid for 1lb. and a di of oringado		3s.	
Paid for twelve pikes, five at 3s. and seven at 2s. 4d.	£1	17s.	6d.
Paid Ffloid per bill for ale, faggots, billets and porters to help	£1	2s.	
Paid for twelve capons at 2s. 6d. the piece	£1	10s.	
Paid for six pullets at 18d. the piece		9s.	
Paid for twenty-four geese at 20d. the piece	£2		
Paid for thirty-six chickens at 7d. the piece	£1	1s.	
Paid for thirty-six ducklings at 6s. per dozen		18s.	

---

[337] Conger: a large sea eel.

Paid for twenty-four rabbits at 8*d.* per piece	16*s.*	
Paid for gooseberries	1*s.*	8*d.*
Paid for eggs di cwt.	2*s.*	2*d.*
Paid the Butler for his pains	6*s.*	8*d.*
Paid for washing the linen	10*s.*	8*d.*
Paid two women for seven days	14*s.*	

f.135r.

Stephen Dallimon[338]	5*s.*	
John Wheatley[339]	3*s.*	
Robert Parker[340]	3*s.*	
Mathew Emrey[341]		
Samuel Beck[342]	3*s.*	
Edward Netherwod[343]	3*s.*	
Robart Gyttynes[344]	2*s.*	
Anthony Stanford		
Bayly, deaf and dumb		1*d.*
John Rockadyne – R. Barnard	3*s.*	
Lewys Ffewtrell	3*s.*	
Richard Popellwell	3*s.*	
Thomas Turnor,[345] White Crest porter	3*s.*	
Robart Carter[346]		
Georg Thorne	3*s.*	
John Browne[347] – R. Barnard	2*s.*	6*d.*
John Basse		
Raph Grannt[348]		
John Bradshaw,[349] Chick Lane	3*s.*	
Richard Popellwell, St. Andrew's Undershaft		
Mitt Lewys		
Rowland Rebyll, St. Michael's Yard	3*s.*	
Abraham Walker[350]	3*s.*	
Persyvall Byngley[351]	3*s.*	
John Lylly[352]	3*s.*	
James Skant[353] with Father [Nursr?]	3*s.*	
John Arthur, St. Martin's	3*s.*	
Mitt Pattenson, Cowcross	3*s.*	
Henry Whitecar	3*s.*	

338 Stephen Dallimond, a Draper. See Boyd, *Roll.*
339 John Wheatley, a Draper. See Boyd, *Roll.*
340 Robert Parker, a Draper. See Boyd, *Roll.*
341 Mathew Emery, a Draper. See Boyd, *Roll.*
342 Samuel Beck, a Draper. See Boyd, *Roll.*
343 Edmund Netherwood, a Draper. See Boyd, *Roll.*
344 Robert Gyttyns, a Draper. See Boyd, *Roll.*
345 Thomas Turner, a Draper. See Boyd, *Roll.*
346 Robert Carter, a Draper. See Boyd, *Roll.*
347 John Browne, a Draper. See Boyd, *Roll.*
348 Ralph (or Raphe) Grant, a Draper. See Boyd, *Roll.*
349 John Bradshaw, a Draper. See Boyd, *Roll.*
350 Abraham Walker, a Draper. See Boyd, *Roll.*
351 Percival Bingley, a Draper. See Boyd, *Roll.*
352 John Lylly, a Draper who practised as a butcher in Rosemary Lane. See Boyd, *Roll.*
353 James Skant, a Draper. See Boyd, *Roll.*

Edward Burrowes	4*s.*	
James Bowers[354]	3*s.*	
Robert Little[355]	3*s.*	
Hall		12*d.*
Dyssell[356]		12*d.*
Garrat[357]		12*d.*
Prudence Lewys, Bech Leyne[358]	3*s.*	
Widow Man,[359] Bech Leyne		
Widow Ffreman, Bech Leyne	3*s.*	
Widow Bowars[360]	3*s.*	
Widow Slanly, Bech Layne	3*s.*	
Widow Bendig, St. Katherine's	3*s.*	
Widow Thorneton,[361] Bech Layne	3*s.*	
Widow Bull, per Aldgate	3*s.*	
Widow Marshall	3*s.*	
B. Squibbe[362]	3*s.*	
Widow Grene		12*d.*
Widow Ould[363]		12*d.*
Widow Richard		12*d.*
Widow Jermyn		12*d.*
Loyd[364]	4*s.*	
Jonas[365]	3*s.*	
Watters[366]	3*s.*	1*d.*
Barnard[367]	5*s.*	
Widow Gaynnfford[368]	2*s.*	6*d.*

[354] James Bowers, a Draper. See Boyd, *Roll.*

[355] Robert Little, a Draper. See Boyd, *Roll.*

[356] Possibly John or Thomas Dyssell, both Drapers. See Boyd, *Roll.*

[357] Possibly William, George or Robert Garrett, all Drapers. See Boyd, *Roll.*

[358] The Drapers' Company maintained almshouses at Beech Lane, intended to accommodate eight widows, though not necessarily always occupied by those 'of the Company'. See W. Archer-Thomson, *History of the Company's Properties and Trusts, 2 Vols.* (London: privately printed, 1940–2), i. 161–4.

[359] Possibly the widow of William Man, a Draper. See Boyd, *Roll.*

[360] Possibly the widow of John or Richard Bowers, both Drapers. See Boyd, *Roll.*

[361] Possibly the widow of John Thornton, a Draper. See Boyd, *Roll.*

[362] Barnard Squibbe, a Draper. See Boyd, *Roll.*

[363] Possibly the widow of John Ould, who died in 1603–4 (DCA, RA 1603–4, f.9v).

[364] Robert Loyd, porter. See Boyd, *Roll.*

[365] Jonas Archer, a Draper, served the Company as a labourer in the early seventeenth century (DCA, RA 1601–2, f.12r; RA 1603–4, f.8r; RA 1607–8, f.15r). He was noted as 'a poor labourer and one of the Company's pensioners' (Boyd, *Roll*).

[366] Possibly John Walter, Clerk of the Drapers' Company for forty years until his death in 1656. See Archer-Thomson, *History,* i. 249–51; Johnson, *History,* iii. 253–5.

[367] Likely William or Richard Barnard, who both served as Beadle of the Drapers' Company in the early seventeenth century (DCA, RA 1606–7, f.11r; RA 1607–8, f.11r; RA 1620–1, f.12r).

[368] Possibly the widow of Thomas Gaynford, a Draper and porter of the Company who was noted as a haberdasher in 1570 (Boyd, *Roll*; DCA, RA 1602–3, f.8r; RA 1603–4, f.8v). Widow Gaynford was an almswoman at Tower Hill (DCA, RA 1607–8, f.19r).

21 JULY 1607,
MR W. COTTON'S[369] FUNERAL[370]

One damask table cloth
One damask towel long
Three dozen damask napkins

Two diaper tablecloths
Two ewery towels, one for the plate
Two dozen of napkins
One shrine cloth
One long officer's cloth

One dresser cloth

---

[369] William Cotton was a Draper (TNA, PROB 11/111/322). He served as Warden in 1600–1 and 1605–6. See Johnson, *History*, ii. 473; iv. 417.

[370] This appears to be a list of napery items employed in a small funeral dinner given for William Cotton, likely held after his burial.

GLOSSARY OF WEIGHTS AND MEASUREMENTS

Bushel Four pecks (or eight gallons)

cwt. A hundredweight (or 112 pounds)

Firkin Half a kilderkin

Kilderkin Half a barrel (or eighteen gallons for beer, sixteen gallons for ale)

lb. A pound

Peck A quarter of a bushel (or two gallons)

Pottle Half a gallon

Quart Two pints (or a quarter of a gallon)

Rundlet A measure of liquid of varying quantity; 'large' rundlets could vary between fifteen and eighteen-and-a-half gallons

Scantling A prescribed size relating to material objects

st. A stone (or fourteen pounds)

Stand A barrel or open tub

APPENDIX

THE ORDER OF THE ELECTION CEREMONIES
IN 1542, 1551, 1559, AND 1575

This appendix contains extracts from the Minute Books of the Drapers' Company relating to the election ceremonies in three different decades. The first, in 1542, took place in the Company's first Hall on St. Swithin's Lane, the others in the second Hall on Throgmorton Street. The spelling, capitalisation, and punctuation have been modernised but original spellings of names have been retained.

THE ORDER OF THE 1542 ELECTION *(DCA, MB1B, f.696)*

And the 21st day at the middle of the second course, Mr William Bowyer, our Master, arising from the outside of the high table went into the parlour, and after a little pause made came out again into the hall along the high table with the minstrels, a Bachelor bearing a cup of hippocras afore him. He did set the garland on the head of Sir William Roche and two or three ladies and then on diverse gentlemen's heads sitting at the north side of the said table and after that set the garland on Mr Sadler's head and drank to him to be Master the year following.

And immediately after the old Master Wardens went into the parlour, past a little pause made, came out again after the ancient Warden with the minstrels and before every Warden a Bachelor bearing a cup of hippocras. They went compass wise to the middle of the hall and chose the new Master Wardens according to the former nomination, and for because Mr Warner and Mr Tull were not here at dinner, Mr Spenser and Mr Askew drank to Sir William Roche for Mr Warner and Mr Tull. And those two being here at dinner were chosen in the hall, the Second Warden at the north table and the Third at the south table.

THE ORDER OF THE 1551 ELECTION *(DCA, MB1C, ff.512v.–513r.)*

Where heretofore it hath been used that the old Master hath on the feast day risen from the table and worn the garland and after hath chosen the new Masters therewith, this year a new order was by Mr

194

Alderman Lamberd, our old Master, in that behalf used. By the advice of Mr Atkyns then being a bidden guest whose mind then Mr Alderman followed on this wise following, saying in other companies, the Master being an Alderman, did not rise, but had the garland brought unto him who commanded the garland likewise to be brought to him. Which then, immediately after the minstrels playing, before Master Wardens following, Mr Tull the eldest Master Warden with a cup borne before him by the eldest Warden of the Bachelors, brought in his hands one of the garlands. He delivered the same unto the hands of Mr Alderman Lamberd, our Master, who then immediately delivered the said garland unto Master John Sadler, sitting on against him at the table, and drank to him to be Master of this Worshipful Fellowship for the next year ensuing. God send him thereof joy. Amen.

Then within a while after went forth after the old custom, Master Tull, Mr Fabyan, Mr Leigh, and Mr Champion, Master Wardens with the minstrels and cup bearers before them wearing each of them a garland on their heads fetching their compass about the hearth as heretofore. Then first, Master Tull trying his garland on certain persons heads at the high table, at length he delivered it unto Master Alderman Lamberd and drank to Mr Giles Brudge for the uppermost Warden for the next year ensuing, by reason he was absent. Then likewise Mr Fabian assayed his garland on certain persons and set it upon Mr Thomas Pettytte's head unto whom he drank to be the second Master Warden for the next year ensuing. Then Mr Leigh likewise on the west side table assayed his garland and at length set it on Mr Richard Askew's head unto whom he drank to be the third Master Warden. After them, Mr Champyon likewise assayed his garland and at length bestowed it on the head of Mr John Calthorp unto whom he likewise drank of a cup of hippocras to be the fourth Master Warden of this Worshipful Mystery of Drapers for the next year ensuing. God send them all much joy and worship. Amen.

THE ORDER OF THE 1559 ELECTION *(DCA, MB7, ff.176–177)*

According to the old ancient custom and laudable order heretofore used, after Alderman Champion (this year Sheriff), supplying for Mr Lowen our Master (being sick and absent), after Master Wardens had at the table required him, did rise from the high table and went into the parlour. With minstrels, the clerk with his hood, the cup bearer before him, proceeded forth into the hall to the high table only and first set his garland on the superiors' head being Mr Alderman Garrat, and after my Lord Giles Paulet and other Aldermen did at length, yielded and set the garland on Master Alderman Chester's head, unto whom he drank for to be our Master for the year ensuing. God find him thereof joy. Amen.

Then within a while, after the three old Master Wardens, minstrels likewise and cup bearers before them, passed out of the parlour into the hall in their hoods, making offering to the high table and compassing about the hall within the hearth and returning to the high table again. Mr Leegh, First Warden, tendering there only his garland, not otherwise upon the superiors' head and others, and to none of the Company but such as have been Chief Wardens or twice Master Warden at the least, and at length drank to Mr Burye to be the First Master Warden, and so stood still at the higher end of the high table. The residue compassing the hall again, Mr Cooke assayed his garland among the other of the Assistants and at length for that Mr Mynors was absent, he repaired unto the high table and proffered and delivered his garland to Mr Alderman Garret superior, and drank to him for Mr Mynors to be the Second Master Warden. Likewise, Mr Brooke assayed his garland among those which had not been Wardens, and youngest Livery this year not touched, and at length delivered his garland to My Lord Giles to whom he drank for Mr Heywar, then being absent, to be our Third Mr Warden. And likewise Mr Barnam tendered and afterwards assayed his garland on the younger sort of the Livery and the new Livery, and returned to the high table again and proffered his garland to Mr Recorder to whom he drank for Mr Chapman, then being absent, to be the Fourth Master Warden. God send them all thereof joy. Amen.

THE ORDER OF THE 1575 ELECTION *(DCA, MB9, ff.19v.–20r.)*

In the dinner time, after the last course was served in, the four Master Wardens in their lined gowns saluted those that sat at the high table and the rest of the tables, which thing done, they required Mr Alderman Pullison, our Master, to rise to the election of the new Master, who tendered his garland first to the ladies and gentlewomen and other strangers, and in the end drank to Mr John Quarles as Master of this Company for the year next ensuing.

Then immediately the four Master Wardens, after the wafers and hippocras were served, proceeded to the election of the new Master Wardens as follows: First, Master Warden Rennoldes having saluted the estate, compassing the hall about, did tender his garland to diverse of the doctors that sat at the high table, and to diverse of the gentlewomen, and of the Assistants sitting at the west table, and in the end drank to Mr Nicholas Whelar as Uppermost Master Warden for the year ensuing. Then Master Warden Calverley, compassing the hall, tendered his garland to diverse of the Assistants and strangers, and for that Mr William Chester was absent, he delivered his garland to Sir Rowland Hayward Knight, who sat in the place of the state, drinking to him in the name of the said William Chester as Second Master Warden for the year ensuing. That done, Master Warden Plackny, compassing the hall and dallying with diverse of the Livery which were never yet Wardens, as well as the west table as at the east, and at the last, for that John Lowen was absent, he tendered his garland to our old Master drinking to him in the name of Mr John Lowen as Third Warden of this Company for the year coming. Last of all, Master Warden Trott compassing the hall round about as the others did, hard to the screen, dallying and tendering his garland to diverse of the Livery, did in the end deliver the same to Mr Laurens Goff drinking to him as the Fourth Master Warden of the Company of Drapers for the year ensuing. God send them all grace well to do and the writer hereof also.

INDEX OF FOOD AND DRINK

Items are indexed in standard modern English. Where fluid spellings have been retained in the text, variants have been noted in brackets in consecutive order as they appear in the original text. *See* Editorial Method.

Genetings (jennetyngs)   122 & n.273, 149,
    156, 160, 164, 170, 181
Ginger   4, 6, 8, 11, 34, 37, 47, 49, 56, 64,
    70, 71, 76, 84, 96, 97, 114, 115, 120, 133,
    138, 146, 150, 159, 161, 165, 171, 183;
    see also comfits
Gooseberries   xxix, 17, 162, 167, 190
Grains   11, 183
Green fish   *see* fish
Greenplover   *see* fish
Gurnet   *see* fish
Guts   *see* blood and guts

Herbs, herblade, salad herbs   xix, xxvii, xxx,
    7, 43, 60, 65, 87, 100, 110 & n.261, 115,
    124, 129, 132, 133, 141, 168, 173, 174,
    177, 189
Herons, heronshaws   *see* birds
Hippocras (ipocrasse, ypocras)   xvii, xx,
    xxviii, xxix, xxxi, xxxiv, 10 & n.28, 18,
    23, 26, 27, 28, 30, 31, 36, 43, 50, 52, 54,
    55, 61, 69, 70, 74, 76, 84, 85, 93, 96, 107,
    110, 111, 121, 130, 131, 149, 152, 165,
    171, 178, 185, 194, 195, 196

Isenglass (isenglas, isinglass, ysanglasse,
    ysonglas)   xxxii, 37 & n.123, 56, 71, 84

Jelly   42, 51, 52, 54, 55, 58, 59, 62, 68, 69,
    70, 71, 74, 75, 83, 84, 85, 86, 87, 93, 123

Katherin pears   *see* pears

Lamb   4, 5, 32, 47; *see also* mutton, sheep
Lamprets, Lampreys   7 & n.19, 65; *see also*
    pies
Lard   5, 41, 74, 86, 100, 122, 139, 150, 161,
    173, 184, 188, 189
Larks   *see* birds
Lemons   xxxi, 17, 49, 61, 187
Ling   *see* fish

Mace   4, 6, 8, 11, 33, 34, 37, 47, 49, 56, 64,
    71, 84, 97, 114, 115, 117, 120, 133, 135,
    138, 146, 150, 159, 165, 171, 183
Malmsey   *see* fortified wine
Marchpanes, parchpanes   xxvii, xxviii, xxix,
    4 & n.7, 6, 9, 18, 26, 27, 28, 34, 36, 43,
    47, 49, 52, 54, 55, 61, 63, 68, 69, 71, 80,
    81, 86, 93, 94, 97, 109, 111, 116, 121,
    130, 131, 133, 134, 139, 152, 157, 158,
    161, 165, 172, 178, 184, 188, 189
Marrowbones (maryebones)   4, 6, 9, 32, 34,
    35, 47, 49, 54, 64, 70, 80, 81, 83, 94, 95,
    113, 116, 119, 134, 137, 145, 148, 160,
    165, 172, 182, 187, 189
Meal, oat, rye, wheat   xviii, xxxiii, 13, 14,
    15, 18, 39, 40, 57, 72, 76, 86, 87, 88, 96,
    99, 101, 120, 123, 138, 140, 141, 151, 152,
    161, 168, 172, 178, 184; *see also* flour
Milk   15, 74, 99, 122, 141, 150

Muscadel   *see* fortified wine
Mustard   xxxi, 5, 14, 33, 40, 50, 51, 53, 62,
    64, 65, 67, 68, 73, 87, 93, 94, 99, 107,
    108, 110, 114, 116, 123, 129, 130, 134,
    140, 145, 151, 157, 158, 161, 178
Mutton, sheep   9, 23, 35, 50, 52, 54, 70, 76,
    83, 94, 95, 108, 112, 114, 119, 129, 130,
    137, 148, 157, 160, 165, 172, 179, 182,
    187, 18; *see also* lamb

Neats Tongue   xxxi, 172, 176, 177, 182,
    184, 187, 188, 189
Nutmeg   11, 37, 56, 70, 71, 84, 96, 97, 120,
    133, 138, 150, 159, 161, 165, 171, 183
Nuts   178

Oats   xxxi, 12; *see also* meal
Oil, salad oil   7, 65, 115, 124, 132, 141
Olives   xxxi, 41, 114
Onions   xxx, xli, 17, 41, 87, 99, 116, 124,
    134, 140, 151, 161, 168
Oranges   xxxi, 5, 7, 17, 32, 47, 49, 61, 64,
    65, 115, 120, 133, 164, 173, 187; *see also*
    comfits
Oringado (orangeado)   188 & n.336

Parsley   7, 115, 117, 124, 133, 146
Partridges   *see* birds
Pasties
    Beef   156
    Red deer   51, 52, 54, 104, 105, 126, 128,
        130, 152
    Venison   xv, xxvii, xxxiii, xxxiv, xxxv,
        16, 20, 21, 22, 28, 29, 45, 50, 51, 52,
        53, 54, 59, 79, 91, 92, 104, 105, 106,
        107, 126, 128, 146, 155, 156, 161, 180
Pears, Katherin pears   xxix, xxx, 15, 23, 30,
    41, 50, 58, 67, 72, 82, 92, 98, 107, 122,
    128, 129, 141, 149 & n.299, 156, 160,
    164, 170, 178, 181
Pewit   *see* fish
Pepper   4, 6, 8, 11, 21, 33, 34, 37, 47, 49,
    56, 64, 71, 75, 84, 96, 114, 115, 117, 120,
    133, 135, 138, 145, 146, 150, 159, 161,
    165, 171, 183, 187
Pies
    Chicken   34, 49, 81, 116, 134, 189
    Eel   133
    Lampern   80, 115, 133
    Minced   4, 47, 63, 80, 113, 146, 188
    Pippin   7 & n.20, 189
    Quince   113, 146, 188
Pigeons   *see* birds
Pikes   *see* fish
Pippin   48, 98, 107; *see also* pies, tarts
Plums   xxix, xxx, 15, 23, 30, 41, 50, 58, 67,
    72, 82, 92, 98, 107, 122, 128, 129, 141,
    149, 156, 170, 178, 181; *see also* prunes
Poultry   *see also* birds
    Capons   xxvii, xxxi, xli, 3, 4, 6, 12, 23,
        26, 27, 28, 32, 34, 35, 37, 38, 47, 49,

50, 51, 52, 53, 56, 63, 67, 68, 69, 70,
80, 81, 83, 93, 94, 95, 107, 108, 109,
110, 114, 116, 118, 129, 130, 134,
136, 146, 147, 157, 158, 161, 165,
171, 182, 187, 189

Chicken 6, 49, 81, 134, 165, 171, 189;
see also pies, pullet

Geese xxxi, xli, 4, 6, 12, 26, 28, 32, 34,
35, 37, 49, 51, 52, 53, 56, 63, 68, 69,
70, 80, 81, 83, 93, 94, 95, 108, 109,
110, 114, 116, 118, 129, 130, 134,
136, 146, 147, 157, 161, 165, 171,
182, 187, 189

Pullets xxxi, 147, 165, 182, 189; *see
also* chicken

Suyte 114 & n.267; *see also* geese

Turkey cock (turkye cocke) xxxi, 4 &
n.6, 5, 32, 47, 63, 80, 146, 187

Porridge, pottage xli, 17 & n.55, 23, 52, 88,
108, 119, 129, 157

Prunes, damson prunes xxx, 4, 6, 8, 11, 33,
34, 37, 49, 56, 64, 71, 97, 114, 115, 117,
120, 133, 135, 138, 146, 159, 165, 171,
183; *see also* plums

Pullets *see* poultry

Pudding 40, 53, 83, 93, 94, 95, 110, 124,
130, 132, 137, 148, 179, 182

Milky 99, 122, 141, 150

Quails *see* birds

Rabbits 6, 12, 23, 34, 49, 81, 114, 116, 134,
190

Radishes, radish roots xxx, 58, 61, 76, 124,
155

Raisins 11; *see also* corinthes

Sack *see* fortified wine

Salad oil *see* oil

Saffron 11, 37, 56, 71, 84, 97, 120, 138,
150, 159, 165, 171, 183

Salmon *see* fish

Salt 5, 6, 7, 13, 17, 29, 33, 40, 48, 61, 64,
65, 73, 87, 88, 99, 114, 116, 117, 122,
123, 126, 134, 135, 140, 141, 142, 145,
151, 161, 168, 178, 189

Sanders, sanders powder 5 & n.11, 11, 33,
37, 47, 49, 56, 71, 84, 97, 120, 138, 150,
159, 170, 183, 187

Saucing drink 95, 114, 137, 145

Sheep *see* mutton, lamb

Smelt *see* fish

Smites 187

Sorrel 115, 132

Spicebread, buns, cakes, spice cakes xxx,
xxix, 13, 18, 23, 30, 39, 43, 50, 57, 61,
67, 72, 84, 85, 92, 96, 107, 121, 128, 138,
149, 156, 160, 164, 170, 178, 181

Spinach xxx, 7, 132

Stag xxxiii, 44, 45, 78, 79, 143, 156; *see
also* bucks, deer

Sturgeon *see* fish

Suet 9, 29, 35, 54, 55, 70, 83, 94, 95, 119,
137, 145, 148, 160, 161, 165, 172, 182,
187

Suyte *see* poultry

Sugar xxvii, xxix, 4, 6, 8, 11, 18, 33, 34,
37, 47, 49, 50, 56, 64, 70, 71, 76, 84, 97,
114, 115, 117, 120, 133, 135, 138, 146,
150, 159, 164, 165, 170, 171, 177, 178,
183, 187

Swans *see* birds

Tarts xxvii, 27, 65, 80, 81, 115

Apple 6, 63, 80

Pippin 7

Tenches *see* fish

Tornesol (tormesall, turnesall) 37 & n.124,
56, 71, 84

Turbet *see* fish

Turkey cock *see* poultry

Veal xxxi, 9, 35, 41, 54, 70, 83, 94, 108,
119, 129, 137, 182

Verjuice (vergewse, vergeus, vergious,
vertious, vertioys, vertgious, veriuce,
vergys, verges, varges) 5 & n.13, 7, 14,
33, 40, 48, 64, 65, 73, 87, 99, 114, 116,
117, 123, 134, 135, 145, 151, 161, 168,
178, 188

Venison xxvii, xxxvii, xxxv, xli, 9, 20, 23,
29, 35, 44, 67, 68, 75, 76, 88, 101, 107,
108, 109, 110, 129, 130, 143, 145, 157,
158, 160; *see also* bucks, deer, pasties

Vinegar 5, 7, 14, 33, 40, 48, 64, 65, 73, 87,
99, 114, 116, 117, 123, 134, 135, 140,
141, 145, 151, 161, 168, 172, 178, 188,
189

Wafers xxix, 7, 13, 18, 26, 27, 28, 30, 40,
43, 52, 54, 58, 61, 69, 72, 86, 93, 97, 110,
111, 120, 130, 131, 139, 151, 159, 165,
173, 178, 184; *see also* biscuit, marchpane

Water 17, 61, 101, 117

Damask, rose, sweet 5, 18, 43, 47, 49,
50, 56, 60, 64, 65, 74, 87 & n.194,
100, 114, 116, 124, 135, 145, 166,
173, 177, 185

Washing 31, 87 & n.194, 100, 166, 173,
124, 166, 173

Wax dish xxviii, xxxi, 127, 129

Wine 6, 7, 10 & n.30, 11, 18, 29, 30, 43,
50, 55, 61, 75, 88, 98, 101, 102, 111, 121,
126, 127, 133, 142, 143, 155, 162, 177,
182, 187; *see also* fortified wine

Claret xxxvi n.133, 5, 7, 8, 14 n.46,
27, 33, 34, 47, 63, 65, 74, 113, 116,
117, 133, 135, 139, 146, 152, 166,
188, 189

French xxx, 10 & n.29, 23, 27, 36, 49,
55, 61, 73, 85, 98, 107, 171

201

Gascon   xxx, 10, 19, 23, 36, 55, 61, 73,
    85, 98, 107, 152, 162, 171, 178,
Red   15 n.46, 74, 85, 121, 142, 152, 162,
    171, 185
Rhenish   xxx, 55, 56

White   4, 7, 8, 10, 33, 34, 36, 47, 49, 55,
    74, 85, 98, 113, 116, 121, 133, 135,
    139, 146, 152, 162, 171, 178, 185
Woodcocks   *see* birds

Yeast   7, 58, 59, 65, 97, 122, 133, 150

INDEX OF PEOPLE AND PLACES

Place names are indexed in standard modern English, with variants noted in brackets in consecutive order as they appear in the original text. For the names of people, original spellings have been retained and used for indexing, with variants listed in alphabetical order. Possible identifications have been noted in brackets

Abchurch Lane (Alchurch Lane) xxx, 13 n.42, 96
Agar's son 106 & n.260; *see also* Thomas Awgar
Aldgate 191
Alford, Mr (Roger?) 79 & n.181
Altham, (James?) 104 & n.237
Apton 21
Arrowsmith, (William?) 101 & n.220
Arthur, John 190
Ashdown Forest (Asshedowne) 103 & n.224
Askew, Richard, warden of the Drapers 194, 195
Asshelyn, Mrs 21 & n.69
Atkyns, Mr 195
Awgar, Nicholas, chandler, warden of the Drapers 106 n.260, 134 & n.292, 135, 140, 151, 164, 169
Awgar, Thomas, chandler, draper 173, 178; *see also* Agar

Bagatte, Mrs 9
Bayly 190
Barnam, Alice, silkwoman 25 & n.102, 78 n.173
Barnam/Barnham, Francis, master of the Drapers 25 n.102, 63, 67, 76 n.167, 78 n.178, 78 n.179, 113, 118, 125, 127, 143 n.295, 145, 147, 154, 155, 196
Barnham, Thomas, draper 78 & n.178
Barnard, William, warden of the Drapers 176 & n.325,
Barnard, (Richard?) 190, 191 & n.367
Barnes, Sir George, master of the Haberdashers, Lord Mayor 46 & n.140
Barnes, John, haberdasher 46 & n.140
Barton 89
Barton, John, cook 179
Bass/Basse, Mrs 60, 100, 124
Basse, John 190

Bates, Mr (Edward?) 185 & n.332
Baxter, Anne 30
Beamond/Beamonde/Beaumond/Beaumonde/ Beaumont, Robert, draper, steward 42 & n.132, 58, 60, 75, 101, 111, 125, 142, 143, 153
Beech Lane (Bech Leyne, Bech Layne) 191 & n.358
Becher, Henry, haberdasher 103 & n.228, 126
Beck, Samuel, draper 190 & n.342
Beddington Park (Bedington Park) 103 & n.227
Bendig, Widow 191
Best, Mr 22
Beswick, Joan, wife of William 25 & n.107
Beswick, William, master of the Drapers 25 n.107, 63
Bingham, Richard, butcher 179
Bishop's Head (Bisshop's Hedd, Bishoppes Head, Bishopp's Hed, Bishoppes Hed, Bishoppes Hedd), the 21 & n.68, 47, 105, 116, 121, 135, 139
Bishopsgate Street 96
Bisshopp, Robert 21
Blackwell Hall, porters of 22 & n.72, 105
Blage/Blagg/Blagge, Mr xxxi, 9 & n.26, 10, 36, 55, 71, 86, 121, 139
Bland, George, butler 179
Blont, (John?) 25 & n.105
Blount, Sir Richard, Lieutenant of the Tower 24 n.82
Blower, Henry, wax chandler 127
Bodeley, John, draper 172 & n.320
Bowars, Widow 191 & n.360
Bowers, James, draper 191 & n.354
Bowers, Henry, butcher 182
Bowyer, William, master of the Drapers 194
Bradshaw, John 190 & n.394
Bradbridge, William, Dean of Salisbury 78 & n.173

207

Richards, Henry, warden of the Drapers   24
  & n.92
Richards, Morgan   61
Richards/Richardes, Robert, rentor of the
  Drapers   106 & n.257, 116, 127, 134
Richard, Widow   191
Roche, Sir William, master of the Drapers,
  Lord Mayor   194
Rockadyne, John   190
Roffe, Thomas, draper   103 & n.224
Rolles/Rowles/Rowlles, John, porter, draper
  167 & n.317, 174, 186
Rombe, Thomas   92
Rookes, Mrs   86
Rydley (Thomas?)   44, 104 & n.242

Sackfield (Sackville), Sir Richard   xxi, 23
  & n.76
Sackville, Sir Thomas, Baron Buckhurst   79
  & n.182
Sadler, Robert, merchant   104 & n.236
Sadler, Roger, warden of the Drapers   80 &
  n.188
Sadler, John, master of the Drapers   195
St. Andrew Undershaft   190
St. Clement's Lane   39
St. Dunstan in the East   143
St. Katherine (St. Katherin, St. Catherine)
  xxxi, 35 & n.35, 191
St. Martin   190
St. Michael Cornhill (Mighell's, Michaell's,
  Mighel's, St Michael's, Mychaells)   xvii,
  xl, 16 & n.52, 22, 42, 75, 77, 90, 96, 100,
  106, 124, 142, 153, 154, 162, 163, 167,
  174, 177, 185
St. Michael's Yard (St. Michells' yard)   190
St. Swithin's Hall   xxiii
Sancheshe/Sanchez, Balthazar/Ballthaser/
  Balthezar, confit-maker   xxix, 36 &
  n.121, 82 & n.192, 86, 121
Sarcefeeld, baker   96
Sawyer, butcher   70, 83, 137
Segar, musician   124, 162
Selby, Robert, porter, draper   60 & n.152,
  75, 89, 100, 142, 153
Sellynger (St. Leger), Sir John   78 & n.175
Semper, (Peter?), porter   42, 60 & n.151
Seyntpere, Richard, chief porter   42
Sharppe, Father   126
Shaw/Shawe, George, porter   125, 142, 153,
  178
Sheford, Thomas, porter   178
Sherbourne Lane   121
Shore, Margery   164
Shorter, (William?)   105
Shorter, Gregory   178
Skant, James, draper   190 & n.353
Skerne, Bartholomew, warden of the Drapers
  3 & n.4, 12, 20, 22, 24 n.83, 29, 30
Skerne, Jane   24 & n.83
Slanly, Widow, almswoman   19

Small/Smalle, steward   16, 22, 28, 42
Smithfield (Smythfield)   xxx n.98, 13 &
  n.43, 85, 97, 122
Smithurst, George   29
Smyth, Doctor   78
Smyth, Margaret   125
Smyth, Peter   19
Smyth/Smythe, Thomas, the Customer   10
  & n.31, 23
Smyth, William, grocer   xxx, 37 & n.122,
  83, 120
Smythe, the Common Hunt   21 & n.66
Southwark   88 & n.199
Spenser, (Nicholas?)   79 & n.184
Spenser, Thomas, warden of the Drapers
  194
Spirling   102
Squibbe, Barnard, draper   191 & n.362
Stanford, Anthony   190
Stanley, Lady Joyce   24 & n.87
Stanley, Thomas   24 & n.86, 24 n.87
Starkey, Mr (Thomas?)   92 & n.211
Star/Starr, Henry, labourer   22, 42, 60, 75,
  90, 101, 106, 127, 142, 155
Stocke, Simon   29
Stokes   22
Storar/Storer, baker   57, 71, 84, 166
Stoughton, Mother   168, 174, 185
Strenell, Otwell   161
Sturdy, Goodwife   164
Sutton, John, warden of the Drapers   132 &
  n.287, 136
Swan, Mr   158
Sweete, Goodwife, provider   122

Tattam, William, porter   125
Tatton, John, warden of the Drapers   105,
  132 & n.288, 136, 143
Taylor, Isaac/Isaack   155, 169
Taylor, John, porter   125, 142, 167, 174,
  178, 186
Thompson, Mr, auditor   43, 45
Thompson, Goodwife   13, 154
Thomson/Thompson, Richard, porter, draper
  75 & n.163, 89, 100, 126 & n.284, 142
Thorne, Georg   190
Thorneton, Widow, almswoman   191 & n.361
Thorowgood/Throwgood, William, warden of
  the Drapers   46 & n.138, 164 & n.314,
  169, 176, 179
Thorowgood, Mrs, wife of William   164 &
  n.314, 168
Tossyer, Mr   78
Tower of London   24 & n.82, 60 & n.154,
  126
Treacle (Tracle/Treagle/Treakle/Treeagle/
  Treegle/Triacle/Triakill/Triegle/Tryacle/
  Tryagle/Tryegle) Stephen, cook   xxxiv &
  n.118, 16 & n.50, 29, 41, 48, 59, 65, 75,
  86, 90, 101, 113, 121, 125, 134, 139, 141,
  146, 152, 153, 161, 167, 173, 179, 184

208

LONDON RECORD SOCIETY

President: The Rt. Hon. The Lord Mayor of London

Chairman: Professor Caroline M. Barron, MA, PhD, FRHistS
Hon. Secretary: Dr Helen Bradley
Hon. Treasurer: Dr David Lewis
Hon. General Editors: Dr Robin Eagles, Dr Hannes Kleineke, Professor Jerry White

The London Record Society was founded in December 1964 to publish transcripts, abstracts and lists of the primary sources for this history of London, and generally to stimulate interest in archives relating to London. Membership is open to any individual or institution; the annual subscription is £25 for UK members and £30 ($45) for overseas members. Prospective members should apply to the Hon. Membership Secretary, Dr Penny Tucker, Hewton Farmhouse, Bere Alston, Yelverton, Devon, PL20 7BW (email londonrecordsoc@btinternet.com)

The following volumes have already been published:

1. *London Possessory Assizes: a Calendar*, edited by Helena M. Chew (1965)
2. *London Inhabitants within the Walls, 1695*, with an introduction by D. V. Glass (1966)
3. *London Consistory Court Wills, 1492–1547*, edited by Ida Darlington (1967)
4. *Scriveners' Company Common Paper, 1357–1628, with a Continuation to 1678*, edited by Francis W. Steer (1968)
5. *London Radicalism, 1830–1843: a Selection from the Papers of Francis Place*, edited by D. J. Rowe (1970)
6. *The London Eyre of 1244*, edited by Helena M. Chew and Martin Weinbaum (1970)
7. *The Cartulary of Holy Trinity Aldgate*, edited by Gerald A. J. Hodgett (1971)
8. *The Port and Trade of Early Elizabethan London: Documents*, edited by Brian Dietz (1972)
9. *The Spanish Company*, edited by Pauline Croft (1973)
10. *London Assize of Nuisance, 1301–1431: a Calendar*, edited by Helena M. Chew and William Kellaway (1973)

11. *Two Calvinistic Methodist Chapels, 1748–1811: the London Tabernacle and Spa Fields Chapel*, edited by Edwin Welch (1975)
12. *The London Eyre of 1276*, edited by Martin Weinbaum (1976)
13. *The Church in London, 1375–1392*, edited by A. K. McHardy (1977)
14. *Committees for the Repeal of the Test and Corporation Acts: Minutes, 1786–90 and 1827–8*, edited by Thomas W. Davis (1978)
15. *Joshua Johnson's Letterbook, 1771–4: Letters from a Merchant in London to his Partners in Maryland*, edited by Jacob M. Price (1979)
16. *London and Middlesex Chantry Certificate, 1548*, edited by C. J. Kitching (1980)
17. *London Politics, 1713–1717: Minutes of a Whig Club, 1714–17*, edited by H. Horwitz; *London Pollbooks, 1713*, edited by W. A. Speck and W. A. Gray (1981)
18. *Parish Fraternity Register: Fraternity of the Holy Trinity and SS. Fabian and Sebastian in the Parish of St. Botolph without Aldersgate*, edited by Patricia Basing (1982)
19. *Trinity House of Deptford: Transactions, 1609–35*, edited by G. G. Harris (1983).
20. *Chamber Accounts of the Sixteenth Century*, edited by Betty R. Masters (1984)
21. *The Letters of John Paige, London Merchant, 1648–58*, edited by George F. Steckley (1984)
22. *A Survey of Documentary Sources for Property Holding in London before the Great Fire*, by Derek Keene and Vanessa Harding (1985)
23. *The Commissions for Building Fifty New Churches*, edited by M. H. Port (1986)
24. *Richard Hutton's Complaints Book*, edited by Timothy V. Hitchcock (1987)
25. *Westminster Abbey Charters, 1066–c.1214*, edited by Emma Mason (1988)
26. *London Viewers and their Certificates, 1508–1558*, edited by Janet S. Loengard (1989)
27. *The Overseas Trade of London: Exchequer Customs Accounts, 1480–1*, edited by H. S. Cobb (1990)
28. *Justice in Eighteenth-Century Hackney: the Justicing Notebook of Henry Norris and the Hackney Petty Sessions Book*, edited by Ruth Paley (1991)
29. *Two Tudor Subsidy Assessment Rolls for the City of London: 1541 and 1582*, edited by R. G. Lang (1993)
30. *London Debating Societies, 1776–1799*, compiled and introduced by Donna T. Andrew (1994)
31. *London Bridge: Selected Accounts and Rentals, 1381–1538*, edited by Vanessa Harding and Laura Wright (1995)
32. *London Consistory Court Depositions, 1586–1611: List and Indexes*, by Loreen L. Giese (1997)
33. *Chelsea Settlement and Bastardy Examinations, 1733–66*, edited by Tim Hitchcock and John Black (1999)

34. *The Church Records of St Andrew Hubbard Eastcheap, c.1450–c.1570*, edited by Clive Burgess (1999)
35. *Calendar of Exchequer Equity Pleadings, 1685–6 and 1784–5*, edited by Henry Horwitz and Jessica Cooke (2000)
36. *The Letters of William Freeman, London Merchant, 1678–1685*, edited by David Hancock (2002)
37. *Unpublished London Diaries: a Checklist of Unpublished Diaries by Londoners and Visitors, with a Select Bibliography of Published Diaries*, compiled by Heather Creaton (2003)
38. *The English Fur Trade in the Later Middle Ages*, by Elspeth M. Veale (2003; reprinted from 1966 edition)
39. *The Bede Roll of the Fraternity of St Nicholas*, edited by N. W. and V. A. James (2 vols., 2004)
40. *The Estate and Household Accounts of William Worsley, Dean of St Paul's Cathedral, 1479–1497*, edited by Hannes Kleineke and Stephanie R. Hovland (2004)
41. *A Woman in Wartime London: the Diary of Kathleen Tipper, 1941–1945*, edited by Patricia and Robert Malcolmson (2006)
42. *Prisoners' Letters to the Bank of England 1783–1827*, edited by Deirdre Palk (2007)
43. *The Apprenticeship of a Mountaineer: Edward Whymper's London Diary, 1855–1859*, edited by Ian Smith (2008)
44. *The Pinners' and Wiresellers' Book, 1462–1511*, edited by Barbara Megson (2009)
45. *London Inhabitants Outside the Walls, 1695*, edited by Patrick Wallis (2010)
46. *The Views of the Hosts of Alien Merchants, 1440–1444*, edited by Helen Bradley (2012)
47. *The Great Wardrobe Accounts of Henry VII and Henry VIII*, edited by Maria Hayward (2012)
48. *Summary Justice in the City: A Selection of Cases Heard at the Guildhall Justice Room, 1752–1781*, edited by Greg T. Smith (2013)
49. *The Diaries of John Wilkes, 1770–1797*, edited by Robin Eagles (2014)
50. *A Free-Spirited Woman: The London Diaries of Gladys Langford, 1936–1940*, edited by Patricia and Robert Malcolmson (2014)
51. *The Angels' Voice A Magazine for Young Men in Brixton, London, 1910–1913*, edited by Alan Argent (2016)
52. *The London Diary of Anthony Heap, 1931–1945*, edited by Robin Woolven (2017)

Previously published titles in the series are available from Boydell and Brewer; please contact them for further details, or see their website, www.boydellandbrewer.com